Flirting With Death

This volume covers a much-neglected topic: the avoidance by psychotherapists and psychoanalysts of the topic of their own mortality and that of their patients. All too often, the psychotherapist or psychoanalyst who is ill is unable to confront this reality in the presence of her patient and fails to prepare the patient for the most permanent goodbye, death. This volume includes nine essays which consider why the psychotherapist and psychoanalyst may find illness, mortality, retirement and termination so difficult.

This volume is a collection of essays by psychoanalysts covering the denial of death amongst psychotherapists and psychoanalysts and the effect on clinical practice, the effect of early childhood confrontation with mortality on the professional development of psychoanalysts, illness in the analyst, the death of patients, and termination and retirement as symbolic harbingers of death.

Corinne Masur is an adult supervising analyst and a child analyst at the Psychoanalytic Center of Philadelphia (PCOP), USA. She has been in private practice in Philadelphia for over thirty years. She is the co-director of the Parent Child Center and a founder of the Philadelphia Center for Psychoanalytic Education and the Philadelphia Declaration of Play, an organization which advocates for the right of all children to have access to free, imaginative play. She has written, lectured and taught on a variety of subjects including early childhood bereavement, mourning, the denial of death, child development and childhood psychopathology. She is on the Faculty of PCOP where she was the recipient of the J. Alexis Burland teaching award several times.

Flirting With Death

Psychoanalysts Consider Mortality

Edited by
Corinne Masur

LONDON AND NEW YORK

First published 2018 by Routledge
2 Park Square, Milton Park, Abingdon, Oxon OX14 4RN
52 Vanderbilt Avenue, New York, NY 10017

Routledge is an imprint of the Taylor & Francis Group, an informa business

© 2018 selection and editorial matter, Corinne Masur;
individual chapters, the contributors

The right of Corinne Masur to be identified as the author of the editorial material, and of the authors for their individual chapters, has been asserted in accordance with sections 77 and 78 of the Copyright, Designs and Patents Act 1988.

All rights reserved. No part of this book may be reprinted or reproduced or utilised in any form or by any electronic, mechanical, or other means, now known or hereafter invented, including photocopying and recording, or in any information storage or retrieval system, without permission in writing from the publishers.

Trademark notice: Product or corporate names may be trademarks or registered trademarks, and are used only for identification and explanation without intent to infringe.

British Library Cataloguing-in-Publication Data
A catalogue record for this book is available from the British Library

Library of Congress Cataloging-in-Publication Data
A catalog record has been requested for this book

ISBN: 978-1-7822-0549-4 (pbk)

Typeset in Times New Roman
by Florence Production Ltd, Stoodleigh, Devon, UK

Contents

Acknowledgements		vii
About the editor and the contributors		viii
Preface		xi
	Introduction	1
1	Mortality and psychoanalysis: the analyst's defense against acknowledging mortality and the effect on clinical practice CORINNE MASUR	7
2	Psychoanalytic reflections on limitation: aging, dying, generativity, and renewal NANCY MCWILLIAMS	25

Early exposure to danger and loss — 41

3	Orphans SALMAN AKHTAR	43
4	Mortality – the inevitable challenge: the development of the acceptance of one's mortality HENRI PARENS	72

Illness — 97

5	Psychotherapy – a life's work RUTH GARFIELD	99
6	Illness in the analyst – thirty years later HARVEY SCHWARTZ	114

When a patient dies   127

7 When a patient dies: reflections on the death of three patients   129
SYBIL HOULDING

When an analyst dies   139

8 Mortality, integrity and psychoanalysis: (who are you to me? Who am I to you?)   141
ELLEN PINSKY

Retirement   159

9 A note on retirement and mortality   161
SYBIL HOULDING

Index   169

Acknowledgements

I would like to thank Salman Akhtar, as it was his encouragement and help that allowed this book to come into being. I would also like to thank Samantha Wertheimer for her invaluable assistance in exploring the literature with me and for me. Additionally I must thank my son, T. J. Fallon, for his invaluable technical assistance. Without him no draft of this book would ever have been edited or saved because of my complete technophobia. Most of all, I would like to thank the chapter contributors: Ruth Garfield, Nancy McWilliams, Salman Akhtar, Harvey Schwartz, Henri Parens, Ellen Pinsky, and Sybil Houlding for their courageous willingness to confront and explore their feelings about this topic in so many of its forms.

About the editor and the contributors

Salman Akhtar, MD, is professor of psychiatry at Jefferson Medical College and a training and supervising analyst at the Psychoanalytic Center of Philadelphia. He has served on the editorial boards of the *International Journal of Psychoanalysis*, the *Journal of the American Psychoanalytic Association*, and the *Psychoanalytic Quarterly*. His more than 300 publications include eighty-three books, of which the following eighteen are solo-authored: *Broken Structures* (1992), *Quest for Answers* (1995), *Inner Torment* (1999), *Immigration and Identity* (1999), *New Clinical Realms* (2003), *Objects of Our Desire* (2005), *Regarding Others* (2007), *Turning Points in Dynamic Psychotherapy* (2009), *The Damaged Core* (2009), *Comprehensive Dictionary of Psychoanalysis* (2009), *Immigration and Acculturation* (2011), *Matters of Life and Death* (2011), *The Book of Emotions* (2012), *Psychoanalytic Listening* (2013), *Good Stuff* (2013), *Sources of Suffering* (2014), *No Holds Barred* (2016), and *A Web of Sorrow* (2017). Dr. Akhtar has published nine collections of poetry and serves as a scholar-in-residence at the Inter-Act Theatre Company in Philadelphia.

Ruth Garfield, LSW, MD, is a child and adult psychiatrist and an adult psychoanalyst who has been in practice for over thirty years. She is on the faculty of the Psychoanalytic Center of Philadelphia and has written, spoken, and taught on numerous aspects of child, adolescent, and adult psychopathology and development.

Sybil Houlding is a clinical social worker and a member of the faculty at the Western New England Institute for Psychoanalysis. She practices in New Haven, CT, treating individuals, couples, and families. She has recently been named faculty chair at the Western New England Institute.

Nancy McWilliams teaches at Rutgers University's Graduate School of Applied & Professional Psychology and practices in Flemington, New Jersey. She is the author of *Psychoanalytic Diagnosis* (1994, rev. ed. 2011), *Psychoanalytic Case Formulation* (1999), *Psychoanalytic Psychotherapy*

(2004), and an upcoming book on overall wellness. Her books are available in twenty languages; she lectures widely both nationally and internationally. She is associate editor of the *Psychodynamic Diagnostic Manual* (2006, 2017), a former president of Division 39 (Psychoanalysis) of the APA, and an honorary member of the American Psychoanalytic Association. She has been featured in three American Psychological Association videos of master clinicians, the most recent being "Three Approaches to Psychotherapy."

Corinne Masur is a clinical psychologist, a child psychoanalyst and a supervising adult analyst who has been in private practice for more than thirty years. She is on the faculty of the Psychoanalytic Center of Philadelphia, is codirector of the Parent Child Center, is a founder and past president of the Philadelphia Center for Psychoanalytic Education and a founder of the Philadelphia Declaration of Play. She has written, taught, and lectured on a variety of subjects including child development, childhood psychopathology, early childhood bereavement, and the denial of mortality and has received the J. Alexis Burland Award for excellence in teaching on three occasions.

Henri Parens, MD is a professor of psychiatry at Thomas Jefferson University, and a training and supervising analyst (adult and child) at the Psychoanalytic Center of Philadelphia. He has been in the private practice of psychiatry and psychoanalysis for more than fifty years. He has held a number of training and professional administrative posts and was director of the Early Child Development Program, MCP/EPPI and was the president of Parenting for Emotional Growth. Dr. Parens is the author of more than 260 publications, including twenty-two books (twelve authored and ten coedited), five scientific films, a DVD documentary, and a TV series for CBS of thirty-nine half-hour programs. His principal research has led him to efforts toward the prevention of experience-derived emotional disorders in children, and he has generated psychoanalytic explanations and strategies toward the reduction, in individuals and in groups, of excessive hostility, violence, malignant prejudice, and war. Dr. Parens is a Holocaust survivor.

Ellen Pinsky is on the faculty of the Boston Psychoanalytic Society and Institute, where she received the Deutsch Prize for writing. She has written numerous articles and reviews which have appeared in the *Psychoanalytic Quarterly, Journal of the American Psychoanalytic Association, American Imago, Salmagundi,* and *Threepenny Review.* Her book, *Death and Fallibility in the Psychoanalytic Encounter: Mortal Gifts,* appeared recently (Routledge, 2017).

Harvey Schwartz, MD is a member and training analyst at the Psychoanalytic Center of Philadelphia and at the Institute for Psychoanalytic Education (IPE), affiliated with the NYU School of Medicine. He served as the chair of the Certification Examination Committee of the American Psychoanalytic Association. He is a member of the Education and Oversight Committee of the International Psychoanalytical Association and he is the coeditor of *Illness in the Analyst: Implications for the Treatment Relationship*.

Preface

In the middle of World War II Gregory Zilboorg wrote an article on the fear of death and the wish for immortality. Ostensibly about morale among the troops, Zilboorg's article turned out to be one of the best things written on death anxiety up to that time – and since. He wrote about the common use of denial saying, "In normal times we move about ... without ever believing in our own deaths as if we fully believed in our own corporeal immortality" (1943).

It is true that we tend to fend off thoughts of death and mortality. We live comfortably inside our bubbles of repression and denial for as long as we can. Inevitably, however, something happens to burst our bubbles. And each of us finds our own way to manage the sudden and powerfully affective awareness of our own mortality. For some, this intrusion, and the resulting awareness, occurs early in life, and for others it does not occur until quite late. For some, the results are long-lasting and for others repression quickly takes over once again. For me, it happened early and often which is what motivated me to create this book.

When I was a young teenager my father died in his bedroom while I sat downstairs. My parents were giving a dinner party that night and as the dessert burned in the oven and the guests rang the doorbell, I sat stock still in the same chair for hours, simultaneously shocked and unable to absorb the shock. How could someone who was here just a minute ago be gone? How could this happen so suddenly and so irretrievably? I just could not take it in.

By this time in my life, thoughts of my own mortality and that of my parents were not unknown to me. Like most children, I had reflected on death a great deal already. Moreover, I had become an existentialist at the age of six when I asked my mother what happens after death and she replied, "Nothing." I spent hours over days and months and years trying to imagine "nothing." I attempted repeatedly to conceptualize the absence of being after death, dumbfounded at the idea of ceasing to exist.

In college I remember going out into the cold western night and staring up at the multitude of stars, wishing I could contact the father I still needed, trying to believe that he still existed somewhere – and failing that, to at least have some sense of a universe that would care for me.

I was not successful.

And years of thoughts and feelings about death and loss and my experience of these followed, culminating in my choosing a dissertation topic related to these thoughts and feelings. Undoubtedly I wanted to master the shock of my father's death and to guard myself against being so suddenly and unpleasantly shocked again. As the composer, Vladimir Shostakovich said, "We should think more about [death] and accustom ourselves to the thought of [it]. We can't allow the fear of death to creep up on us unexpectedly. We have to make the fear familiar, and one way is to write about it" (Barnes, 2008, p. 27).

I studied the history of psychoanalytic thought on the topic of mourning in adults and children and wrote about these subjects in an effort to master my own feelings about my losses and my own anxieties about death. This helped, but of course it did not work entirely.

However, most closely related to the conceptualization of this book is the fact that at age forty-six, with a three year old at home, I actually died.

Lucky for me, I was in the emergency room when this happened and I was brought back to life by the application of CPR and cardioversion. For the next several years death anxiety was my constant companion.

I was at a dinner party three months after my heart attack when the man sitting to my left asked me what it was like to be dead. How do you answer a question like that? The truth was that I had been struggling with the fact that I had actually died, so much so that I could think of little else. All day, every day, since the heart attack I wondered if I would have a second heart attack – in a minute, in an hour, or perhaps tomorrow. And, as my worry intensified, I wondered if the next time it would be final. In the grocery store, walking down the road, driving in my car with my three year old, I wondered. Every odd feeling in my chest, every ache or pain seemed to auger sudden death. And the fact was that I remembered everything. Memory of tragedy is strange – some people describe a sequence of events in slow motion, some people remember a series of distorted images but I remember my heart attack as if it were on a television screen. And this show was playing over and over again in my head, generally when I least wanted to watch it. I had returned to my practice part time and working with patients was one of the only times that I was free of those thoughts.

During this time I tore myself away from my own preoccupation over my health to wonder how to help my patients with their feelings about my sudden abandonment of them. I wondered how to talk to them about my illness, my absence, my altered appearance and energy level – *and* I wondered how to help myself to regain my professional identity, to regain confidence in my competence and, perhaps most difficult, to regain my sense of ongoing being.

It took several years for me to truly recuperate, physically and psychologically, although of course I was irrevocably altered. My proximity to death had been terrifying both in the moment and for the subsequent months and years – and my prolonged fear of reoccurrence equally so. But gradually, as I felt more my old self, I became interested not only in how I was coming to terms with what I had experienced and what I continued to experience in terms of my feelings about my near death and my eventual certain death, but also in how other clinicians in our field do so. I wondered how I could help my patients come to terms with their own mortality and how others were working with the same question. Even more compelling for me was my observation that while I had been and continued on a lesser scale to be bombarded with thoughts of death and of my own mortality, others, especially certain colleagues, seemed less concerned with this matter, even when issues regarding their own morbidity and mortality became prominent in their lives. Moreover, I failed to find sufficient interest in this subject – in the literature or within my institute – to satisfy my increasing concern that many patients and many therapists and analysts were or are avoiding this topic, using a myriad of defensive maneuvers for a multitude of personal, cultural, and professionally sanctioned reasons.

It is to this end that this book is devoted: to the exploration of how those of us entrusted with the innermost thoughts and feelings of others can examine our own denial and confront our own fears of death so that we can help our patients to cease denial and avoidance and confront their own.

Corinne Masur
April, 2017

References

Barnes, J. (2008). *Nothing To Be Frightened Of.* New York: Vintage.
Zlilboorg, G. (1943). Fear of death. *Psychoanalytic Quarterly*, 12, p. 465–475.

Introduction

In his article, "Death Is Nothing At All: On Contemplating Nonexistence," Martin Frommer notes that even the relational school, one of the most recent and most vibrant offshoots of psychoanalysis, has yet to come to terms with the psychic mind's struggle with its ultimate extinction. He says, "I feel the impact of this absence . . . psychoanalysis has been a steady companion providing ballast for many aspects of my psychic life, [however] my relationship with death is not one of them. In this regard psychoanalysis has been like the close friend who is not to be found when death takes center stage" (2016, p. 374). I am with him on this matter. And it is for this reason that this book exists.

I, like many fellow analysts and even more fellow human beings, search for a way to come to terms with mortality – my own and that of my patients. When I was forty-six I suffered a heart attack and in the emergency room I experienced cardiac arrest. When later I came to consciousness in the ICU, despite the comforts of morphine and others sedating drugs, I soon realized how close I had come to death and began to suffer intractable anxiety. Several days later, when I was well enough to sit up, I grabbed my chart which had somehow been left out, and read that I was described as a "highly anxious" patient. I was shocked. Was there such a thing as too much anxiety in response to having almost died – or rather, too much anxiety in response to having died and having been lucky enough to have been revived? Had I reacted incorrectly to my near death? What other way would there be to react?

I have contemplated this question in the years since and I have wondered at the writer of this note, a young cardiology fellow. What were his ideas about what might be the "normal" way to react to death? I have wondered how cut off and dissociated he must have had to make himself in the face of death and how difficult he might have found it to confront his own feelings, let alone those of his patients.

Since that time I have treated innumerable young mothers facing breast cancer diagnoses, wondering what to tell their young children, slightly older mothers with life threatening illnesses contemplating the idea of leaving adolescent children, older adults working through losses of spouses, siblings, and others, as well as a full range of situations in which patients have had to grapple with loss and death. I have also worked with a number of children as they faced their nascent feelings about death. Three and four year olds are especially vulnerable as they first discover death. As a child therapist I listen to young children as they try to understand that death will befall their mothers and fathers, and even more perplexing, that they themselves will one day die.

I remember one three-year-old boy whose mother had committed suicide. On his first visit to my playroom he sat down in front of the dollhouse and threw the mother doll behind the house. When I asked where she had gone he picked her up and put her on the roof of the house. He had been told by his father only that Mommy was "up there." As far as he was concerned, being "up there" meant that Mommy was now living on the roof of their house. This little boy truly believed that his mother still lived; she just lived elsewhere. And later in the treatment, as we worked through his painful feelings of yearning and searching for Mommy, he asked me quietly, "Are you the mommy on the roof?"

I was a newly minted therapist at the time and I simultaneously felt deep pain and confusion when I heard his question and saw the look on his face. How badly he wanted to find his Mommy and how much he hoped that I was she. Here I was, a nice young woman who played with him and cared about his thoughts and feelings. Perhaps I could be his mother? And he was not the only one to wish this. In the inevitable confusion that one can feel in the face of the desperate need of a patient, simultaneously with one's own desire to help and to comfort, I myself wished that I could replace his mother, to make him feel safe, to ease his pain. After all, he was so young, too young for such a grievous loss. But of course I could not replace her and even as inexperienced as I was, I knew that this temptation was one not to be given in to.

In the softest, kindest voice I could muster (while trying not to cry myself) I said, "I know you wish I could be your mommy but we both know that Mommy died and it is very sad for you and for your daddy."

Was this the right thing to say? Was it the thing that would make him feel that I understood his terrible missing feelings for his mother?

Actually, in the long run, I have learned that right or wrong was not the point. At that moment this child needed to deny his mother's loss. He persisted in locating her on the roof, on the moon, on airplanes that flew overhead, and perhaps in me, his therapist. This was his interpretation of "up there" and he was sticking with it. Only months and years of painful reminders could convince him that Mommy was truly gone and that she could not come back.

Bearing witness to the full expression of sadness, terror, injury, loss, religious crisis, and terrible anxiety, that is, to the feelings that come with loss, is hard work. We are tempted to assuage the sadness, calm the anxiety, and, in general, try to be "the mommy on the roof" for our patients.

Memories of our own losses, our own illnesses and near death experiences are inevitably brought up by patient material. At these times we acutely experience our own vulnerability. Sometimes this may leave us wanting to defend against our raw openness and we may unwittingly wall off our own subjective experience in order to manage our patients' expressions of pain and loss. This defensive distancing from our own fears and vulnerability in the face of death results in vastly reduced accessibility to and empathic attunement with our patients' struggles around these issues. The unconscious upsurge of defensive function when faced by enormous affect is ubiquitous but it is not necessarily inevitable. And it is to this subject that this book is dedicated: How do we work to become more open to our patients' feelings and fears about death and loss when they evoke such terror both in them and in ourselves?

Contemporary analysts vary with regard to the value they place on the handling of existential material within the framework of analytic treatment. Frommer (2016) recounts a discussion which took place between him and Robert Stolorow in which Stolorow argued that "Human beings pay dearly for their illusions of invulnerability and invincibility that shield them from deadlining with their finitude." Paul Lippman, also in the discussion, commented that while human beings know that they die, they don't really believe it and that is a good thing. Lippman argued for the protection of fantasy regarding death, as Frommer says, "echoing the Nietzschean conceit that human beings need their illusions to get by" (p. 387). And this raises an extremely important point: It may well be that certain patients and indeed, certain analysts, do need their illusions to get by. It may be that an intense examination of and confrontation with mortality might prove too much to bear for some. Among the characteristics needed for working with the most difficult existential issues are solid ego strength and good defensive capacity. Solid defensive functioning is needed not to allow the individual to deny death, because we are discussing the confrontation of our own mortality here, but to pull back from full recognition when necessary, to self soothe and reduce affect when the confrontation with mortality and other potentially overwhelming realities becomes too anxiety provoking. One needs to have solid ground on which to stand, after all, while contemplating what it would be like to fall off the cliff – and likewise, one needs to be able to stop thinking now and then about that abyss while hiking along its edge. So it is for analysts: Some may not be suited for this work while most of us will wax and wane in regard to our ability to engage with these matters, depending on our own ego state and sense of solidity versus vulnerability on any particular day.

As Frommer (2016) said,

> Psychoanalytic work frequently requires ... that we intimately engage with all-too-real potentially overwhelming aspects of living and dying.

> This work begs us to extend ourselves beyond comfort, bypassing defense to confront what is unknowable, sometimes fearsome and often taxing. Our efforts to be with our patients in the immediacy of their attempts to confront mortality and death require us to confront our own feelings and fantasies. While I appeal to all analysts and therapists to consider this subject more actively and consciously, I also appeal to us as a community to talk more about this subject, to care more for one another when we are overtaxed by a particular patient and to reach out to each other to provide support in our clinical work around these issues. (p. 387)

Furthermore, Frommer says that we need "... to develop a more fully articulated and elaborated communitarian ethos and existential framework that can hold the analyst securely as s/he serves the analytic endeavor in relation to the human condition. The scaffolding for this framework requires a psychoanalysis that theorizes death as central to psychic life; a psychoanalysis that is committed to exploring the ways that mortality shapes subjectivity" (p. 388).

And what of the analytic community's attention to its own members' illnesses and deaths? We spend our lives caring for patients, examining their every feeling but do little for one another even in the face of great suffering, let alone allowing ourselves to be known in our own suffering and vulnerability. When we face our own real death – whether in a partial sense through retirement, illness, or disability or in the fullest sense we rarely call on colleagues or our professional community to help and support us. So often members of our community fade away, attending fewer and fewer meetings, sitting on fewer and fewer committees until they are no longer around at all – and often we let that happen, relying on their friends and family to sort out. But what if we as a community were to actively engage with our retiring, ill, and dying members? What might this look like and how might we do it?

This book is meant to engage the reader in these issues as well as in contemplating how mortality and the defenses against its recognition affect all of us – in our quiet moments alone, in our clinical work and in our instituuinal participation.

There are so many ways that death visits the consultation room: when a patient suffers the illness or death of a loved one, when a patient is ill or dying, when the analyst is ill or dying, when termination of treatment is near, when retirement of the patient or the analyst is thought about or as it approaches, or when the analyst and patient confront any one or any combination of these issues in the imaginative space of the therapeutic endeavor.

The clinician-authors who have generously contributed their most private thoughts and feelings on the topic of illness, mortality and death in these chapters challenge our management of these issues both on a personal and a professional level. And they have a great deal to teach us. We are reminded that death evokes all or specific other losses: When our patients talk about their losses, we cannot help but think of our own. We learn from Salman Akhtar and Henri Parens that early exposure to danger or loss can affect a clinician's later attitudes and work with patients around these issues. We are told by Nancy McWilliams, Harvey Schwartz, and Ruth Garfield that the analyst's feelings about his or her own illness is too often defended against to the detriment of both patient care and self care. We are reminded by Sybil Houlding that termination is a loss which evokes death and that retirement is both a loss and an event which presages or indeed symbolically represents death. She also helps us to consider what it is like to have a patient die. She describes that experience as often being a lonely one, confined as we are by the rules of confidentiality, and reminds us of how rarely this is acknowledged and how typically we are unsupported by our professional community in this event. Ellen Pinsky talks about the extremely difficult experience of having one's analyst die while in treatment with that analyst and about the ways in which we as a community do and do not face this inevitable eventuality squarely. These are all subjects too infrequently discussed and about which too little has been written.

References

Frommer, M. S. (2016). Death is nothing at all: on contemplating nonexistence. A relational psychoanalytic engagement of the fear of death. *Psychoanalytic Dialogues*, 26: 373–390.

Chapter 1

Mortality and psychoanalysis
The analyst's defense against acknowledging mortality and the effect on clinical practice

Corinne Masur

To paraphrase Avery Weissman (1977), psychoanalysts like other people are afraid of death. This fear leads to the development and use of myriad defensive activities (including avoidance, denial, repression, and intellectualization) to ward off thoughts and feelings related to mortality. When overused, these defensive activities may interfere with three aspects of the analyst's role: 1. the personal exploration of her inner experience of her own mortality, 2. the ability and willingness to facilitate her patients' exploration of mortality, and 3. the external reality of the need to prepare for the disposition of the practice in the event of her death.

Sigmund Freud refused to give mortality psychic significance (Frommer, 2016). His views on the subject shaped a long-standing relationship between psychoanalysis and death that nullified the human struggle with mortality. And despite profound post-Freudian changes in psychoanalytic theory and practice, "[T]he human awareness of mortality continues to be treated as if it were not a defining psychic issue" (Frommer, 2016, p. 374).

Regarding the general psychoanalytic literature, Hoffman noted in 1979 that relatively little attention has been paid to the process by which the individual anticipates, reacts to, and comes to terms with his own death. De Masi in 2004 stated that "Psychoanalytic literature, in spite of its thorough exploration of the pain of mourning, has not focused its attention in an equally systematic manner on the bewilderment we feel at the thought of our own death." Or as Weissman (1977) succinctly observed, ". . . psychoanalysts have avoided the whole subject."

In 1955 Eissler wrote, "Since Freud . . . made death a central concept of his psychological system one would have expected that psychoanalysis would devote more effort to the study of death itself. Strangely enough, this has not happened. In general, death is still viewed as a purely biological phenomenon . . ." The overall thrust of Freud's writing on death was in the direction of discounting awareness of death as a psychologically important variable in human development and psychopathology (Hoffman, 1998). To the extent that there was a discussion of this area in the literature (up until recent years) much of it was devoted either to tracing death anxiety in Freud's theory or discussing how defensive functioning relative to the acknowledgment of mortality does or does not fit within developing psychoanalytic theory. As Hoffman (1998) noted, the opportunity to construct a much-needed bridge between the existential and the psychoanalytic perspectives on the psychological impact of awareness of death has been missed. Historically, psychoanalytic approaches have emphasized the ubiquitous human need to deny death. This perspective is derived largely from the conflict based metapsychology of psychoanalysis as well as from the limitations imposed by the study of largely healthy patients who reported death anxiety (Rodin & Zimmerman, 2008).

It is tempting – even for clinicians – to "pretend that it is not going to happen to us" (Akhtar, 2011, p. 86). This attitude is common among many of our patients as well. And for those of us who deal with people on a daily basis who struggle with the meaning of existence, who may in fact be physically ill or dying, we find that we must sometimes allow ourselves to be painfully vulnerable to being drawn into these emotional worlds precisely because of the profoundly reverberating existential issues in this material (Rodin & Zimmerman, 2008). In such cases, the opportunities for effective therapeutic process are unique. For the patient who has suffered loss whether recent or past, for the patient who has faced illness or is facing illness or end of life, in other words, for any and all patients, the recognition of the finite nature of life may be acute – and this idea and the feelings associated with it must be able to be tolerated by the analyst in order to facilitate the patient's ability to tolerate those feelings herself.

In the last several decades, greater attention has been paid to this subject. The psychoanalytic literature now includes some articles on the death of the analyst (Garcia-Lawson & Lane, 1997; Rendely, 1999; Traesdal, 2005; Ziman-Tobin, 1989), the illness and death of the analytic patient (Buechler, 2000; Chassey, 2006; Coltart, 1996), the death of a patient's spouse or child (Chasen, 1994; Gerson, 1994; Mayer, 1994, Mendelsohn, 1991), and the analyst's own illness or impending death (Dewald, 1982; Fajardo, 2001; Feinsilver, 1998; Morrison, 1990; Pizer, 1997; Schwartz & Silver, 1990).

This chapter is not devoted to the topic of the history of thought about death in psychoanalysis, or the debate over the existence of the death instinct, but to the impact which the denial of death (versus the conscious awareness of the finite nature of life) has on the psychoanalyst herself and on the clinical practice of psychoanalysis and psychoanalytic psychotherapy.

It is important to consider this subject not in the realm of past or present theory building but inside the consulting room. In that space the therapist ultimately faces herself and her patient and, in so doing, faces certain very basic existential issues. Both the therapist and the patient vacillate between conscious acknowledgement and defensive retreat from a variety of issues including the universal struggle to accept the reality of one's own death.

Death is "the most fundamental and terrifying problem of human life" (Stern in Lord, Ritvo and Solnit, 1978, p. 2) and if the feelings related to death cannot be experienced, expressed, and understood within the confines of the analytic experience then where (other than church, mosque, or synagogue) is the patient to deal with them? Harold Searles held the conviction that every psychoanalytic therapy should help the patient to explore the deep meaning that the patient attributes to his or her own death. Furthermore, he believed that as psychoanalysts we should not limit ourselves to exploring issues related to death with those rare patients who face a serious illness, but we should help every patient to develop her capacity to tolerate the thought of the transience of human life (De Masi, 2004). It is to this end that this chapter, and indeed, this volume is devoted.

In this chapter, three aspects of the therapist's role in regard to confronting her own feelings regarding death and those of her patients will be discussed. The therapist's defensive reaction to the exploration of her own mortality will be examined first. Second, the difficulties facilitating the patient's exploration of the subject will be looked at, and third, the external reality of having to prepare for the disposition of the therapist's practice in the event of her own death will be delineated.

The therapist's relationship with her own mortality

The limited nature of human existence is a topic which generates anxiety in both patient and analyst. It is a phenomenon which is painfully difficult to approach directly. As such, patients in analysis often avoid the matter. Therapists, and analysts who once were analytic patients themselves may have experienced the wish to avoid this material – or they may have done so without having been aware of their avoidance and their analysts may have permitted this avoidance in a process of mutual collusion. I am describing a process of transgenerational transmission in which avoidance is allowed by the analyst in part because she was allowed to do so in her own analysis. This is not to say that issues of loss, sadness, mourning, and the like are not common material in analyses, especially during the termination phase, but rather that the issue of one's own death – as patient – and that of one's analyst – may be different and more difficult to confront than the loss of others in one's life. Similarly, the loss of individual functions or parts of oneself must be mourned despite the temptation by analyst, patient, or both to circumvent these issues.

In 1915 Freud observed that it is impossible to imagine our own death. But how can this be? Many have fantasized their own deaths and dreamed their own death. Rather, what Freud may have been suggesting is that what is difficult or impossible to imagine is what it is to actually cease to exist. This is what is inconceivable and horrifying. The idea of ceasing one's existence evokes anxiety, panic, and immeasurable grief. Moreover, as Akhtar states (2011), death is the greatest narcissistic injury, the most profound humiliation we can imagine experiencing. Human beings live in the moment, experiencing a multiplicity of sensations at any one time and to cease to experience these sensations, the pleasure and the pain of life – well, *that* is unimaginable.

Freud suggested that the unconscious is "convinced of [its] own immortality" (1915b). As such, immortality would be a basic, primitive tenet of human life. In so doing, Freud reified and universalized what may have been his own personal failure of imagination (Frommer, 2016). Instead, I suggest that, in general, the human being (ego and id, conscious and unconscious) is aware of the finiteness of being and defends mightily against the awareness of this fact in order to avoid the tremendous anxiety, terror, sadness, and other potentially overwhelming affects which would be experienced if this were acknowledged. To cease to experience, to lose the capacity to love and be loved, to smell, taste, feel, breathe, remember the past, imagine the future, to learn, to be productive, to create, and to be is to lose everything. And to acknowledge the inevitability of this enormous loss, to admit that we will inevitably lose consciousness forever – is something so difficult to accept, so narcissistically injurious, that man has had to create a variety of ways to avoid the acceptance of this inevitability.

Religious belief is only one of a variety of such ways which have been constructed to cope with the reality of the finite nature of man's existence. Hoffman (1979) believes that the concept of immortality is a restitutive response to the impact of a cognitive appreciation of the meaning of death. If we can believe that we continue to live on after death, albeit in different form, then we need not fear death or contemplate the finite nature of existence. Life is not finite, after all, if there is an afterlife. Those who believe in an afterlife need not fully confront the temporal limitations imposed on the lifespan. The cessation of consciousness is no longer at issue. The religious person reassures herself that there is a continuity of consciousness after death. As Akhtar (2011) says, "Anxiety about the limited nature of our existence delivers us to the cushion of handed down magic. We open our windows to dreams of heaven and hell, reincarnation or the continuation of our 'souls' in one way or another" (p. 88).

For those who do not hold a strong belief in the continued existence of the soul or who do not believe that the soul maintains a continuity of consciousness, there can still be a narcissistically comforting belief that immortality is maintained through creation and procreation. Some believe that we live on through our children and some believe that we live on through the creative work we leave behind, whether that work be academic, architectural, or artistic. The creation of art or music, of institutions or the production of written work can feel like a substitute for the continued existence of the corporeal or spiritual self.

As such, the motivations for creative and professional accomplishment are myriad but most fundamental is the complaint against mortality. Human beings want desperately to live on. And if we accept that immortality is not actually possible then we can strive to make it partially so, enjoying the feeling that our work will live on beyond our own life spans. We take pleasure in the fantasy of being remembered. Behind this idea is the unconscious and irrational belief that we will be present to watch as others read our work, look at our art, sit in the auditoriums named for us, or walk in the buildings we helped to create. And further comfort is supplied by the thought that those who do so will remember us. As Becker (1973) says in his comprehensive book, *The Denial of Death*, "The idea of death, the fear of it haunts the human animal like nothing else; it is the mainspring of human activity, activity designed largely to avoid the finality of death, to overcome in some way that it is the final destination for man" (p. ix). The books and articles we write, the schools and departments and hospitals we build up, live on in journals and bookshelves and libraries, in our colleagues' and students' memories, in universities and cities after we are gone. Or so we hope and fantasize. We strive to be published in better journals and by bigger publishing houses and to speak to larger audiences, for the greater the audience, the more likely we are to be remembered and the less we have to fear disappearing entirely. Belief in a literal afterlife softens the blow of mortality as does the belief in a professional afterlife, a written record of our existence, a collective memory of our work.

The recognition of the finite nature of life is a goad for productivity and creativity. Just as understanding that there is only one more day before an important examination can motivate us to study longer and harder than on previous days, the understanding that our lifetime is limited can motivate us to move forward productively with creative work. As Akhtar (2011) says, "The horrid witch of mortality becomes the maudlin muse of our creativity" (p. 88). Similarly, Shabad, in his discussion of Frommer's paper said, "I have faith that if I am able to feel my death, I will also feel an urgent mandate to realize my life to its fullest potential" (2016, p. 394). Maintaining a knowledge of death, of keeping our mortality in mind also puts life into better perspective; petty spats are just that and each day takes on greater value.

Moreover, as Thomas, Soloman, and Pyszczynski (2015), describe in their terror management theory, the hope for symbolic mortality is offered by culture in the sense that we are part of something greater than ourselves that will continue on after we die. This is why human beings strive to be part of meaningful groups which have a lasting effect on the world – whether the group be civic, religious, academic, etc. This, they say, gives people a sense of reality with order, meaning, and permanence.

Similarly, they say that the path to symbolic and literal immortality also requires that we each feel some degree of self-esteem. They argue that self-esteem shields us ". . . from the rumblings of dread that lie beneath the surface of everyday experience. Self-esteem enables each of us to believe we are enduring, significant beings rather than material creatures destined to be obliterated" (p. 9).

Defenses against mortality

The yearning for immortality is universal. The need and desire to defend against an ongoing awareness of mortality affects all mankind including the psychoanalyst. Zilboorg (1938) states, "If the fear of death were constantly conscious, we should be unable to function normally. It must be properly repressed to keep us living with a modicum of comfort" (p. 17). He continues, "Man could not possibly be productive or content while simultaneously experiencing, at every moment, the awareness of his own death. While he understands that he will one day cease to exist, he puts that aside through repression to concentrate on the act of living" (p. 18). Zilboorg's statement reflects his own feeling that ongoing functioning and productivity would be interfered with more than a universal reality. Akhtar (2011) suggests that this is not so. In cultures other than the Judeo-Christian, for example, in Eastern societies, death is not kept so far from personal awareness. Those from a Judeo-Christian background may have greater difficulty accepting the inevitability of death than those in the Muslim, Hindu, and Buddhist worlds. Akhtar suggests that it is, in fact, not impossible to live with a knowledge, indeed, a feeling of our impending end, and that denial may be culturally sanctioned and influenced.

The psychoanalyst in Western culture, like individuals of certain other professions (clergy, for example), bears a responsibility not only to herself but to her patients to keep in mind the reality of death, the fear of death, and all the feelings associated with acknowledgement of death. So, while repression and denial are understandably tempting responses to the anxiety created by the acknowledgement of death, what is the analyst to do when confronted by material involving the patient's feelings and questions regarding his or her own mortality and, indeed, the analyst's mortality?

Clearly, many individuals resort to repression and denial. There are some for whom it is especially hard to avoid such defensive maneuvers. In those individuals for whom narcissistic omnipotence is a component of the character, the acknowledgement of limitations of any sort including those temporal limitations imposed by the finite nature of the lifespan may be particularly difficult (Hoffman, 1979). As Kohut stated, the acknowledgement of death requires maximal relinquishment of narcissistic delusions (in Hoffman, 1979, p. 269) and those with more narcissistic characteristics, those who are prone to the use of omnipotent, grandiose, and manic defense may be most vulnerable to the temptation to utilize defensive maneuvers in the face of so injurious a reality.

For those therapists for whom narcissism and omnipotent grandiosity are not prominent character features, the job of remaining conscious of the proximity of death and all the affects associated with this reality while not being overcome by the anxiety associated with this knowledge is also a difficult one. Indeed, we might return to Zilboorg's question, is it possible to be constantly aware of death and yet to continue to live fully and enjoyably? The psychoanalyst, like all human beings, has the desire to quell the inevitable existential anxiety generated by the conscious awareness of mortality, paired with the professional responsibility to maintain this awareness in order to be open to her own feelings regarding this subject and those of her patient. At the same time she will have the normal human desire to live life in the most comfortable fashion possible.

Research which may shed light on this dilemma has been done by Rodin and Zimmerman (2008). In their study of 300 patients with metastatic cancer they observe that death awareness is not necessarily intolerable. They found that such patients experience fluctuating and contradictory self states, ones in which the knowledge that death is real and immanent alternates with the denial that death is coming. Can this state be applied to the psychoanalyst? To some extent, can the analyst herself not strive for such alternating states on behalf of the need for an awareness of death and for the possibility for resonance with one's patients? Can the analyst not allow such contradictory and alternating self states or modes of awareness?

The dichotomous view that death is either accepted or denied is a remnant of the "horizontal split" implied in Freud's psychic mode (Rodin & Zimmerman, 2011). However, in more recent work by the relational analyst Stephen Mitchell (1993) self experience has been described as multiple, shifting, and fluid. As early as 1961 Weisman and Hacket suggest that there can be a "middle knowledge" of death in which states of awareness and denial may alternate, fluctuate, and coexist. This is consonant with the research cited above.

Furthermore, in contemporary psychoanalytic thought, dissociation rather than denial is seen as the more fundamental mechanism of defense (Rodin & Zimmerman, 2011). And this fits here. Dissociation is a defense which is often used in the face of intolerable anxiety or threat. Confrontation with death and acknowledging mortality both raise such feelings, and as such may create a dissociative reaction in some analysts, or perhaps, in most analysts at some times. The question here is, how do we combat our automatic and often unconscious use of dissociative mechanisms?

In their study Rodin and Zimmerman hypothesize that death awareness may be more easily tolerated by cancer patients in treatment centers that provide adequate emotional support to face death in an open and direct fashion. Furthermore, they state that anxiety about death and the capacity of individuals to modulate and process it may be as much a reflection of the relational context as it is of the individual patient's psychology.

This work suggests that we as psychoanalysts may also need adequate emotional support if we are to face death in an "open and direct fashion." Our own relational context may need to include more professional acknowledgement, support, and discussion in order for us to be able to tolerate the difficult and frightening confrontation with mortality that we are called upon to experience with our patients and within ourselves when our patients' situations and material stir up our own existential issues.

The facilitation of patient material regarding mortality and death

A professional man in his late thirties presented for psychotherapy several years after the termination of a long analysis. He reported being bothered by frequent anxiety regarding death. He described having spoken at length during his analysis regarding his anxiety about his own mortality only to be met with the analyst's silence. He spoke in his analysis of the childhood fantasy that he would wake up one day to find out that his life to date had been a dream and that he was still a baby. He understood this fantasy as having been a way to reassure himself that death was still a long way off. He remembered ruminating over the meaning of existence, lying in bed night after night trying to imagine no longer being alive and repeatedly asking himself "Is this really real?", "Is life really real?", "Am I really real right now?", and becoming anxious when he would think "It *is* really real and that means I am going to die." Throughout adolescence he continued to struggle with a variety of anxieties with the fear of death predominating. He developed fears of food poisoning, botulism in particular, tetanus, and flying in airplanes, and understood these as derivatives of the fear of death. And when his father died suddenly when he was fifteen from a rapidly advancing cancer, his worries intensified. He reported talking in his analysis as an adult about his fear of dying, his persistent efforts to imagine ceasing to exist, and his horror of this idea. Not once, he stated, did the analyst actually engage around any of these issues nor did he interpret them as derivatives of other conflicts or anxieties. The only interpretation he could remember his analyst making regarding any of these feelings revolved around his fear of flying to which his analyst suggested that his problem was one of trust, saying that it seemed the patient did not trust the pilot. The patient felt so left alone with his worries about death and mortality, he was so dissatisfied with this aspect of the analysis, and he continued to be so troubled by these anxieties that he sought out further treatment a few years after the termination of his analysis in order to address these feelings.

This case illustrates the difficulty one patient experienced in the context of his analysis in regard to his analyst's inability to accompany him in the exploration of material regarding death. Acknowledgement by the analyst of his or her own mortality is difficult and may be interfered with by the analyst's own denial and repression. When left unanalyzed in the analyst such use of defensive maneuvers can interfere with the analytic function in the presence of material related to death and mortality in general. As such both analyst and patient will be deprived of the free exploration of the reality of death and all its associated feelings, meanings, and ramifications. In such cases, the analyst may not be capable of facilitating the full exploration of the patient's material regarding death and the loss of self. In these cases, it is the analyst's limitation which hampers the productive use of the patient's material and forecloses on the experience of patient and analyst exploring the multiple meanings and feelings around life's ultimate limitation together.

But why might the analyst be hesitant to approach such material? Personal history, character traits, and the history of the profession pertain. There is a reluctance in many in the profession to accept the limitations of the therapist. As healers, we are there to help, not to be helped. Analysts started out as physicians (for the most part) and it is well known that physicians are "loathe to come to terms with the actuality of death" (Lord, Ritvo, & Solnit, 1978, p. 2). Traditionally, many have felt that their job has been to cheat death in their patients and to put forward an image of strength and invulnerability to their patients. In 1978, when Lord, Ritvo and Lord published the first empirically based paper on the reaction by patients to the death of their analyst, little material existed about the feelings of physicians toward their own mortality or even their vulnerability to illness (p. 2). Since then more has been written but the area is still one of sensitivity. Kasper (1959) stated that the doctor is expected to be above personal sickness and wishes to believe this fiction himself. The very motivation for becoming a physician, psychologist, or social worker often involves the wish for mastery over personal trauma, illness, or loss with resulting defenses against vulnerability in the identification as helper over that as patient.

Historically, psychoanalysts have preferred to revise the inexorability of death into a more acceptable form which can then be analyzed as a symptom of something else and whisked away (Weissman in Hoffman, 1998, p. 112). Fear of death by patients has, in the analytic literature, been referred to as the ultimate castration fear and as the most profound narcissistic insult to the ego. While one can see the possibilities in this type of understanding, the question remains whether these interpretations are actually helpful to the patient or whether they are avoidances by the analyst of the powerful affects and associated material related to the patient's – or the analyst's – actual mortality. There may be times when the fear of death is representative of another fear but there are also times when the fear of death represents just that.

When the analyst confronts the patient's fear of death, she must consider her own. Counterreaction and countertransference to this material is ubiquitous and inevitable. Primitive emotions and projections are inherent in any analytic work; patient material inevitably resonates with the analyst's past and present emotions, experiences and conflicts, both conscious and unconscious. This is just as true when it comes to the analyst's mortality and her own feelings about the finite nature of life as it is to all other patient material. Patient material regarding these matters involve powerful affects and these in turn evoke similar feelings within the analyst, simultaneous with defenses in the analyst who may not be conscious of her own wish to "avoid the entire subject."

The analyst's countertransference must be attended to, as always, but perhaps more so in this case; her own fear, anxiety, and frustration with her own limitations and the limitations inherent in being human may all be aroused by material regarding death. The analyst must be able to overcome the powerful defenses set in motion to maintain "sufficient emotional resonance" with the patient (Baradon et al, 2005). Without this there is no way for the analyst to empathically recognize her patient's real affective state and human dilemma. The matrix of transference and countertransference is extremely complex and raises minute by minute questions of technique. Depending on the analyst's theoretical perspective (relational, intersubjective, ego or self psychological or drive oriented) differing degrees of empathy, reflection, self revelation, and interpretation are called for. But regardless of orientation, the maintenance of self-monitoring for defensive reaction is required (ibid., 2005). It is painful to be brought to awareness of our own finiteness and for some analysts it may be awkward to be brought into a shared experience of this feeling with the patient. In this matter, patient and analyst are on equal terms. Perhaps the shared nature of the inevitability of death is one more obstacle to its full exploration in the analytic field for some analysts.

Ironically, one reaction to the idea that the analyst may deny her own mortality may be to deny this very possibility. "I don't do that!" the analyst may think. "I explore death wishes and death fears with my patients every day and moreover, I know very well that I am going to die." Intellectualization is perhaps the most common defense among highly educated professionals. Of course we know that someday we will die and we appreciate that this is true for our patients as well; frequently we treat patients who have recently lost a loved one or who are themselves ill, and routinely we traverse the material brought up by the termination phase of treatment and its inevitable confrontation with loss. In intellectualization, however, we bind the feelings associated with death, and especially our own death, in order to exert control over the anxiety generated by this unpleasant reality (Moore and Fine, 1990, p. 101). We separate the idea of death from the feelings associated with it, thereby sealing off those feelings, leaving us able to interpret and provide insight to our patients without the possibility of experiencing in a feelingful way our own inner experience of the meaning of death – including our own fear, anxiety panic, and terror as well as the patient's similar feelings.

Knowledge of one's own death is not just an intellectual concept but a dynamic factor involved in coming to know and accommodate to the boundaries of self and other. The acknowledgement of mortality is attainable only by those with a truly differentiated sense of self (Hoffman, 1979). Slater said, "The fear of death is not . . . primitive, elemental or basic. Animals have no such (conscious) fear . . . It depends on rather advanced and sophisticated awareness of the self as a separated entity . . . It is only when he comes to see himself as a unique and differentiated entity, with an existence which is separable and apart from other men . . . that he can begin to have anxiety about the termination of that existence" (Hoffman, 1998, p. 25). Both Kohut (1966) and Erikson (1959) view coming to terms with transience as among the highest achievements of human development. Acceptance of our limits requires abandoning narcissistic and omnipotent defenses involving delusions of infinite existence, time, and energy. The acknowledgement of the limits of the self and the finiteness of the life span is a victory of reality over wish. As humans, but particularly as analysts, it is necessary to struggle against the unconscious wish for gratification of the infantile wish for limitless supplies – in this case of time – in favor of the acceptance of the boundaries of reality (Kohut, 1966, p. 219).

The problem here is that acceptance of the temporal limitations of life, for many, can feel devastating. Doing so threatens to divest things of their value although, paradoxically, it can lend them value at the same time (Hoffman, 1979, p. 248). The confrontation with transience and mortality gives rise to an intrapsychic conflict with the ego, both sides of which may be conscious. On one side it is felt that life derives meaning and value from the fact that it is destined to end. Impetus and momentum are gained for achievement and accomplishment. Many find that they work better and more purposefully with a deadline, and death of course is the ultimate deadline (hence the word itself). On the other side, the inevitability of death may engender a feeling that life is meaningless. Why bother to accomplish anything if eventually we are going to die anyway? This is the side taken in depression. The helplessness felt in regard to our inability to combat death results in hopelessness and a loss of motivation. Questions regarding the very meaning of existence are raised by the knowledge of death and the finite quantity of time we each have to be alive.

So is it possible for anyone – therapists and analysts included – to fully recognize the finiteness of life while continuing to live joyfully and with fulfillment? Is it possible to tolerate those alternating and contradictory self states referred to at the beginning of this chapter? Or does this acknowledgement inevitably lead to depression and hopelessness? Hoffman explores these questions in his book, *Ritual and Spontaneity in the Psychoanalytic Process* (1998). He quotes postmodern philosophy regarding the limits of free will and existentialism. What is immutable, transcultural, and transhistorical, he says, is that human beings create their worlds and their sense of meaning in the teeth of the constant threat of nonbeing and meaninglessness. For most this is just too painful to bear fully.

But how can the therapist embody the search for inner truth without doing so? The postmodern philosopher Thomas Nagel suggests a simultaneous distancing and acknowledgement for this "is the opposite of self-denial and the result of full awareness" (Hoffman, 1998, p. 15). This is similar to the dying patient's alternating acknowledgement and denial of imminent death. In the study of childhood mourning, children are said to have a "limited grief span," that is, they are said to have a limited tolerance for their sad feelings leading to periods of sadness followed by periods of denial and happy play. Is this not true for all adults and for us as analysts, as well? Many of us are, of course, capable of tolerating the anxiety and indeed the outright fright associated with the thought of ceasing to exist – at least for periods of time. The question remains as to whether, with conscious effort, we are able to allow those periods of time to take place during the patient hours that require us to do so.

In his article, "Death is Nothing At All," Martin Frommer discusses the case of a young woman whose father had recently died. She came in and sobbed for the good part of a session before saying, "Please, I need you to answer this one question . . . where is my father?" Frommer found himself frozen, wishing to take shelter within the analytic stance by asking where she thought her father was or by retreating into omnipotence as the all-knowing analyst. He answered, using some self psychological concepts, saying that her father was within her and that she would come to see this. In a later session she spoke of sitting by her father's grave, talking to him about her life and Frommer realized that his intervention had fallen flat. He understood that he had not been able to tolerate staying with his young patient in her feeling of bewilderment over her father's disappearance. He could not admit to her – or to himself – in that clinical moment that he did not know where her father was and that we, as humans, all struggle with this question.

This is just the sort of moment we all face over and over again in our work (as well as in our lives in general). Can we allow ourselves to be present for the patient in this moment – and for ourselves? Can we bear to come into the room as a fellow human with our patient rather than staying aloof as the one who knows? Adrienne Harris called the type of omnipotence to which we retreat in these moments a part of everyday narcissism. This way of understanding is important as it portrays the commonplace and habitual nature of this sort of retreat. As Frommer says, "We dissociate the vulnerability of our . . . human condition in the service of maintaining emotional stability" as well as a way of maintaining a sense of being in charge of ourselves and our clinical work.

Frommer presents another case, that of Karen, a woman in her sixties who had always been frightened of death. Once well into the treatment he describes having discussions regarding death and mortality that were more like those one might have with an intimate friend, noting that even with friends these discussions are rare. Recognizing how much he derived from these discussions, he felt guilty for desiring this dialogue with Karen and wondered if she was trying to please him by continuing this topic sensing *his* need for it. He also wondered if perhaps she was gratifying her own desire for closeness with him by spurring a dialogue which seemed to promote closeness between them.

Frommer's openness to the discussion of his patients' terror of death, his ability to experience his own vulnerability in regard to this subject, and his rigor in examining his feelings regarding both the content and the process occurring around this material serves as one example of how an analyst can be available for the discussion of mortality and the attendant feelings surrounding it. Similarly, Salman Akhtar suggests what he calls a novel perspective in which the analyst allows him- or herself to avoid the temptation to rely on the classical interpretation of anxiety about death being a derivative of the fear of something else (castration, abandonment, etc.) and to actually talk with the patient about death. As he says, "All human beings think about their death(s): young or old, consciously or unconsciously. Having such a perspective . . . allow[s] the analyst to see that the patient is making an effort to bring this topic up for consideration" (2011, p. 113). For example, he says, when a patient is in the termination phase he may bring up the subject of death not just as a metaphor for termination but in the attempt to address this important topic before the treatment ends. Akhtar makes a plea that the analyst courageously take this material on at its manifest level.

Akhtar, Frommer, I myself, and others write and speak on this topic in an effort to counterbalance the temptation to hide behind defensive and dissociative processes which operate unacknowledged within psychoanalysis and within psychoanalysts to protect not only the patient but the analyst too. The loss of omnipotence, the narcissistic injury, the vulnerability we all suffer when we realize that we do not have a remedy for mortality either for ourselves or for our patients are enormous and immensely difficult to tolerate (Frommer, 2016).

The denial of death and the analyst's practice

Finally, I would like to look at the effect of the denial of death on the practical aspects of the analyst's practice and on how this may impact our patients.

Case I

A young woman in her twenties visited an analyst for a consultation. Several days after the third session she was shocked to read in the morning paper that the analyst had been struck and killed by a car. She had not received any notification of this event nor did she subsequently. No one called her to refer her elsewhere but she did seek treatment with another analyst whom she found on her own.

Case 2

Some time ago a friend called me. I had referred her to an analyst in the city where she lived who I did not know personally but whose name had been given to me by a prominent analyst in that city whose judgement I trusted. I was told that this man was smart and kind. He was well known and well loved in the local analytic community. My friend had begun psychotherapeutic treatment with the analyst and had been with him for five years when she called. She had become very fond of him, she relied upon him, and trusted him. She had tried different treatments over the years and was very happy to have found this analyst and to have established a steady alliance with him. She found him warm, humorous, and flexible. Her dilemma was that she had gone for her session several weeks before only to find the door locked. She called the analyst again and again only to hear the familiar message. After a while a new message replaced the old one. It was delivered in a woman's voice and stated that the analyst had become ill and that further information would be provided when it was available. Again my friend waited, calling occasionally to see if she would hear new information on the message. For a couple of weeks the same message was heard and then finally, there was no message at all. She asked me if I could find out what had happened to her analyst and whether there was anything she could do for him. It was only when I contacted the analyst who had originally given me this man's name that I was able to find out and tell my friend that her beloved analyst had died.

While it seems obvious to say that analysts need to prepare themselves for possible sudden illness or death and to set up office practices in keeping with this possibility, this is not routinely done. What explanation can there be for this other than the analyst's avoidance and denial of a troubling eventuality? The problem stands, and it is a serious one, that our patients suffer more than they ought to when we do not have a plan in place.

What can be done? First, a written document can be prepared and distributed to a lawyer and several colleagues specifying crucial aspects regarding patient notification and the disposition of cases and records in the event of the analyst's sudden incapacitating illness or death. A plan can be developed for how patients are to be notified and how their records are to be accessed and dealt with. Passwords for computer files can be given to the aforementioned lawyer and colleagues. Moreover, detailed recommendations can be specified and periodically updated concerning to whom individual patients are to be referred in order to continue their work and to work through their feelings regarding the loss of a uniquely important figure in their lives.

At some analytic institutes member analysts are encouraged to choose a "buddy" with whom they not only exchange important information regarding the eventual disposition of their patients and their files in the event of sudden illness or death but they also agree to monitor one another for signs of impairment, another issue which is often poorly dealt with among those in our profession.

It is interesting that we, who pay such close attention to the smallest details of content and nuance in our patients' material and inner lives, would neglect such obvious and important aspects of their care. We endeavor to provide for our patients while we are working with them and yet, as the case examples above demonstrate, we so often leave them completely in the lurch when we suddenly become ill or die.

There are a variety of ways to handle the practical details of the practice in the event of the illness or death of the analyst. A professional will can be made out and, as stated, given to several individuals including a lawyer, a spouse, and a relatively dispassionate colleague, capable of quickly instituting notification of patients without too much affective involvement. Less formally, as mentioned above, detailed instructions can be left with a similar set of trusted individuals with all computer access pass codes, patient names and numbers, and updated referral recommendations included. Ethical/legal guidelines for the disposal of records must be researched so that appropriate instructions can be left regarding this matter.

Conclusion

While it is true that in many people great anxiety is generated by the acknowledgement of the reality and inevitability of death, and defensive mechanisms are activated to ward off this anxiety, it is important for the effective practice of psychoanalysis and for optimal availability to the patient that the psychoanalyst be able to struggle against the routine implementation of defense in order to be able to explore both her own conflicts and feelings regarding her own mortality and those of the patient. As Frommer (2016) noted, the analyst's personal relationship with mortality is a critical variable in how the fear of death is engaged psychoanalytically. The ability to tolerate the awareness of the inevitability of death in concert with the feelings that accompany this acknowledgement represents an advance in personal development of the individual. Feelings of intense fear and unassuageable sadness are to be expected in the anticipatory grief and mourning that one must experience with the acknowledgement of the finite nature of being – but these are the emotions of life and health as opposed to those of pathology. As Thomas Nagel said, "It is better to be simultaneously engaged and detached . . . for this is the opposite of self denial and the result of full awareness" (Hoffman, 1998, p. 13). That is, it is necessary to allow ourselves to alternate between states of acknowledgement of death and states of denial so long as we are aware of this fluctuation. This is by far preferable to the use of defensive mechanisms to obscure the awareness of death for prolonged periods of time while sitting with our patients.

Coming to terms with transience is among the highest achievements of human development (Erikson, 1959; Kohut, 1966) which is only possible after the process of differentiation of self and other has been reached. Both analyst and patient stand to benefit when the analyst is capable of facilitating the mutual exploration of all aspects of the feeling and experience of coming to terms with one's own mortality and, as Nagel says, "to come as near as we can to living in the light of truth" (Hoffman, 1998, p. 13).

Furthermore, the development of theory to support the analyst's attempts to tolerate "the truth" of mortality is yet to be developed. Here I will quote Frommer who said about his own experience,

> While psychoanalysis has been a steady companion, providing ballast for many aspects of my psychic life, my relationship with death is not one of them. In this regard, psychoanalysis has been like the close friend who is not to be found when death takes center stage. . . . Despite profound changes that have taken place in psychoanalytic theory and practice over the last several decades, the human awareness of mortality continues to be treated as if it were not a defining psychic issue. While contemporary psychoanalysis has helped us to appreciate the fundamental role played by intersubjective engagement in helping minds formulate and metabolize diverse and often potentially overwhelming realms of psychic experience, the relational turn has yet to consider the need of the solitary mind to be joined in grappling with its own eventual extinction. (2016, p. 374)

Clearly more work needs to be done.

References

Akhtar, S. (2011). *Matters of Life and Death*. London: Karnac.
Baradon, T., Broughton, C., Gibbs, I., James, J., Joyce, A., & Woodhead, J. (2005). *The Practice of Psychoanalytic Parent-Infant Psychotherapy*. London: Routledge.
Barnes, J. (2008). *Nothing To Be Frightened Of*. New York: Vintage.
Becker, E. (1973). *The Denial of Death*. New York: Free Press.
Buechler, S. (2000). Necessary and unnecessary losses: the analysts' mourning. *Contemporary Psychoanalysis*, *36*: 17–90.
Chasen, B. (1996). Death of a psychoanalyst's child. In: B. Gerson (Ed.), *The Therapist as a Person* (pp. 3–10). Hillsdale, NJ: Analytic Press.
Chassey, S. (2006). Death in the afternoon. *International Journal of Psychoanalysis*, *87*: 203–217.
Coltart, N. (1996). Endings. In: L. Rangell & R. Moses-Hrvshovsk (Eds.), *Psychoanalysis at the political border: essays in honor of Rafael Moses* (pp. 117–129). Madison, CT: International Universities Press.

De Masi, F. (2004). *Making Death Thinkable*. London: Free Association.
Dewald, P. A. (1982). Serious illness in the analyst: transference, countertransference and reality responses. *Journal of the American Psychoanalytic Association, 30*: 347–363.
Eissler, K. (1955). *The Psychiatrist and the Dying Patient*. New York: International Universities Press.
Erikson, E. H. (1959). *Identity and the Life Cycle*. New York: International Universities Press.
Fajardo, B. (2001). Life threatening illness in the analyst. *Journal of the American Psychoanalytic Association, 49*: 569–586.
Feinsilver, D. B. (1998). The therapist as a person facing death: the hardest of external realities and therapeutic action. *International Journal of Psychoanalysis, 29*: 1131–1150.
Freud, S. (1915b), Thoughts for the times on war and death. *S. E., 14*: 275–300. London: Hogarth.
Frommer, M. S. (2016). Death is nothing at all: on contemplating nonexistence. A relational psychoanalytic engagement of the fear of death. *Psychoanalytic Dialogues, 26*: 373–390.
Garcia-Lawson, K. A., & Lane, R. C. (1997). Thoughts on termination: Practical considerations. *Psychoanalytic Psychology, 14*: 239–257.
Gerson, S. (1994). Psychoanalytic engagements with death: Discussion of Martin Frommer's "Death is Nothing at All: On Contemplating Nonexistence." *Psychoanalytic Dialogues, 26*: 400–440.
Hoffman, I. Z. (1979). Death anxiety and adaptation to mortality in psychoanalytic theory. *Annals of Psychoanalysis, 7*: 233–267.
Hoffman, I. Z. (1998) *Ritual and Spontaneity in Psychoanalysis*. Hillsdale: APA.
Kasper, A. M. (1959). The doctor and death. In: H. Feifel (Ed.), *The Meaning of Death* (pp. 259–270). New York: McGraw Hill.
Kohut, H. (1966). Forms and transformation of narcissism. *Journal of the American Psychoanalytic Association, 14*: 243–272.
Lord, R., Ritvo, S., & Solnit, A. (1978). Patients' reactions to the death of the psychoanalyst. *International Journal of Psychoanalysis, 59*: 189–197.
Mayer, G. L. (1994). Some implications for psychoanalytic technique drawn from the analysis of a dying patient. *Psychoanalytic Quarterly, 63*: 1–19.
Mendelsohn, F. M. (1991). More human than otherwise: Working through a time of preoccupation and mourning. In: B. Gerson (Ed.), *The Therapist as a Person*. Hillsdale, NJ: Analytic Press.
Mitchel, S. (1993). *Hope and Dread in Psychoanalysis*. New York: Basic Books.
Moore, B., & Fine, B. (1990). *Psychoanalytic Terms and Concepts*. New York: American Psychoanalytic Association Press.
Morrison, A. I. (1990). Doing psychotherapy while living with life threatening illness. In: H. J. Schwartz & A.-L. S. Silver (Eds.), *Illness in the Analyst: Implications for the Treatment Relationship*. New York: International Universities Press.
Rendely, J. (1999). The death of an analyst: The loss of a real relationship. *Contemporary Psychoanalysis, 35*: 131–152.
Rodin, G., & Zimmerman, C. (2008). Psychoanalytic reflections on mortality: a reconsideration. *Journal of the American Psychoanalytic Association, 36*: 181–196.

Schwartz, H. J., & Silver, A.-L. S. (1990). *Illness in the Analyst: Implications for the Treatment Relationship*. New York: International Universities Press.

Shabad, P. (2016). Will you miss me when I'm gone? Death and our significance to others: A discussion of Frommer's "Death is nothing at all." *Psychoanalytic Dialogues*, 26(4): 391–399.

Traesdal, T. (2005). When the analyst dies: Dealing with the aftermath. *Journal of The American Psychoanalytic Association*, 53: 131–152.

Weisman, A. D. (1977). The psychiatrist and the inexorable. In: H. Feifel (Ed.), *New Meanings of Death* (pp. 107–122). New York: McGraw Hill.

Weisman, A. D. and Hacket, T. P. (1961). Prediliction fo death. Death and dying as a psychiatric problem. *Psychosomatic Medicine*, 61, 23: 232–256.

Zilboorg, G. (1938). The sense of immortality. *Psychoanalytic Quarterly*, 7: 171–199.

Zlilboorg, G. (1943). Fear of death. *Psychoanalytic Quarterly*, 12: 465–475.

Ziman-Tobin, P. (1998). Consultation as a bridging function. *Contemporary Psychoanalysis*, 25: 432–438.

Chapter 2

Psychoanalytic reflections on limitation
Aging, dying, generativity, and renewal*

Nancy McWilliams

When I was asked to give the talk that would eventually become this chapter, mortality was on my mind. I was about to turn three score years and ten, and I was going through a health crisis. A tiny spot on my right cheek had been diagnosed as Merkel carcinoma, a rare, aggressive skin cancer with a bad prognosis. Mercifully, it had been caught early enough that my own prognosis was deemed excellent, provided I had immediate surgery and then a long course of daily facial radiation. I was lucky. I had a good dermatologist, a fiancé (now husband) who pushed me to see the doctor sooner than I had intended, and a pathologist who knew enough to check for the unusual Merkel tumor. Because my face was visibly damaged by the surgery and then by the radiation, my health issues immediately invaded my clinical work, ready or not. Just as when I was diagnosed with an aggressive (and also ultimately treatable) breast cancer twenty-two years ago, I was shaken by this cameo appearance of the Grim Reaper. I had virtually no risk factors, and I was assuming my good health habits were somehow protecting me.

My patients were upset, too. Several of them, even those in my age range who had been with me for years, had not thought much about my inevitable decline and death—or their own—at least not in a realistic, clear-eyed way. Although I am optimistic about recovering this time around, I can now see my funerary writings on the wall, and so can they. Thinking about mortality at seventy is different from thinking about it at three, when I first learned about death and greeted the new knowledge literally kicking and screaming, or at nine, when I lost my mother, or at thirty-five (the year John Updike referenced as our "midpoint"), or when I reached the respective ages at which my parents had died, or when I lost my husband of forty years. And no doubt different still from thinking about it at eighty or ninety-five.

A different kind of experience also went into my deciding to talk about this topic. A couple of years ago, a student in my graduate school supervision group directed a general question to her twenty and thirty-something classmates, asking advice from any of them who had worked with geriatric populations. What had they learned about doing psychotherapy with the elderly? Several students engaged in the discussion. I began to notice that they were giving me furtive glances as they pooled their knowledge, and I asked if they were feeling self-conscious about talking about the aged with an aged professor.

With some embarrassment, they nodded. I began talking about both the up- and the downsides of the years past sixty-five, the point Erikson (1950) originally denoted as the beginning of old age. Incidentally, in his later years, Erikson stated more than once that if he were *then* writing his developmental theory, he would have subdivided the years after sixty-five rather than lumping together the psychology of ninety-five year olds with that of sixty-five year olds. Accordingly, half a century later, Joan Erikson added material to their book *The Life Cycle Completed*, addressing the stage of the "old-old" and the concept of "gerotranscendence" (Erikson & Erikson, 1997). And in 2001, Marcia Spira and Barbara Berger, in yet another needed correction of the historic masculine tilt of psychoanalytic theories, and a protest against the cultural consignment of postmenopausal women to the developmental dustbin, postulated a "penultimate" phase in women between fifty-five and seventy in which generativity predominates.

Some weeks after our discussion in the supervision group, my students told me it was eye-opening to learn of the positive aspects of getting old—the increased self-acceptance and acceptance of others, the relief in not being pushed around so much by hormones, the loosening of the grip of vanity, the easing of competitiveness, the pleasures of grandchildren, the enjoyment of age-mates with shared memories, the serenity, the sense of proportion. I told them about Hedda Bolgar who, at one hundred and four, commented on how nice it was to have nothing to prove now, to be more deeply comfortable with herself and more tolerant of other people. Contemporary Western culture had given my students very little in the way of a vision of late-life gratifications. No one had ever talked to them about a positive side of aging.

And finally, another event in the past decade, one I found quite amusing at the time, prompted me to think and write about mortality and limitation in general. In 2007, just after Stanley Greenspan published the first edition of the *Psychodynamic Diagnostic Manual* (PDM) (PDM Task Force, 2006), he and the leaders of the project's committees asked readers for feedback, both about anything they found useful in the PDM and also about what seemed wrong or lacking. One of the first responses was from a geriatric psychiatrist in Los Angeles, Daniel Plotkin, who queried, "You frame this as a biopsychosocial, developmentally sensitive document, and you cover issues of infancy, childhood, and adulthood. What about the elderly?" The main architects of the PDM turned to one another in clueless surprise, as if to say, "The elderly? What elderly?!" Not an uncommon reaction to such an omission, given how little attention there has been in *any* taxonomical system to those who are well along in years, but a particularly arresting one in this case, given that the modal age of the people involved in leading the PDM effort was, by my calculation, about seventy-five, and several were pushing ninety. We were a study in denial.

Mortality, limitation, and psychoanalysis

At this age, as I hear the waterfall in the distance, the shortness of time frames all my plans and expectations in new ways. As you can imagine from reading a bit about my childhood, I have thought about mortality and its ramifications for a very long time. Now I have a large cohort of psychoanalytic age-mates who, whatever their early histories, are also thinking about it, and in perhaps similarly new ways. It occurred to me that as psychoanalytic professionals, we should be talking together, as analysts traditionally do, about topics that are hard to keep in consciousness and that are not welcomed by our social conventions. And we should be talking in the presence of colleagues of all ages—about getting old, dying, and other unalterable realities.

Increasingly, I notice that we are doing so. At a recent conference in New York City, Martin Stephen Frommer, Malcolm Slavin, Sophia Richman, and David Newman engaged with questions of mortality and psychoanalysis. At this meeting, even though the conference theme seems to invite topics more in the area of eros than thanatos, there has been repeated attention to the relationship between limits and creativity; for example, in Yudit Jung's masterclass on perversion as dying in order to live, and in the panels on aging within psychoanalysis, on termination, trauma and creativity, sex in the elderly, loss and resilience, and illness in the analyst.

I see no evidence, though, that psychoanalysts as a group are any more comfortable with the reality of death than anyone else, as is evident in the anecdote about the PDM. Still, it is a core part of our professional ego-ideal to get our minds around the implications of all disturbing human experience. Several decades ago, Ernest Becker (1973) took Freud to task for not fully engaging with the consequences of the human terror of no longer existing— a reality that Freud, probably rightly, believed was not comprehensible to the vast unconscious part of the mind. I remember Erik Erikson once commenting on what he called the "ego chill" by which one is afflicted when one tries to put aside other thoughts and think specifically about not going on being. Try it: it's terrifying.

In the early 1980s, considerably before there was much psychoanalytic literature about serious illness in the analyst (e.g., Pizer, 1997), my colleague Peggy van Raalte (1984) wrote a doctoral dissertation on what happens to people whose analysts die during their treatment. One of her most arresting findings was that in cases of an analyst's long and eventually terminal illness, those bereaved clients who had noticed a change in their analyst and whose questions been answered honestly tended to do better after the loss. Those whose analysts had tried to continue as usual, without addressing their health issues with the patient, tended to have difficulty trusting any therapist after their analyst's death and were also more likely to struggle with self-blame for the loss ("If only I had been more interesting . . ."). In the case of the sudden demise of the analyst, some went afterward to another professional, whom several then devalued and left (perhaps out of identification with the aggressor, abandoning that therapist as their analyst had abandoned them); most of these settled more or less comfortably with a third person, who helped them with their grief. Overall, the analysands who did the best after the loss were those to whom an "intermediary person" had reached out to offer a consultation in the wake of their bereavement.

Such findings have important clinical implications. Psychoanalysis establishes a powerful attachment. We need that power in the therapeutic relationship in order to help people free themselves from profoundly overdetermined suffering. But the relational power necessary for healing has just as much potential to do harm. Given that our death risks traumatizing those who have depended upon us, I was particularly interested in an ancillary set of conversations that van Raalte had with several very elderly analysts, whom she interviewed about their attitudes toward their mortality. Most of them emphasized that they didn't have to worry about that yet; they were healthy, they ate well, they exercised . . .

So it is pretty evident that a central way that all of us, analysts and non-analysts alike, deal with death is by dissociating any self-state in which it is visible. Additional evidence for this avoidance may be seen in our reluctance, which I can see in myself and numerous colleagues who have admitted a similar procrastination, to make plans for our patients if we should die or become unable to work with them. Periodically, we all hear from the American Psychological Association (APA) that we should have a professional will. "A very good idea," I always find myself thinking, as I keep transferring that task from one to-do list to another.

Another way human beings historically have dealt intellectually with the certainty of their eventual demise is to claim that our knowledge that we will die is a distinctively human insight and curse. One example, among many, of that assumption is a statement that my friend George Atwood is fond of making, attributing it to Pascal: "Man is the most magnificent creature in the universe because he is the only one who perceives his own wretched destiny to be extinguished."

Such beliefs offer the consoling conceit of human exceptionalism. Our species has a long history of trying to find *the* way" in which we differ qualitatively from other animals—it seems to be important to our species-narcissism to protest our uniqueness. Many qualitative differences have been suggested—use of tools, use of language, use of symbols, capacity for abstraction, theory of mind—all of which have been eventually shown to be differences of degree, not differences of kind, from at least some other creatures. Are we the only ones who have a concept of death, of the inevitability that we all die? I doubt it. Elephants clearly grieve, and crows take turns sitting with a mortally ill bird in their flock until the bitter end. We will have to look for other consolations.

Aging

Putting aside temporarily an explicit focus on dying, what about the aging process? It may begin at birth, but it certainly becomes harder to ignore at my time of life. The physical decline is a nuisance, but it is the mental part I find most distressing. I somehow never expected not to be able to depend on my own mind. I could not have imagined this loss at a younger age—my mind is "me" and feels ongoing. But now, I am an exemplar par excellence of Billy Collins's poem "Forgetfulness," which I cannot resist quoting in its entirety for anyone not familiar with it:

> The name of the author is the first to go
> followed obediently by the title, the plot,
> the heartbreaking conclusion, the entire novel
> which suddenly becomes one you have never read,
> never even heard of,
>
> as if, one by one, the memories you used to harbor
> decided to retire to the southern hemisphere of the brain,
> to a little fishing village where there are no phones.
>
> Long ago you kissed the names of the nine Muses goodbye
> and watched the quadratic equation pack its bag,
> and even now as you memorize the order of the planets,
>
> something else is slipping away, a state flower perhaps,
> the address of an uncle, the capital of Paraguay.
>
> Whatever it is you are struggling to remember,
> It is not poised on the tip of your tongue,
> not even lurking in some obscure corner of your spleen.
>
> It has floated away down a dark mythological river
> whose name begins with an L as far as you can recall,
> well on your own way to oblivion where you will join those
> who have even forgotten how to swim and how to ride a bicycle.
>
> No wonder you rise in the middle of the night
> to look up the date of a famous battle in a book on war.
> No wonder the moon in the window seems to have drifted
> out of a love poem that you used to know by heart.

For me, it is names that I cannot always depend on surfacing, nor can I count on retrieving nouns in general. I have "senior moments." I lose my watch, my glasses, my car keys. I forget whether I have turned down the heat or sent a thank-you note. I cannot recall why I came upstairs. I have to ask my students if I've already told them a favorite story or joke. When I see at this meeting people I've known and liked for years, their names sometimes make a terrifying pause before percolating from my underground storage tank to my tongue (thank God for nametags). Only a young Freud could have ascribed all forgetting to unconscious conflict.

I used to remember the patient that a supervisee presented a week or two ago, but now I have to ask for a nutshell recap before the descriptors of the client kick in and activate the constellation of knowledge, images, and associations that were starting to make sense in my mind of his or her suffering and how it was appearing in the intersubjective space of therapist and patient. I wonder how many years I have before these small, accumulating deficits become a qualitative detriment in my capacity to do effective psychotherapy, teaching, and supervising. (Already I try not to schedule patients at 3 pm, because I need a nap.) And yet at the same time, I see ongoing evidence of the usefulness of my knowledge base to the people with whom I consult.

I am reminded of a supervisor I had in the mid-Seventies who was disturbed by a colleague's mental deterioration, probably from Alzheimer's, and alarmed by her insistence on continuing to practice. He entreated his students to let him know when he should be put out to pasture. We felt dismayed by that request; we idealized him and couldn't envision him as mentally deteriorating. But we learned something valuable in his anticipating both an eventual loss of function and his probable loss of judgment about its most painful implications. He is still practicing, by the way, at ninety, and like many analysts we have all known, is still able to make brilliant, intuitive, therapeutic connections despite whatever mental limitations he is managing.

The idea that wisdom is somehow the consolation prize for getting older, and that it compensates for the less benevolent effects of aging, is not entirely a wishful fantasy; neuroscientists are beginning to describe for us in biological and chemical terms the specifics of that trade-off. We are unusually fortunate in our field in that, unlike most professions in a rapidly changing global technological culture, analysts are generally considered by their colleagues to be more rather than less useful as they get older. And, on average, analysts (at least male analysts—females have not been studied) live longer than other people, including other professionals (Jeffery, 2001). Not all loss of function equates with total loss, and some loss may even leave room for newer capacities. And yet I think we should be talking together about late-in-life practice issues such as whether and when and for what reasons to retire, or cut down, or continue working with minor adaptations to our infirmities—all individual decisions with individual pluses and minuses that nevertheless can profit from some communal attention.

Limitation is an old emphasis for psychoanalysts, going back at least to Freud's framing of maturation in terms of giving up the pleasure principle for the reality principle, the ultimate prototype of which is the reality of death. His attention to limits is consistent with a temperate, cautious, mature European intellectual perspective very much at odds with more adolescent American sensibilities that can include, as we have seen all too clearly in the 2016 presidential election season, a sense of exceptionalism, invincibility, and baseless optimism about how everything will come out okay if only we apply a can-do attitude.

As George Makari (2015) is only the most recent scholar to argue, the United States was founded on a radical Lockean metapsychology that assumed unlimited resources, boundless potentials, the inevitability of progress, and a confidence that all problems can be solved with common sense and individual ingenuity (and, one might add, with denial about the genocides necessary to support that mythology). We Americans burden our children with the psychotically omnipotent message that they can be anything they want to be, can accomplish anything they set their minds to do—a setup for depression when the reality of one's limits becomes clear.

Another way of depicting our cultural surround, and noting the divergence of psychoanalysis from the mainstream, is that most Americans subscribe to a version of the comic rather than the tragic vision of human life, the pursuit of happiness rather than the coming to terms with inevitable pain. Many of you know Messer and Winokur's (1984) helpful distinction in comic-versus-tragic terms between the mindset of psychologists from the American behavioral tradition, on the one hand, and that of European-influenced psychoanalytic thinkers, on the other. In the comic narrative, limits are challenged and overcome, complex difficulties resolve themselves in the end, and people live happily ever after. Give us a symptom, and we'll apply a technique that will fix it. Problem solved. Steven Reisner (2016) has memorably called this phenomenon the "commodification of the symptom" and noted how it obliterates the possibility of seeing any larger meanings in suffering. Not exactly the vision of the ancient Greeks, who venerated the constraints of time, fate, and acts of the gods, and ascribed the most painful life outcomes to hubris, the human tendency to deny limitation.

Temperamentally, most analysts are skeptical about comic visions and prefer either the tragic sensibility, or, as Frank Summers (2011) has articulated, the romantic view, which has also emphasized limitation.

All of this is intimately connected with our cultural attitudes about mortality. If we have scant shared language for our essential limitation, and we also surround dying and death with practices that embody various versions of denial (as Jessica Mitford, 1963, and many others since have noted), there is not much room for appreciating what our limitedness might *offer* us psychologically, or what space the ultimate closing off of life might open up. It occurs to me that part of our problem is that we have no lived experience of a contrast class or "control group" to mortality. We have no emotional sense of what we would be in a world in which we lived forever. But I suspect that James Grotstein (quoted in K. Gentile, 2016) was right in speaking of the "agonizing sense of the infinite." Immortality just might be unbearable. And we do occasionally get a glimpse of the idea of death as deliverance. When one gets sufficiently old, or tired, or is in pain, death may be greeted as a blessing. I am told that when the playwright Arthur Miller was asked, in his advanced years, if he would like to live forever, he replied in the negative, saying that eternity would give him "nothing by which to measure my life."

The individualistic ethos that pervades American mythology is a problem for our relationship to mortality. In cultures whose members venerate ancestors, or keep the tribe's oral traditions alive generation after generation, or have more geographical stability than our restless, rootless civilization, there is presumably some sense of the continuity of the larger human group when particular selves exit the scene. In contrast, in a society that organizes its politics according to individual rights and offers little language about communal obligations, much less about sacrificing for the common good, people tend to think of themselves as isolated, entitled units. The prospect of death is consequently the loss of everything valuable.

The consumerism that has dominated American economic life since the middle of the twentieth century has exploited our tendency to think in terms of unlimited gratifications. Public discourse is replete with the implication that getting what one wants—what one is "entitled to," what one "deserves"—equates with life satisfaction. This appeal to our allegedly insatiable drive and limitless narcissism, which is especially striking in commercial ads and other efforts to get us to buy things, has been fed by both behavioral assumptions and psychoanalytic ones. For example, John Watson (1930), after losing his academic position at Johns Hopkins because of a personal scandal, became an executive in the J. Walter Thompson ad agency, where he participated enthusiastically in efforts to shape the preferences of the American consumer via conditioning. Freud's nephew Edward Bernays (1928), often called the Father of Public Relations, was the original advocate of selling products via their implicit promise of more and better sex. As a contrast with this American consumerist pathology, consider the Japanese adage that true happiness is not getting what you want, but coming to want what you have—not a naturally resonant observation to most Westerners, but not an unfamiliar concept to most analysts, given what we witness again and again in our offices.

How do these musings bear on our functioning as psychoanalytic therapists, supervisors, consultants, scientists, and teachers? Although many contemporary researchers in psychotherapy define progress in terms of measurable behavioral changes, analytic therapists are distinctively interested in helping people to accept what *cannot* be changed. While the American positive psychology movement puts most of its emphasis on attaining happiness, psychoanalysts believe that a critical element of psychological health is the capacity to bear suffering. Freud was not joking when he defined psychoanalytic healing as the replacement of neurotic misery with ordinary human unhappiness. Surrender to what is larger than we are is, as Emmanuel Ghent (1990) elegantly elaborated, a necessity of human life that is not entirely devoid of satisfaction.

This appreciation runs across all the major psychoanalytic orientations, from Freud's recurrent reminders that our mortality stimulates our creativity, through Kernberg's work (e.g., 2008) on how the healing of disabling narcissistic pathology involves the acceptance of death and the finiteness of time, through Lacan's (1989) concept of the "name" or "no" of the father (punning "*nom*" and "*non*"), to the concept of the "third" that interferes with the doer-done to polarity and opens a transformative space (Benjamin, 2004), to Lichtenberg and Wolf's (1997) self-psychology manifesto, whose first principle connects a strengthened sense of self, the development of creativity, and the acceptance of mortality. Carlo Strenger's (2009) writing on midlife similarly relates creativity to the acceptance of death and limitations. So does Spyros Orfanos's (2006) exploration of the Prometheus myth; and Leanh Nguyen's (2007) reflections on victims of trauma and torture who have obliterated mortality and the creativity that goes with it. We find this sensibility in collected writings of diverse psychodynamic authors, such as in the 2007 book edited by Brent Willock, Lori Bohm, and Rebecca Curtis, *On Death and Endings*.

Analytic therapists understand the process of accepting what cannot be changed as involving the creation of a relationship in which we can name our desires, rage about the gratifications we may have deserved but did not get, and go through a grief process that culminates in moving on to satisfactions that *are* possible—rather than staying frozen in either resentment or chronic victimhood. When our patients respond to adversity with the complaint, "Why me?" we may be sympathetic, but we also tend to convey, "Why *not* you? Bad things happen to us all." Freud is the first writer I know of who framed mourning as "work"—to my mind one of his most brilliant insights. The "mourning labor" is a kind of toil that we both resist and seek out when we engage in the process he called "working through."

Martha Stark (1994) and others have gone so far as to say that psychoanalytic therapy itself is an extended process of grieving. In an earlier era, Hendrik Ruitenbeek (1983) talked about the task in analysis of mourning one's own eventual death–bringing that issue out of the unconscious where he believed it blocks one's emotional maturity. We therapists may foster acceptance of limitation in trivial ways, such as via offhand comments to patients like, "Yes, I suspect your husband is never going be very good at picking up after himself," and also in dramatically consequential ways, such as the frank admission to a multiply traumatized man that although he can look toward having a good-enough life, he will never again be the self he was before the disasters.

And we now seem to agree that, in contrast to beliefs suffused with the comic mentality to the effect that mourning is "resolved," or that people facing loss come to "closure," mourning never ends. Peter Shabad (2001) has made this point, as has Marilyn McCabe (2003) and many other analytic writers. Unless we stay persistently in the paranoid-schizoid position, sadness about limits stalks every developmental accomplishment. Instead of coming to an eventual halt, mourning becomes the background of the capacities for gratitude, empathy, and generativity. Rupture generates possible repair.

Creativity and generativity

The great spiritual and religious wisdom traditions have emphasized the gains that come out of loss, the appreciation for what *is* that results from the mourning of what *is not*, the serenity that comes with not striving after what *cannot be*, and the ways that creative phoenixes can arise from the ashes of devastation. Acceptance of limitation, via the grief process, seems to be the best cure we have for narcissistic fantasies of omnipotence and boundlessness. We are probably doing even our most talented children no favors when we emphasize their unlimited potential. Limitlessness is too vast a frame for structuring a meaningful life.

In very practical clinical ways, disappointment can benefit people. This is not an easy lesson to learn for those of us with big hearts who hate to disappoint our patients. As I grew as a therapist, I had to learn to become comfortable with confronting patients with limits and tolerating their rage and grief. Initially, I tended to see neurotically unhappy or traumatized people more as hungry children needing to be adequately fed than as angry, aggressive ones needing to react to realistic limitation with pained protest that had to be accepted and even embraced—especially when I was the target of their enraged protestations.

Parenthood helped me with what the cognitive behavioral therapists call a "cognitive reframe." For example, when one daughter was about seven, I told her she'd have to clean up her room by the end of the day. She flounced angrily out of the house into the backyard, yelling that she hated me. I called after her, "You can hate me, but you still have to clean up your room." She came back to the kitchen door, stuck her head in, and announced, "And what's more, I've *never* liked you!" and slammed the door behind her. But she did clean up her room. More important, she seemed to feel a new pride in how she decided to organize her belongings.

I was also helped in my maturation toward more comfort in setting realistic limits by psychoanalytic writing, perhaps especially Winnicott's (1968) idea that young children need to "destroy" the mother and then to absorb emotionally the fact that she survives their destructiveness—one of his most vivid depictions of the relationship between limits and maturation. The growth that comes with giving up the fantasy that one can have everything, including mutually exclusive things, is precious.

Michael Balint (1979) believed that the area of creation is essentially objectless, and hence, because it cannot be studied in the context of the transference, is more mysterious than either the oedipal area or the area of the basic fault, which present themselves directly in the clinical interpersonal space. I agree about the mystery, but I'm not sure that Balint was right about that objectlessness. If my own sojourns in the area of creation are typical, they involve a clear, ongoing relationship with an internalized object, my idealized dead mother, whose "mission" I am carrying on, a process characteristic of normal mourning described in depth by Otto Kernberg (2010) in a touching paper written after the death of his wife, Paulina. The limit of death created a space for something reparative and ongoing.

There are empirical grounds as well for inferring a connection between early experiences of the reality of death and later creative activity. My former student Annalisa Erba, who wrote her doctoral dissertation (2003) on the relationship between childhood parental loss and creative activity, discovered an *American Psychologist* article (Eisenstadt, 1978) and a later coauthored book (Eisenstadt, Haynal, Rentchnick, & De Senarclens, 1989), in which J. M. Eisenstadt reviewed massive evidence that childhood bereavement correlates with creativity in the older years. In this context, by the way, I recommend also the book by Phyllis Cohen and Mark Sossin: *Healing after Parent Loss in Childhood* (2014).

In losing a major love object at any age, survival guilt kicks in, and one carries on, on behalf of the dead person as well as the self. Undoing guilt is certainly part of why bereavement can foster vital activity. If a child believes that his or her hostile fantasies have somehow killed a love object, there would be some need to atone by compensatory good deeds. This effort at atonement is perhaps especially true when there is realistic as well as unconscious omnipotent, neurotic guilt. Adlai Stevenson was once prevailed upon to comfort a boy who had accidentally shot and killed a young friend. He had been asked to do so because he had had a similar experience: Stevenson, at the age of twelve, accidentally shot and killed a sixteen-year-old friend of his sister at a party at his home with a gun that was thought not to be loaded. His comment to the mother of the boy with a similar story was to tell her devastated son, "He must live for two" (McKeever, 1991).

And there is also the simple fact that without a living parent, one has to sort of "make it up"—a very practical kind of creativity necessitated by the absence of a model for one's life. My own generation, now living, on average, an unprecedentedly long and healthy life, finds itself having to make it up in a comparable way. There are enough of us charting this new territory of health and vitality beyond seventy that we may find we have something to say about what the good life looks like in the advanced years.

But I think that the largest contributor to the creative mobilization of resources in response to loss and limit is the indelible lesson that life is capricious, that anything can happen to anybody at any age. Live now, for tomorrow, quite literally, you may die. Death of beloved friends and relatives may cause some survivors to feel that life is meaningless—we often see such depressed people in treatment—and yet it seems to impel others to conclude that one had better live fully in the truncated time one has. And when we can work with the more deadened survivors of what feels to them like unbearable loss, the mourning process may restore them to vitality.

In a similar phenomenon, individuals diagnosed with terminal illnesses often say that they now enjoy life with a heightened sense of its preciousness. Or they have a burst of creativity like the one we recently witnessed from David Bowie. Eric Fair, the National Security Agency intelligence officer who just published a searing memoir, *Consequence*, about his involvement with torture in Iraq (2016), has a serious heart problem from which he almost died, and a consequent heart transplant that extended his life but probably at most for a couple of decades. The looming sense that "the clock is ticking" created in him a deep urgency to get his book done in the time he had.

One wonders what have been the complex psychological consequences for people in our era of, for the first time in human history, not living in a world with high mortality for women bearing children, or with the predictable loss of offspring to childhood illness, or with the much shorter life spans of the pre-penicillin generation. One consequence is a sense of relief and safety, but is there also possibly more ennui, sense of existential despair, and lack of a sense of urgency to live life to the fullest? None of us would likely trade our long average life span for the mortality rates of a previous era, and yet few changes are entirely without some loss.

Most of us have treated patients who may not have obviously suffered in crippling ways but who get stuck psychologically and seem to feel an odd absence of pressure to get on with their lives. They may passively wait for us to tell them how to do so, or spend their sessions complaining about the unfairness of life, or get lost in questions of "What if?" rather than "What *is*, and what options are possible, given that reality?" They wait for something external to change. They destroy time. They drag on in therapies that sap both parties of their vitality, in the hope that the gratifications they should have had at a younger age will spontaneously come about in treatment, and they experience us as hostile, depriving, and/or incompetent when we tactfully suggest that this is not going to happen. Despite the fact that time may be the only nonrenewable resource we have, they seem to have no sense of time as passing.

Until such clients get some kind of wake-up call—until they "bottom out" in some way, or suffer an unexpected illness, or become inspired by a different narrative from the standard American version of getting and spending as salvation—they seem to be very hard to help. In contrast, some patients with calamitous histories and disabling limitations can use therapy in the service of remarkable progress in adapting to their considerable challenges. Our depressed patients often say to us, "What does it matter? We're all going to die anyway." And yet it may be precisely the fact that we are all here on borrowed time that gives our lives meaning.

It is a time-honored task for elders to try to pass on their wisdom to their successors. I find myself thinking about what my own cohort of analysts has contributed, and about the ways in which we are now generative, in that newer way of fostering the capacities of the next generation. Many of our own accomplishments began in a context of limitation: Those of us who are psychologist-analysts were originally not acceptable to the reigning powers in organized psychoanalysis. Instead of licking our wounds, we founded our own creative spaces, and ultimately, we opened psychoanalysis up beyond an insular, self-reinforcing medical community.

In addition, psychologist-analysts founded the "relational turn," a school of thought which normalized countertransference, called for a new appreciation of the intersubjective, democratized the tone of analytic treatment, and attested to the inevitability of enactment. They challenged the pathologizing of sexual difference and opened up new ways of thinking about gender, desire, and sexuality. They critiqued the logical positivist bias of academic psychology and looked at psychoanalysis from new angles of vision: phenomenology, hermeneutics, postmodernism, fallibilism, constructivism, general systems theory, field theory, neuroscience, and numerous philosophical perspectives. They rejected a metapsychology that excludes the arts, literature, and humanities from the legitimate sources of our knowledge and practice.

Even by a narrow definition of science, those who were limited by being psychologists in a medically dominated specialty have accomplished a lot. Psychoanalytically impelled investigations into attachment have had a significant impact on academic thinking about both development and psychotherapy, and ultimately on our general cultural understanding of what young children need. We have created, tested, and improved short-term psychodynamic models of treatment, and we are empirically testing long-term models of therapy for personality disorders. And it has been preponderantly our members who have relentlessly attacked organized psychology's latest descent into the narcissistic attractions of colluding with the powerful at the expense of the weak. We have insisted that our own professional organization, the APA, acknowledge crimes committed in the name of psychology, and we continue to try to hold their feet to the fire.

We have kept alive the moral vision of analysts who have insisted that psychotic patients deserve sensitive therapy, not just medication for their "chemical imbalance." We have developed services for the poor, the disenfranchised, the addicted, the homeless, trauma survivors, veterans and their families, and those in foster care. We have integrated Buddhism and other Eastern disciplines with Western psychoanalysis. Although we have a long way to go in this area, our meetings look a lot more diverse than those of most other psychoanalytic bodies, or, for that matter, of our own organization at its inception, which was overwhelmingly dominated by white, putatively heterosexual, older, urban, Jewish males.

All of the above notwithstanding, it is only fair, I think, to admit to some ways in which we have failed the next generation. We have not sufficiently preserved a psychoanalytic presence in academia, agency practice, counseling centers, hospitals, accrediting procedures, and the differentiation of professional ethics from risk management, as Stephen Soldz (2016) has eloquently noted. We have been blind to many dimensions of majority privilege. We have preferred to talk to one another, and to fight with one another, over talking to the wider world and fighting for the value of an overall psychoanalytic sensibility. We have sometimes behaved with the smugness about our superiority as psychologists that we used to resent when psychiatrists treated us with similar arrogance. Boomer narcissism has been indulged and fed for decades by companies trying to sell us things, from records in the 1950s to Botox more recently. We like to see *ourselves* as the creative generation—after all, we're the ones who "invented" sex, drugs, and rock 'n' roll. People who see themselves as perpetually young may pay insufficient attention to the needs of those who follow.

It is my fervent hope, though, that despite our failings, my generation has passed on to the next era of psychoanalysts the fire in the belly that ignited all the areas of creativity of which we can be legitimately proud. Analysts have been justifiably accused of being highly individualistic, like the culture in which we have grown up. But we are *also* part of a community, a set of social links, a historical movement, and from that larger perspective, not everything about us dies when we die as individuals. I hope that those of us in my own generation of analysts have been generative enough to leave behind a legacy of lasting value to our younger colleagues.

Note

* This chapter was published previously as Nancy McWilliams (2016). Psychoanalytic reflections on limitation: Aging, dying, generativity and renewal. *Psychoanalytic Psychology* 34(1).

References

Balint, M. (1979). *The Basic Fault: Therapeutic Aspects of Regression*. London: Tavistock.
Becker, E. (1973). *The Denial of Death*. New York: Free Press.
Benjamin, J. (2004). Beyond doer and done to: An intersubjective view of thirdness. *Psychoanalytic Quarterly*, *LXXIII*: 5–46. http://dx.doi.org/10.1002/j.2167-4086.2004.tb00151.x

Bernays, E. (1928). *Propaganda*. New York: H. Liveright.
Cohen, P., & Sossin, K. M. (2014). *Healing after Parent Loss in Childhood: Therapeutic Implications and Theoretical Considerations*. Lanham, MD: Rowman & Littlefield.
Eisenstadt, J. M. (1978). Parental loss and genius. *American Psychologist, 33*: 211–223. http://dx.doi.org/10.1037/0003-066X.33.3.211
Eisenstadt, J. M., Haynal, A., Rentchnick, P., & De Senarclens, P. (1989). *Parental Loss and Achievement*. Madison, CT: International Universities Press.
Erba, A. (2003). Paradise lost: Potential long-term sequelae of early maternal death in two exceptionally creative people in history. (Unpublished doctoral dissertation.) New Brunswick, NJ: Rutgers University Graduate School of Applied and Professional Psychology.
Erikson, E. H. (1950). *Childhood and Society*. New York: W. W. Norton.
Erikson, E. H., & Erikson, J. (1997). *The Life Cycle Completed: Extended Version with New Chapters on the Ninth Stage of Development*. New York: W. W. Norton.
Fair, E. (2016). *Consequence: A Memoir*. New York: Henry Holt.
Gentile, K. (2016). Generating subjectivity through the creation of time. *Psychoanalytic Psychology, 33*: 264–283. http://dx.doi.org/10.1037/a0038519
Ghent, E. (1990). Masochism, submission, surrender—Masochism as a perversion of surrender. *Contemporary Psychoanalysis, 26*: 108–136. http://dx.doi.org/10.1080/00107530.1990.10746643
Jeffery, E. H. (2001). The mortality of psychoanalysts. *Journal of the American Psychoanalytic Association, 49*: 103–111. http://dx.doi.org/10.1177/00030651010490011001
Kernberg, O. F. (2008). The destruction of time in pathological narcissism. *International Journal of Psychoanalysis, 89*: 299–312. http://dx.doi.org/10.1111/j.1745-8315.2008.00023.x
Kernberg, O. F. (2010). Some observations on the process of mourning. *International Journal of Psychoanalysis, 91*: 601–619. http://dx.doi.org/ 10.1111/j.1745-8315.2010.00286.x
Lacan, J. (1989). *Ecrits*. London: Routledge.
Lichtenberg, J. D., & Wolf, E. (1997). General principles of self-psychology: A position statement. *Journal of the American Psychoanalytic Association, 45*: 531–543.
Makari, G. (2015). *Soul Machine: The Invention of the Modern Mind*. New York: W. W. Norton.
McCabe, M. (2003). *The Paradox of Loss: Toward a Relational Theory of Grief*. Santa Barbara, CA: Praeger.
McKeever, P. (1991). *Adlai Stevenson: His Life and Legacy*. Columbus, GA: Quill (Harper).
Messer, S. B., & Winokur, M. (1984). Ways of knowing and visions of reality in psychoanalytic theory and behavior therapy. In: H. Arkowitz & S. B. Messer (Eds.), *Psychoanalytic Therapy and Behavior Therapy: Is Integration Possible?* (pp. 63–100). New York: Plenum. http://dx.doi.org/10.1007/978-1-4613-2733-2_5
Mitford, J. (1963). *The American Way of Death*. New York: Simon & Schuster.
Nguyen, L. (2007). The question of survival: The death of desire and the weight of life. *American Journal of Psychoanalysis, 67*: 53–67. http://dx.doi.org/10.1057/palgrave.ajp.3350007

Orfanos, S. (2006). Mythos and logos. *Psychoanalytic Dialogues, 16*: 481–499.
PDM Task Force (2006). *Psychodynamic Diagnostic Manual*. Silver Spring, MD: Alliance of Psychoanalytic Organizations.
Pizer, B. (1997). When the analyst is ill: Dimensions of self-disclosure. *Psychoanalytic Quarterly, 66*: 450–469.
Reisner, S. (2016). *How the APA became the sorcerer's apprentice.* (Unpublished panel talk.) Spring meeting of the Division of Psychoanalysis (39), American Psychological Association, Atlanta, GA, April 7.
Ruitenbeek, H. M. (Ed.) (1983). *The Interpretation of Death*. New York: Jason Aronson.
Shabad, P. (2001). *Despair and the Return of Hope: Echoes of Mourning in Psychotherapy*. Northvale, NJ: Jason Aronson.
Soldz, S. (2016). *How the APA became the sorcerer's apprentice.* (Unpublished panel talk.) Spring meeting of the Division of Psychoanalysis (39), American Psychological Association, Atlanta, GA, April 7.
Spira, M. S., & Berger, B. (2001). The penultimate. *Psychoanalytic Social Work, 8*: 27–42. http://dx.doi.org/10.1300/J032v08n01_03
Stark, M. (1994). *Working with Resistance*. Northvale, NJ: Jason Aronson.
Strenger, C. (2009). Paring down life to the essentials: An epicurean psychodynamics of midlife change. *Psychoanalytic Psychology, 26*: 246–258. http://dx.doi.org/10.1037/a0016447
Summers, F. (2011). Psychoanalysis: Romantic, not wild. *Psychoanalytic Psychology, 28*: 13–32. http://dx.doi.org/10.1037/a0022558
Van Raalte, P. (1984). The impact of death of the psychoanalyst on the patient: Theoretical considerations and clinical implications. (Unpublished doctoral dissertation.) New Brunswick, NJ: Rutgers Graduate School of Applied and Professional Psychology.
Watson, J. (1930). *Behaviorism*. New York: W. W. Norton.
Willock, B., Bohm, L. C., & Curtis, R. C. (Eds.) (2007). *On Death and Endings: Psychoanalysts' Reflections on Finality, Transformations and New Beginnings*. London: Routledge.
Winnicott, D. W. (1968). The use of an object and relating through cross identifications. In: D. W. Winnicott (Ed.), *Playing and Reality* (pp. 86–94). New York: Basic Books.

Early exposure to danger and loss

Chapter 3

Orphans*

Salman Akhtar

> Our patients, who teach us so much of what we get to know, often make it clear that they met disillusionment very early indeed. They have no doubt of this and can reach deeper and deeper sadness connected with the thought.
>
> Donald Winnicott (1939, p. 21)

Words matter. They help us express and convey or hide and camouflage our thoughts and inner experiences. For us psychoanalysts, this is an issue of paramount importance. We depend upon 'associations' – a river-like, undulating chain of words – to deduce the psychologically elusive layers of striving and fear in our patients. Words are our allies. We listen to them and use them with utmost care. As yet we remain vulnerable to collusion with the public at large in avoiding the use of words felt as too anxiety-provoking or deemed 'politically incorrect.' We refer to the external female genitalia as 'vagina' instead of the medically correct 'vulva,' lump all militant uprisings as 'terrorism', and recoil from calling anyone 'mentally retarded' or 'handicapped.' Under the guise of updating our vocabulary, we renounce powerful and direct communication. We struggle to think and speak fearlessly but Freud's (1897) *matrem nudam*[1] is the outer wall of our lexical prison.

These introductory remarks, long-winded though they might seem, are intended to underscore the noticeable absence of the word 'orphan' from our literature. Indeed, the word 'orphan' does not appear in the index to the standard edition of *The Complete Psychological Works of Sigmund Freud* nor is it mentioned in any of the twenty-seven glossaries published over the 120 years history of our profession (Akhtar, 2009). A quick search of PEP-Web, the computerized compendium of the contents of twenty-nine psychoanalytic journals[2] reveals that although there is much written about those who have suffered parental loss during childhood, only two papers (Gordon and Sherr, 1974; Carveth, 1992) with the word 'orphan' in their titles. This can be attributed to fashions of the times and to our well-intentioned desire to avoid hurtful labels. However, one wonders whether there is some anxiety resulting in such linguistic avoidance. An attempt to explore the origin of such unease might begin from examining the word itself.

The word 'orphan' has its roots in the Latin *orphanus* meaning destitute or without parents, and the Greek *orphanos* meaning bereaved, comfortless, and one who has lost parents during childhood. Somewhat greater latitude in the connotation of the word 'orphan' evolved over time (e.g. in its application to animals, unpopular technology, and a single line of a paragraph appearing at the end of the page) but the most prevalent meaning continued to be a child whose parents are dead. Two quibbles arise in this context. Does one have to lose both parents to qualify as an orphan? And, what is the cut-off point, age-wise, after which the death of a parent does not lead to one being considered an orphan?

A quick look at Spanish, Chinese, Hindi, and Arabic, the four languages that are collectively spoken by more than half of the world's population, reveals varying answers. Spanish and Chinese have only one word, *huerfano* and *gu'er*, respectively, for orphan, and restrict its use to children who have lost both parents to death. Hindi too has only one word, *anath*, for orphans, but its origins do not refer to the death of parents. The word actually means 'not protected by anyone', or 'not belonging to anyone.' Moreover, the word is used only for those who have lost their fathers; there is no specific word for children who have lost their mothers. In contrast, Arabic shows a remarkable latitude and sophistication. Not only does it have different words for those who have lost a father (*al yateem*), a mother (*al munqateh*), or both parents (*al la lateem*) during childhood, it implicitly suggests a continuum of the trauma's severity. *Al yateem* translates roughly into 'one has no identity or no self of his own', *al munqateh* into 'one who has been severed and lacerated', and *al la lateem* into 'one who is in utter despair'. Fascinatingly the Arabic distinction between paternal and maternal loss centers upon conflicts of individuation versus the rupture of a fused self-object representation (see the section on mental pain below).

Linguistic and cultural variations aside, the common custom is to restrict the use of the word 'orphan' for those who have lost at least one parent before ceasing legally to be a minor. The word thus has inherently painful and helpless connotations. There is also an air of immutability associated with a designation of this sort and the nihilism that this can portend makes one recoil from it.[3]

At the same time, the background of deprivation and of being raised by people other than parents allows rich avenues for writers' imaginations. Orphans are therefore often chosen as protagonists of literary fiction. Gordon and Sherr (1974) provide a comprehensive list of novels and plays where the main character has lost one or both parents.[4] While familiarity with the fictional characters in their list can enhance empathy for such individuals, it is the step-by-step deconstruction of the intrapsychic vicissitudes of this trauma that truly enlightens the clinician.

The lifelong impact of childhood parental loss

The impact of parental loss during childhood is life-long. Its myriad manifestations can be broadly grouped under the following categories: (i) continued intrapsychic relationship with the dead parent(s), (ii) mental pain and defenses against it, (iii) narcissistic imbalance, (iv) disturbances in the development of aggressive drive, (v) problems in the realm of love and sexuality, (vi) disturbances in the subjective experience of time, and (vii) attitudes towards one's own mortality. In what follows, I will address the phenomenological and psychodynamic aspects of these areas in some detail.

Continued intrapsychic relationship with the dead parent(s)

In *Mourning and Melancholia*, his seminal contribution to the topic of loss and grief, Freud (1917b) declared that

> Reality testing has shown that the loved object no longer exists, and it proceeds to demand that all libido shall be withdrawn from its attachments to that object. This demand arouses understandable opposition – it is a matter of general observation that people never willingly abandon a libidinal position ... normally, respect for reality gains the day. Nevertheless, its orders can not be obeyed at once. They are carried out bit by bit, at great expense of time and cathectic energy, and in the meantime, the existence of the lost object is psychically prolonged. Each single one of the memories and expectations in which the libido is bound to the object is brought up and hyper-cathected, and detachment of the libido is accomplished in respect of it . . . . When the work of mourning is completed, the ego becomes free and uninhibited again (pp. 244–245).

This stance became the centerpiece of the psychoanalytic perspective on mourning and only recently has come under question (Meyers, 2001; Masur, 2001). Rather than undergoing decathexis, the lost object is now seen as getting psychically relocated. It continues to have an existence in the mind but the relationship between it and the self is altered and carries a lesser degree of affect. Freud, who had originated the decathexis idea, took this latter position elsewhere. In a 1929 letter to a friend whose son had died, Freud spoke of grief in the following terms:

> Although we know that after such a loss the acute stage of mourning will subside, we also know we shall remain inconsolable and will never find a

substitute. No matter what may fill the gap, even it be filled completely, it never-the-less remains something else. And actually this is how it should be. It is the only way of perpetuating the love which we do not want to relinquish (Letter to Ludwig Binswanger, cited in Fichtner, 2003, p. 196).

Such an outcome is even more marked in children. Though there are individual variations, generally the cathexis of primary love objects is maintained for years after loss and decathexis occurs slowly and painfully in toddlers (e.g. Spitz, 1946, 1950, 1965; Bowlby, 1960, 1963, 1969; Furman, 1974). With somewhat older children, the opposite seems to be the case; there is an inability to decathect the object representation of the deceased (Pollock, 1961; Wolfenstein, 1966; Nagera, 1970). This is due to a developmental lack of tolerance of mental pain and the deeply disturbing threat of narcissistic imbalance; a parent has after all been a 'self object' (Kohut, 1977) in addition to being a separately experienced object. Thus a split in the ego is established. One part knows that the parent is dead. The other part holds on to the internal representation of the parent, intrapsychically 'behaving' as if he or she were fully alive. Even when they know that the parent is dead, children often show intense distress and make all sorts of actual and imaginary efforts to bring the dead parent back to life.[5]

Pollock (1961) observed approximately similar phenomena in three adult patients who had lost a parent before the age of six. He noted that:

> Throughout the years there had been a retention of the deceased parent in the form of a fantasy figure who was in heaven; to whom the patient could talk and tell whatever he or she wished; who never verbally or actively responded to the patient; and who was always all-seeing and omnipresent (p. 350).

Cournos (2001) comes very close to this in describing her life-long reactions to the loss of her father at age three and mother, at age eleven. She notes that she "could certainly recite the fact that my mother was dead and never returning. This belief existed side by side with the fantasy of remaining in an on-going relationship with her" (p. 141). Echoing Furman (1974), she emphasizes that a child has limited choice in seeking a substitute parental figure and thus finds an adaptive value in maintaining a living image of the deceased parent.[6] The parent might appear to 'spiritually' accompany the child, and later, the adult, everywhere. Or, the belief in his or her being alive might be betrayed by a dream image.

Clinical Vignette

During his late teens, Charles LeRoy, who had lost his mother at age seven, felt a sudden sense of discomfort while watching the scene where the protagonist's mother is hiding in the Valley of Lepers in the movie,

Ben Hur (Metro-Goldwyn-Mayer, 1959). Two days later, he woke up from sleep in an emotional turmoil that had elements of shock, regret, and sadness. He had dreamt that he was walking on a street and a construction worker invited him to see what was hidden under the ground. With great effort, the latter unscrewed the manhole and lifted it. When Charles looked inside, his found his mother fully alive. Apparently she had not died at all and had been living under ground for several years. Charles was shocked by the discovery and felt deeply regretful that he had not known this before.

Less dramatic evidences of a life-long internal tie to the deceased parent come in myriad forms. Aimless wandering that is unconsciously intended as a search for the lost love object is another manifestation. 'Agoraphilia' (Glauber, 1955), involving an inordinate fascination for outdoors, especially ruins and wilderness, is a specific variation of such aimless wandering. Here "the love of the dead mother and the need to master the fears of her, have become the love and mastery of, or triumph over, the petrified aspects of Mother Nature" (p. 703).

Mental pain and defenses against it

While they might not have consciously experienced or registered it as such during childhood, adults orphaned as children remain forever vulnerable to separation anxiety, or to use Fred Pine's (1979) more evocative term, 'separateness anxiety'; this involves discomfort and disorientation over the sense of separateness from others. However, it is the emergence of mental pain, with its characteristic admixture of hurt, disbelief, bitterness, and anger that forms the greatest threat for their ego stability. The dysphoric experience can readily emerge at the slightest of betrayals.

Since the nature of this affect is elusive and literature assessing it is meager, it might not be out of place to elucidate the concept here at some length. Freud (1926) introduced the concept in psychoanalytic literature under the rubric of *Seelenshmerz* (literally, soul-pain). He acknowledged that he knew very little about this affect and fumbled in describing it. He referred to a child's crying for his mother and evoked analogies to bodily injury and loss of body parts. He also mentioned a sense of "longing" and "mental helplessness" (pp. 171–172) as being components of mental pain. In the *Project* he suggested that mental pain resulted from a marked increase in the quantity of stimuli impinging upon the mind. This caused "a breach in the continuity" (1895, p. 307) of the protective shield. Pain was a direct result of such shock trauma. In *Mourning and Melancholia*, Freud related pain to object loss and said that the complex of melancholia behaved like "an open wound" (1917, p. 253). It was, however, not until an addendum to *Inhibition, Symptoms and Anxiety* (1926, pp. 169–172) that Freud linked his economic explanations to his object-related hypothesis regarding the origins of mental pain. He suggested that where there is physical pain, in increase in narcissistic cathexis of the afflicted site occurs and the same is true of mental pain. In illustrating his ideas through the situation of an infant separated from his mother, Freud implied that the object loss leading to mental pain occurred at a psychic level of ego-object non-differentiation. Weiss (1934) made this explicit by stating that:

> Pain arises when an injury – a break, so to speak, in the continuity – occurs within the ego . . . Love objects become, as we know, libidinally bound to the ego, as if they were parts of it. If they are torn away from it, the ego reacts as though it had sustained mutilation. The open wound thus produced in it is just what comes to the expression as mental pain (p. 12).

Thus was born the notion that mental pain is not an accompaniment of any object loss by only of the object loss that leads to an ego rupture. It is perhaps in this spirit subsequent analysts used words such as "pining" (Klein, 1940, p. 360) and "longing" (Joffee and Sandler 1965, p. 156) in association with mental pain. They also resorted to somatic analogies and metaphors. Indeed, in mapping out the affective world, Pontalis (1981) placed pain "at the frontiers and juncture of body and psyche, of death and life" (p. 131). In a recent effort at bringing these and other scattered writings (Khan, 1979; Joseph, 1981; Kogan, 1990) on this subject together I stated:

> Mental pain consists of a wordless sense of self-rupture, longing, and psychic helplessness that is vague and difficult to convey to others. It usually follows the loss of a significant object or its abrupt refusal to meet one's anaclitic needs. This results in the laceration of an unconscious, fused self-object core of the self. Abruptly precipitated discrepancies between the actual and wished-for self-states add to the genesis of mental pain. Issues of hatred, guilt, moral masochism, as well as fantasies of being beaten can also be folded into the experience of mental pain. The feeling is highly disturbing and is warded off by psychic retreat, manic defense, induction of pain into others and changing the form and function of pain. Each of these can have a pathological or healthy outcome depending upon the intrapsychic and social context upon whether they ultimately permit mourning to take place of not (Akhtar 2000, p. 223).

Among the defenses mentioned above, 'manic defense', with its trio of idealization, denial of dependence, and omnipotence (Klein, 1935; Winnicott, 1935), is especially suited for warding off mental pain. *Idealization* tenaciously retains an 'all good' view of the world and oneself which, in turn, defends against guilty recognition of having injured others in fact or fantasy. *Denial* is aimed at erasing the awareness of dependence upon others. *Omnipotence* is utilized to control and master objects, but without genuine concern for them. Excessive reliance upon 'manic defense' depletes the capacities for mature aloneness, self-reflection, and genuine attachment. Mild, transient, and focal (i.e. only in one or the other area of psychosocial functioning) deployment of manic defense, on the other hand, can safeguard mental stability, and, in a paradoxical fashion, permit gradual acceptance of current and childhood losses.

Narcissistic imbalance

A frequent result of parental loss during childhood is lowering of self-esteem. Not having someone to belong to and nobody to call one's own result in a sense of existential shame. One feels different from others, sensing that something is missing that should have been there in one's environment (and in its internalized representative, one's psychic structure). This feeling of being different is more marked in association with pre-adolescent parental loss and tends to persist throughout the later course of life. Ameliorative impact of substitute caregivers (i.e. grandparents, step-parents) helps but does not wipe out this inner shame completely.

Such narcissistic imbalance has many consequences. Idealization of parents, parenthood, and parenting is common. Envy of friends and relatives who did not lose parents in childhood is often evident and so is the tendency to overprotect one's own offspring. Hunger for belonging and narcissistic demonstration of finally having someone to call one's own extends to the marital context, leading, at times, to behavior patterns that could be annoying to the spouse.

Clinical Vignette

Sharmila Ghosh, a thirty-five year old school teacher, was in psychotherapy with me. Having married a somewhat older man who was an internist, she had expected to receive a sense of protection and support besides financial security from him. He was known to be a generous man and, for all external appearances, lived an opulent life. Soon after marriage, Sharmila saw the real picture. Her husband chronically spent beyond his means and his indulgent attitude towards others had a driven quality. She and her husband began to argue about household expenses, among other things. This led to marital strife and, later, to her seeking my help.

As our work unfolded, an interesting detail of their interaction emerged. This involved her husband's handing over the telephone to her whenever a family member or a friend called him or even when he had initiated the call. He somehow appeared incapable of carrying out a phone conversation from the beginning to end on his own. I initially thought that Indian cultural emphasis upon communal togetherness (Roland, 1988) was responsible for this behavior of his. However, when I learned that he had lost both his parents during early childhood, I surmised differently. His handing over the phone to her now appeared his way to tell others that he did have someone in his life, and that someone did belong to him. When I shared this insight with Sharmila, she instantly understood and experienced a sense of tenderness toward her husband. Her telling this experience to him led to a softening of the tension between them.

Narcissistic imbalance consequent upon early parental loss might not remain restricted to such 'minor' psychopathology, however. A tendency to view oneself as an 'exception' (Freud, 1916) might also develop, leading to egregious violations of societal limits and taboos. Arrogance, promiscuity, stealing, embezzlement, and near-incestuous cross-generational sexual activity may all arise out of such an unduly entitled attitude.

Disturbances in the development of aggressive drive

A frequent concomitant of early parental loss is the disturbed development of the aggressive drive. Three kinds of problems can occur. In the order of decreasing severity, these include the aggressive drive undergoing atrophy, splitting, and repression. In order to understand the first of these concepts, namely the atrophy of aggression, one has to re-visit Anna Freud's (1972) statement that a coherent aggressive drive can only evolve if there is certainty of a libidinal object being available. In simpler words, one can be meaningfully angry only if there is someone there to be angry with. This is precisely what is lacking in the life of orphans. Ever uncertain of their belonging to anyone, children without parents fail to develop the normal entitlement to be angry. They lack a 'healthy capacity for indignation' (Ambassador Nathaniel Howell, personal communication, April 4, 1996). As adults, they either do not adequately register conflict with others or readily withdraw inwards; instead of confrontation, there is mere resignation. Commonly seen in schizoid (Akhtar, 1987, 2009b) and 'as if' (Deutsch, 1942) personalities, such striking absence of reactive aggression is not based upon repression. No displaced and disguised forms of resentment and anger can be found. This distinguishes atrophy of aggression from repression of aggression since the latter is inevitably accompanied with derivative (e.g. via dreams and parapraxes) or displaced expressions.

The second type of disturbance in the metabolism of aggression involves its splitting-off from the libidinal and affectively neutral sections of personality. This results in a personality organization that is essentially 'borderline' (Kernberg, 1975) in structure. Self-and object-constancy do not develop if the parental loss has occurred during the first two years of life or are retrospectively weakened if the parental loss has occurred after that period. In either case, the resulting arrest of separation-individuation process perpetuates excessive dependency, keeping the individual psychologically in the position of a child. Splitting-off of aggression also depletes the central core of the ego of the assertive energy required to negotiate the adolescent passage. Of course, this is not an all-or-none matter. Ameliorative presences in the environment may help the orphaned child muster enough strength to separate from primary objects and form an autonomous identity. Yet, in most instances, some tendency toward splitting remains at the core and leads to the persistence of idealized and hated objects in the inner world.

If, however, the love-hate economy in the external surround is in favor of the former, a more integrated self can emerge. Even under such circumstances, one sees evidences that much of aggression has undergone repression and finds only limited expression in rational ways.

> Aggressive feelings are not confronted, labeled, mutually managed, and brought under modulated ego regulation by the child. Instead, they remain unchanged in the unconscious mind and are subjectively felt to be a potentially dangerous, internal liability. When stimulated by loss or threat of loss in a current important relationship, the repressed aggression threatens to breach the defense of repression and erupt in an uncontrolled aggressive act. Other defenses are then evoked to reinforce repression (Settlage, 2001, p. 62).

Prominent among such defenses are turning against the self (leading to self-neglect, self-sabotage, and self-destructiveness), projection (leading to fear of others), undoing (leading to superstitious and compulsive rituals), and reaction formation (leading to inordinate generosity and pathological altruism).[7] All in all, atrophy, splitting, and repression are mechanisms that form a hierarchy in the inner processing of early aggression in parentally deprived individuals. Keeping this spectrum in mind has implications for the treatment of orphaned adults (see details below).

Problems in the realm of love and sexuality

Developing and sustaining attachments, especially in the realm of romance and marriage, are difficult for those who have lost parents in their childhood. The anxiety inherent in intimate bonds (e.g. abandonment, loss, mobilization of aggression) can tax their egos and lead to a reflexive avoidance of attachment or tenacious clinging to loved ones. Often there are oscillations between these poles. Or, the closeness-distance conflict (Akhtar, 1992b) is displaced upon family pets, who are overindulged, or upon inanimate objects which are omnipotently controlled; deep discomfort at any change in their location or, conversely, constant re-arrangement of furniture and art work on the wall, betray the underlying difficulties of attachment.

While there is no one-to-one correlation, the earlier the parental (especially maternal) death, the greater is the vulnerability of developing an 'oral fixation', i.e. a hungry, yearning, and, mostly, passive orientation towards life with an entitled desire to be fed and taken care of. To escape from such dependent needs and fine alternate gratification, intense sexual strivings might develop prematurely. Kernberg (1975) emphasizes that such development powerfully reinforces oedipal fears by pregenital fears of the mother. Under these circumstances, a positive Oedipus complex is seriously interfered with. Adult sexuality is then characterized by either sexualized dependency or prominent negative oedipal trends. These manifest in greedy promiscuity and orally derived homosexuality among men, and among women, in an intensified penis envy, flight into promiscuity to deny penis envy, or a sexualized search for the gratification of oral needs from an idealized mother, leading to homosexuality.

Disturbances in the subjective experience of time

Individuals who have lost a parent (especially the mother) during early childhood also display subtle – and sometimes, not so subtle – disturbances in the subjective experience of time. Now, we know that the origins of the sense of time are intricately bound with infantile experience of intervals between need and its gratification (Orgel, 1965; Arlow, 1984, 1986; Meissner, 2007; Birksted-Breen, 2009). And, we know that the mother's gratifying and frustrating responses are accompanied by intense emotions of pleasure and disappointment to that the "mother becomes the conveyor of time and timelessness" (Erikson, 1956, p. 246). In the Kleinian idiom,

> the baby endures and tolerates the separation because he/she can count on a good object that is firmly established inside himself; therefore, being able to identify with some aspects of this object. The ego builds up concomitantly to the initial notions of the present (which is based on the memory from the past) and it develops the ability to wait for the reappearance of the object in the future. The future emerges as a possibility of representing and waiting (instead of despairing), of repairing and affectively finding again the same emotional state of the contact between nipple and mouth (Bornholdt, 2009, p. 101).

Among other factors that contribute to the consolidation of a sense of passing time are the "forward projection of narcissism" (Chasseguet-Smirgel, 1984, p. 28) on the older generation and the associated injunction to wait (to marry, to be an adult) the oedipal children receive from their parents. All in all, it sees that parental availability and 'good-enough' parental functioning is essential for the evolution of a proper and realistic time sense in the child.

All this falls apart with the death of a parent. Not only the subtle structuring functions are lost, the child's ego is split between a developmentally pressured and inescapable forward movement in time and a stunned clinging to the object before it was lost. The former might go through post-trauma development with variable degrees of authentic participation and accruing of structure. The latter remains fixated upon a nostalgic longing for the now idealized past or a desperate conviction that the tragic loss can and will be totally undone. The former tendency is embodied in an 'if-only . . .' fantasy that claims that life would have been conflict-free were it not for the childhood parental loss. To be sure, there is some truth to this idea but the embellish-ment resides in feeling that life was devoid of all problems before the parental death and that everything would have turned out well had the tragedy not occurred.

A variant of the 'if-only . . .' fantasy is the 'someday . . .' fantasy whereby the orphan relentlessly expects to find and re-unite with the parent whom, in a separate section of his mind, he recognizes to be dead. The manner in which such individuals seek a "fantasied reversal of a calamity that has occurred" (Renik, 1990, p. 234) and strive to materialize this 'someday' varies greatly (Akhtar, 1996). Some pursue it actively while others simply wait and turn towards spirituality. Abraham's (1924) observation, though made in a different context, is pertinent in this regard as well.

> Some people are dominated by the belief that there will always be some kind person – a representative of the mother, of course – to take care of them and to give them everything they need. This optimistic belief condemns them to inactivity (p. 399).

Frequently the 'if only . . .' and 'someday' fantasies (Akhtar, 1996) coexist and form a tandem theme. "If only this had not happened, life would have been all right, but someday this will be revealed and life will (again) become blissful." Such attitudes push the individual out of the present time; he shuttles between past and future, feeling nostalgic at one moment and hopeful at another but always out of tune with the calendar of actual life.

Attitudes towards one's own mortality

The adult orphan often displays an attitude towards his own mortality that differs from his more fortunate counterparts in life. He is either inordinately afraid of dying or, equally likely, is idealizing of death and fascinated by the idea of his own mortality. Referring to the first constellation, Settlage (2001) declares that his

> clinical experience suggests that the inadequate structuring of object and self constancy is an important factor in the fear of facing one's eventual mortality. Impairment of these structures deprives the individual of the

inner sense of being loved and cared about that underlies emotional equanimity and being at peace with oneself. When present, this inner sense makes it easier to accept the reality of one's own death (p. 64).

I agree with this observation. However, I think that there is both a quantitative and qualitative difference in the fear of death experienced by normal persons and that felt by maternally deprived individuals. In the former, fear of death draws affective tributaries from the deepest remnants of annihilation anxiety, fear of separation from love objects, and castration fantasies (for details, see Chapter 5). In those who have experienced childhood parental loss, all these factors are operative. In addition, there is a repudiated pressure to identify with the dead parent, give up the human aspects of identity, and return to an inanimate status (Lichtenstein, 1963). Having, at times, been treated as inanimate by callously inattentive or enraged substitute caretakers has also blurred their inner boundaries between the animate and inanimate, and resulted in their fear that the latter will take over their entire existence. Finally, the despair at dying without having joyously lived is far more, as one would imagine, than at expecting death after having lived well.

The second outcome of having lost a parent in childhood is a tendency to be over-involved in thoughts about death and dying. Death can become idealized and, unconsciously, personified as a beckoning mother or lover (Wheelis, 1966). One might pursue it actively (via gross or subtle self-destructive acts) or await its arrival with inordinate eagerness. The following poem by an East Coast-based psychotherapist eloquently captures the latter sentiment.

> The train of death has started towards my city.
> Only, it is at some distance right now.
> Or, is it?
> Thinking of death at thirty-seven,
> Waiting on the train station,
> I sense the aching of the tracks for the
> Crushing embrace of oversized wheels. Can smell
> The perspiration of the engine.
> Am awed
> At its dark surefootedness.
> Yet, the cold certainty is familiar.
> For thirty years,
> I have waited on this station.
> The pile of newspapers besides me growing each day
> All the news of the world, cross word puzzles,
> Cartoons, editorials, ads
> My luggage for the journey to come.

The poem is titled *Thinking of Death at Thirty-Seven*, the age at which the individual (who prefers to remains anonymous, though has given permission to include this poem) wrote it. What became evident to him much later is that in writing "for thirty years/I have waited on this station", he had revealed that he was seven years old at the time of his mother's death.

Some caveats

The foregoing description of the psychopathological consequences of childhood parental loss needs 'softening' by a reminder that the outcome of such calamity is far from uniform. Many variables have to be taken into account with each having its own pathoplastic impact upon the inner goings on.

- The resemblance of what has been described above with certain features of severe character pathology (Kernberg, 1975; Akhtar, 1991, 1992a) should not lead one to conclude that childhood parental loss always results in such disorders. The fact is that grown up orphans give evidence of a wide-range of personality functioning, ranging from severe to mild psychopathology and even mental health.[8] At the same time, it is true that a sector of their minds remain wounded forever, especially if the parental loss has occurred very early in life.
- Like all traumas, being orphaned may, at times, become the basis of personality strengths as well. Character traits of stoicism, ambition, and generativity especially can be intensified. Diminished fear of death, in some adults with childhood parental loss, can result in remarkable acts of courage and sacrifice.
- As a follow-up to the point above, the presence of 'God-given' talents (e.g. artistic inclination) and superior intelligence can greatly modify the impact of being orphaned. A healthy and ambitious nucleus of personality can get organized around such extraordinary abilities and lead to great fame and social success.[9]
- The impact of a parent's death varies with the child's age at the time of such loss (Bowlby, 1961, 1963; Wolfenstein, 1966; Furman, 1974). The degree of psychic autonomy achieved, the particular developmental conflicts active at the time, and the level of ego maturity together determine how and to what extent would the trauma get adequately 'metabolized' and the nature of meanings that would be assigned to the tragedy.
- The death of a mother might have a greater or, at least, different effect upon a growing child than the death of a father. Provided all other variables remain the same, maternal death tends to deprive the child of 'a secure base' (Bowlby, 1988) and a source of emotional refueling and the father's death robs the child of firm investment in external reality and the outer rind of the ego.

- The gender of the child might also play a role in the impact of parental loss. In general, girls tend to be more adversely affected by the loss of the mother than boys. The loss of mother deprives them not only of the primary love object and symbiotic partner but of a role model and scaffold for the elaboration of core gender identity. The same applies to the boy's losing a father during childhood.
- A major role in determining the outcome of parental loss is also played by the nature of relationship the child had with the parent before his or her death. Unresolved conflicts, especially those laden with aggression, tend to complicate the healing of the wounded psyche by adding a sense of guilt and responsibility for the parent's death (Volkan, 1981).
- The socioeconomic status of the family can also impact upon what final shape the trauma of childhood parental loss would take. The availability of ample monetary resources can shield the child from the harshness of external reality while also providing access to better educational resources and institutions.
- The role of ameliorative influences is of paramount importance vis-à-vis childhood parental loss. The auxiliary ego support provided by the substitute parents (e.g. stepparents, grandparents) can go a long way in helping the orphaned child mourn, salvage self-esteem, and retain a sense of purpose in life. Extra-familial figures like housekeepers, nannies, neighbors, school teachers, and clergy can also be of considerable help in mitigating the deleterious impact of such trauma. Much more important than all this is the behavior of the surviving parent. If he or she remains stable, continues the appropriate development-facilitating role, and attempts to compensate for the child's loss while also empathizing with it, the child can show remarkable resilience. A non-clinical anecdote captures this point very well. Recounted by a Pakistani colleague, Naeem Jaafri, the story goes like this:

> I was a little over seven when I lost my mother. It had a devastating impact upon me. But my father, an internist with a large private practice, was kind and loving and helped me a lot. A year or two later, he remarried. My step-mother was also good to me and yet I felt something was not quite right. I felt she never gave me sufficient food to eat. When I told this to my father, he did something remarkable. He told me that I could go and eat whatever and how ever much I liked at the corner restaurant down the street from his office, free of charge; he would pay the bill on a monthly basis without ever questioning me. I was at first flabbergasted, then thrilled, by this newfound power. I visited the restaurant at all sorts of times, ordering this and that item on the menu. The bills were always paid and no one raised an eyebrow. Within a few months, I got tired of the whole thing and stopped going to the restaurant.

The complaint I had against my step-mother also withered away. Matters seemed more manageable and peaceful to me (personal communication, December 2009).

While it can be argued that my colleague's father should have sat him and his wife down and chatted about whatever was going on between them, such an expectation from a busy physician in 1950's Lahore is merely a psychoanalyst's dream. The fact is that the father intervened to restore the loss sense of omnipotence in his boy, most likely knowing (at least, on an unconscious level) that the matter had little to do with actual food. In doing so, he did help his child.

What this anecdote as well as the foregoing caveats demonstrate is that simply knowing that someone is an orphan is not enough. A larger number of biopsychosocial variables and their complex interplay with each other must be taken into account in order to grasp the deep psychological significance of childhood parental loss. In the words of Anna Freud (1974):

> It is on the one hand the total character and personality of the child and on the other hand the totality of environmental circumstances which determine the outcome of the experience. Here, as in all other areas of the child's life, the interaction between internal and external forces decides between the possibility of normal developmental progress and the incidence of pathological developmental distortion or arrest (p. vii).

Armed with such nuanced empathy, one can approach the treatment of adult orphans in a meaningful manner.

Guidelines for treating orphaned adults

Based upon my clinical experience with adults who have suffered the loss of one or both parents in childhood, I have delineated six technical guidelines for working with them. I must emphasize, though, that I am not recommending specific strategies, only a background for the "evenly suspended attention" (Freud, 1912b, p. 111) that is customary in our work.

Providing a greater amount of 'illusion' and 'holding'

Those who have lost a parent in early childhood have been introduced to 'reality' in a brutal manner. The illusion of absolute safety, afforded by parental 'holding' (Winnicott, 1960), has been prematurely ruptured. Infantile omnipotence, instead of being renounced gradually and in a piecemeal fashion, has had to be given up abruptly. All this results in a longing – however dormant and disguised it may be – for a type of interpersonal relatedness in which one can truly relax and express oneself with little worry about the dyadic partner's needs. All one desires is to be fully accepted, cared for, and treated with exquisite empathy and devotion. Not that there is no aggression, hostility, and revenge fantasies contained in the patient's psyche but at the beginning stage of treatment, these are not fully accessible for the patient to experience and explore. That work will emerge but only after the patient has experienced an illusory 'dual unity' (Mahler et al, 1975) for a sufficiently long period of time.

The predominant therapeutic task with orphaned adults is therefore to create and sustain a proper 'holding environment' (Winnicott, 1960). Besides the physical comfort and stability of the office where the two parties meet (for details see Akhtar 2009c), this includes a psychological ambience of trust, safety, non-judgmental acceptance, and containment of affects while helping the patient's growth potential to be activated. To be sure, such provision is important in the treatment of all patients but it acquires greater valence in those with a background of childhood parental loss.

A concrete expression of such therapeutic attitude resides in seeing the patient in a face-to-face position. The availability of visual contact with the actual person of the analyst subliminally gratifies the 'real' object hunger of these patients to the extent that it becomes possible to discuss it. Even when a more traditional psychoanalytic treatment is undertaken, an initial period of sitting up for at least a few weeks is helpful; this leads to a certain amount of internalization of the analyst and diminishes the impact of the visual loss upon beginning to lie down on the couch (Akhtar, 1992b). During the analytic treatment also, an atmosphere needs to be created whereby the patient feels comfortable to sit up from time to time; such departures from the recumbent position might be interpreted or benignly accepted depending upon the analyst's empathic sense of what is going on and how to handle it best. Celenza's (2005) recommendation that "every analysis should, at some point, include both modalities [sitting up and lying down] for some period of time" (p. 1656) is important to remember in this context. She notes that both lying down on the couch and sitting up on the chair have their own pros and cons and each can facilitate dialogue, even self-revelation, though in different ways.

Individuals who have suffered childhood parental loss also need a greater leeway with physically settling in the office and making it their own, so to speak. They often borrow magazines from the waiting room and, indeed, should be readily allowed to do so without making any interpretations. Abrams' (1978) concept of 'developmental intervention' is pertinent in this context. This refers to the analyst's supportively 'permitting' or underscoring the progressive trend when a hitherto thwarted capacity has emerged as a result of the analyst's 'holding' or interpretive activity. From this perspective, an orphaned adult's taking things from the office or the waiting room is seen as the resumption of the healthy sense of entitlement (over parents) that had been ruptured by the parental death. The analyst's upholding this newly acquired ability of the patient facilitates the emergence of experiential building-blocks necessary for further development.

Validating the importance and the 'unfairness' of the loss

The therapist must offer empathic resonance to the adult orphan's loss and its profound effects upon him. If the patient asks whether it was 'fair' that his mother or father died when he was a little child, the therapist should not hesitate to say that it was certainly 'unfair'. Somewhat later in their work, the therapist might also point out that the question of something being 'fair' or 'unfair' is itself a concern of childhood; adult life is replete with randomness and unfairness both against and in favor of oneself. Subsequently, the therapist might add that, given the vantage point of a developing child it *is* unfair to have lost a parent and be left bereft of support and belonging. Such 'mirroring' (Kohut, 1977) and 'affirmative' (Killingmo, 1989) interventions can have healing effects of their own. Pine's (1997) remark that, at times, the seemingly non-specific elements of technique acquire high individualized therapeutic effects is relevant in this context.

In working with such patients, one often comes across the fact that significant adults in their background did not help them mourn the death of the parent. In fact, they avoided the topic and acted as if everything had returned to normal very soon after the child's parent had died. The true subjective experience of the orphaned child was not validated. This, in turn, led to the child (and, subsequently, the adult) feeling even more lonely and isolated. The longing for genuine recognition became intensified and, at times, quite blatant.

Clinical Vignette
Charles LeRoy (see Clinical Vignette above) had lost his mother at the age of seven and was soon abandoned by his father. Raised by aging grandparents and sundry relatives, Charles had no memory of any adult every talking to him about his mother's death. Everyone treated him kindly but this in itself was far removed from the shattered inner experience that he was going through. Charles once visited a remote uncle who worked as a superintendent of an old style orphanage. Upon seeing the place and the collective life of the institutionalized children, Charles felt a sharp pang of longing to be enrolled there. The environment mirrored his true self and held the promise of a authentic identity for him.

Listening to this kind of experience teaches us the importance of genuine mirroring and validation while dealing with orphaned adults. Any attempt to minimize the long-term, indeed life-long, impact of childhood parental death negates the patients' subjectivity and erodes therapeutic alliance with them.

At the same time, it should be underscored that validation is not restricted to verbal remarks. The well-timed raising of an eyebrow, the attuned leaning forward in the chair while talking to the patient, and a confirming nod of the head often carry more weight than the therapist's words. Even a respectful acceptance of the patient's silence can make the patient feel deeply understood. The following observation of Klein (1963) eloquently captures this point.

> However gratifying it is in later life to express thoughts and feelings, to a congenial person, there remains an unsatisfied longing for an understanding without words – ultimately for the earliest relations with the mother. This longing contributes to the sense of loneliness and derives from the depressive feeling of an irretrievable loss (p. 301).

That this longing is much more intense in individuals who have lost parents (especially the mother) goes without saying.

Discerning the defenses against the awareness of the pervasive impact of the loss

Not infrequently, adults who have been orphaned as children enter psychotherapy and psychoanalysis for reasons that are overtly unrelated to their childhood trauma. They know the facts of their loss but do not realize how deep and pervasive its impact has been over them. The following cases illustrate how a background of pain pervades their lives and, in unconscious ways, contributes to their presenting symptoms.

Clinical Vignette

Sol Ackerman, a thirty-five year old internist, became symptomatic a few months after the birth of his son. He was madly 'in love' with the baby and reacted with intense pain to the slightest in-attention of his wife towards the child. This led to friction between them which was fueled by Sol's repeatedly calling home from work to check on his infant son's welfare. The marital tension was not all, though. Sol was aware of some gnawing anguish that was threatening to break through his otherwise composed persona, a pain the true origins of which he could not fathom.

In the second session of his treatment, Sol reported the following dream: "I am flying a small plane, solo. Its engine is having some trouble. I land the plane on the North Pole and come out seeking help. There is snow everywhere. I walk. And then suddenly I come across this woman sitting on a bench. But there is something very peculiar about the woman. She is made entirely of small icicles. She is brittle and can not move. Just as I am looking at her, my good friend Bob appears on the scene. He and I help the woman to rise up and begin walking.

The scene changes. Now I am in Spain, a country I have never visited in reality. I am in a tavern. There is red wine being served. And, there are lively and beautiful women everywhere."

Sol's associations led to the memory of his mother's developing scleroderma when he was four years old and, over the next two years, developing contractures of skin and joints. She died, when Sol was six, in an immobile and 'frozen' state. Amidst sobs, Sol began to see how the dream revealed his wish to be helped by his analyst (represented by his friend, Bob) to thaw this frozen grief and move on with his life to more enjoyable activities. The analysis of this dream not only opened up the floodgates to the memories of his childhood loss (and how it had always remained with him) but also to associations that provided links between his maternal loss and his anxious insistence upon his wife remaining constantly available to his baby son.

Such stirring up of childhood loss at the time of becoming a parent is understandable. However, events that can trigger the trauma of orphanhood are diverse and, at times, far removed from the realm of parent-child interaction.

Clinical Vignette
Mary Thompson, a retired librarian in her mid-sixties, sought my help for panic attacks which interfered in her ability to function optimally. She had received ongoing but ultimately unhelpful treatment for the past twenty years. Mary had managed to function but her anxiety attacks had never gone away. She grew increasing disenchanted, angry, and depressed as she found herself unable to maintain the lifestyle that she had in the past.

Her symptoms appeared twenty years ago when she was bitten by a venomous snake while vacationing with her friends. She was treated by the local doctors with the appropriate anti-venom and flown home. However, upon her return she suffered a toxic reaction, which affected her body such that it swelled up and she was unable to move. Her medical doctor, unfamiliar with the particular anti-venom administered, put her through a series of tests that caused further incapacitation and left her feeling helpless and furious. Though the situation was eventually rectified, it precipitated the onset of her anxiety-related symptoms.

During the initial sessions of the treatment, Mary revealed the details of a tragic childhood. She lost both parents at three years of age. Her father bludgeoned Mary's mother to death. He then took a shotgun to his head and killed himself as his young daughter (Mary) and his infant son lay in a crib in the next room. The children were soon placed in an orphanage and, over time, adopted by different families. Mary, at age five, was sent from her native state to live with adoptive parents.

Mary grew very fond of her adoptive mother though she cared little for her adoptive father who was abusive both towards her and his wife. Mary moved out of the house during her late teens, when her adopted mother died. She then pursued a semi-professional degree and found a job, which earned her a decent income. An avid sportswoman, she became active in the local women's soccer team. She also enjoyed writing poetry and had over the years written a fair amount of it. Though Mary had maintained some connection with her brother, spending her summer holidays with him, it was only after she became an adult did she have the freedom and flexibility to develop family ties of her own choosing. This consisted of a female lover with whom she had been living for over forty years.

Though Mary knew of her early parental loss, it was only during our work together that she began to connect that trauma with her current symptoms. Initially, she spoke of these losses through clenched teeth and tense posture, and responded with anger to my inquiries. I decided to stop asking questions and simply listen as her narrative unfolded. Mary was skeptical of any treatment and angry at the world of doctors. I listened patiently, affording her the space that she needed yet maintaining a neutral yet empathic stance towards her. I did not offer immediate relief, just the sense that that in time we would understand all this together.

In time, both Mary and I were able to link the onset of her symptoms to her early childhood trauma. The loss of her parents, which left her an orphan, introduced her to a profound sense of helplessness. She recalled hearing her father bludgeoning her mother and then the sound of the shotgun. While she attempted to run out of the house (at age three!) with her baby brother, the sense of being overwhelmed and without any support remained inside her. This feeling of helplessness emerged repeatedly during her stay in the orphanage. Such was the case when she had to abide by ideosyncratic 'house rules' and, more importantly, to witness her brother (and the little friends that had made there) being sent away for adoption. Mary could now begin to understand why the immobility following the snake bite episode had stirred a deep sense of anxiety in her. As she developed a deeper insight into the nature of her current symptoms and the childhood narrative that lay hidden in them, Mary began to feel less anxious and resumed some of her earlier activities.

While both foregoing cases portray anxiety-related symptoms as the presenting features that gradually led to the discerning of the long-term effects of childhood parental loss, the clinical picture in such situations varies greatly. At times, patients seek help because they have become depressed in the face of a current loss which triggers the earlier but dormant trauma.

At other times, the clinical picture is one of self-destructive acting out that turns out to be a desperate cry for help.

Clinical Vignette

Susan King, an attractive college student in her mid-twenties was referred to me following a sudden onset of depression precipitated by the death of her maternal grandmother. Despite a trial of antidepressants by her family physician, Susan's symptoms did not lessen. Instead, she found herself abruptly ending a relationship of five months. Her uncontrollable crying and inability to study finally brought her to my office.

I gathered that Susan had lost her mother in an automobile accident, when she was five years old. Following this, her father remarried and Susan was placed in the care of caretakers who came and went as the family struggled to deal with their departures. Susan later moved away from home to attend college. Following this, she procured a job in the adjoining state where I had my practice.

Later, Susan narrated a more complex history of her childhood and adult life. She had terminated a relationship of five months describing it as nothing but sexual and one that could not be sustained anyway. Prior to that, she had ended a meaningful relationship with a young man that had lasted five years. Though she described this relationship as being 'ideal' in many ways, she nevertheless engaged in destructive behaviors, including sexual promiscuity, that were bound to destroy the bond.

A picture of early childhood neglect also emerged. After her mother died, Susan was placed in a new school. Too ashamed to talk about her loss, she kept silent. She often went to school with a disheveled appearance receiving little supervision from her stepmother or the ever-changing cadre of housekeepers. The youngest of five siblings, she was often in the company of teenagers who overlooked her need to be supervised. She soon became a participant in their sexual play and this dominated most of her adolescent life.

As our work deepened, the pattern of self-destructive behaviors became more apparent. On one occasion, she, along with a girlfriend, went on a trip and 'played a game of roulette with the drug Ecstasy.' What this essentially entailed was taking the drug without knowing the vendor, off the street – an extremely dangerous thing to do. Susan had a history of some drinking and doing drugs but this was certainly out of character for her. At another time, she 'crashed 'party in her neighborhood wearing a short leather skirt, boots and a sexy top.' Again, this was out of character for her, as she frequented the church on weekends and was a devout Christian. Besides such dangerous enactments, there was a deepening attachment to me. Susan now began to have enormous difficulty leaving the office. She cried in almost every session as she recalled painful memories of her deceased mother. As a child, she was numb but clung to her housekeepers, becoming distraught when they would leave. This part was now present in my office.

Susan could now begin to connect her symptoms to her early childhood loss of her mother. It became clear that her counterphobic risk-taking was an unconscious cry for help; it betrayed a wish that I (as a parent) protect her from all dangers. The hitherto unrecognized and yet dominant role of the number five (e.g., her breakups at five months and five years, her going to the fifth floor of my building even though my office was located on the fifteenth floor) could be seen as a magical attempt to return to age five (when she lost her mother) in order to thaw the frozen grief within her.

Besides the sort of interpretative linkages described in the three vignettes above, the analyst must keep his ears attuned to listening for the subtle ways in which the death of a parent in childhood is denied and the full moving over it postponed. Here, the disarmament of the 'if-only' and 'someday' fantasies (Akhtar, 1996b) acquires a central technical role. It is as if what the child could not mourn, the adult is refusing to mourn. That this needs holding, containing, unmasking, and interpreting goes without saying (for details of technique vis-à-vis such fantasies, see Akhtar, 1996b).

Additionally, an eye must be kept on the vicissitudes of aggression in such patients. If one suspects a mal-development and atrophy of aggression in them, gentle questioning about it and encouragement to be more expressive might be indicated. Also useful might be unmasking the patient's lack of entitlement. With patients whose aggression has become split off from the main sector of the personality, it might help to make 'bridging interventions' (Kernberg, 1975) that involve the analyst's display (by gentle verbal reminders or a subtle shift in the tone of voice) that he, at least, has not forgotten the transference configuration that is opposite to the one currently active. Finally, with patients in whom aggression has undergone massive repression, the customary work of defense analysis and transference interpretation is indicated.

Interpreting the defensive uses of one's status as an orphan

Another important task in the treatment of orphaned adults involves discerning the moments when the lament of loss is serving a 'screen' (Akhtar, 2009, p. 253) function and keeping even more troubling intrapsychic matters in abeyance. Often the 'pre-death' family environment has not been as tranquil as initially portrayed by the patient. In the case of one particular patient, for instance, there had been many shifts of family residence, the death of a beloved aunt, and a painful separation from the biological father *before* the patient lost his mother at age seven. The traumatic effects of the preceding incidents had, however, been glossed over by the patient who attributed all his difficulties to the death of his mother. Certainly there is little reason to regard this case to be exceptional in clinical practice.

Given the fact that orphanhood has diverse consequences and there is a dialectical relationship between the direct and indirect damage that has occurred as a result, it is hardly surprising that patients can use one as a defense against the other. Take, for instance, the patient's need for validation that he or she has suffered a major loss and this indeed has been a very unfortunate occurrence. This can acquire a sadomasochistic coloration. One who asks over and over again if it was 'good' or 'fair' that his parent(s) died during childhood is hardly looking for a mirroring confirmation. Such 'interrogation' is better responded to by clarifying its affective tone, unmasking the denial (of the therapist's having already stated that it was 'unfair') implicit in it, and interpreting the sadistic ('you do not believe me') and masochistic ('see how fate has dealt me a cruel blow') transferences inherit in it. The desperate object hunger, the near-addictive masochism, and the unconscious sadism can only then come to surface. Endlessly patient listening to repetitive material and going on and on with 'affirmative interventions' (Killingmo, 1989) is not technically appropriate under such circumstances. Here I wish to reiterate an earlier comment of mine.

> Listening is good. Listening patiently for a long time is better. But listening forever to material that is all too familiar constitutes a collusion with the patient's sadomasochism and narcissism. Such listening is contrary to the purposes of psychoanalysis (Akhtar, 2007c, p. 13).

Paying special attention to termination and post-termination phases of the treatment

Though it is not possible to generalize, there is ample foundation to the thought that terminating treatment might be harder for those with a background of childhood parental loss. Letting go of the nurturing and development-enhancing relationship provided by psycho-analysis (or intensive psychotherapy) is likely to re-awaken the wound of childhood loss. This can be mitigated by the judicious use – in varying and individually tailored combinations – of the following measures:

- Arriving at the decision to terminate more slowly than usual and with much greater attention to the patient's vulnerability in this regard.
- Having a longer interval between the day one agrees to terminate and the day one decides the actual date of termination.
- Setting the date of termination fairly in advance, i.e., at least 6 months or so still left to work together.

- Following Martin Bergman's (2005) recommendations, conducting the last few hours of treatment with the patient sitting up and with the analyst and patient assessing what has been accomplished and what further work might still be there to do on one's own. "During this time, the two partners are speaking to each other more as equals than they did during the analysis itself" (p. 251).
- Following Joseph Schachter's (1990, 1992) recommendations, bringing up the possibility of post-termination contacts though leaving the choice to exercise this option and to initiate it to the patient.

These five guidelines seek to provide auxiliary ego support for the patient for whom separation and loss are especially painful. However, these are only pointers, not rules. Their use has to be tailored to individual situations, keeping the strengths and 'soft spots' of each particular patient in mind.

Managing the countertransference experience

Working with adults who have lost one or both parents in childhood can evoke powerful countertransference responses. Pertinent in this context is the following observation by Parens (2010), even though it is made in the context of children grieving over the death of a parent.

> Many empathic adults find it difficult to tolerate a young child's experiencing intense psychic pain. We know in our field that helping such a child deal with his/her feelings, thoughts, and fantasies is extremely painful not only for the remaining sensitive parent, but also for such teachers, and it is even taxing for therapists. Yet, we know that we cannot help a child cope with painful experiences without empathetically allowing the child's affects to resonate within our own psyche, with our own experiences of object loss, an experience unavoidably painful to a greater or lesser degree for each of us (p. 43).

Similar difficulties can arise in the treatment of adults who have suffered childhood parental loss. Their desperate hunger for the deceased parent, their wistful longing for the analyst to provide the guidance expected from the parent who is no more, their soul-wrenching pain at the inability to turn the clock back, and their recurring reminder about the unfairness of what happened, can together strain the analyst's work ego. The fact that the transferences of these patients have a markedly 'real' quality can also compromise his interpretive skills. The difficulty is compounded if the analyst has also suffered a similar childhood loss.

The resulting countertransferences can lead either to a defensive recoil from the patient's anguish or to an overidentification with the consciously-avowed 'traumatized child' self. The former tendency can lead to viewing the patient's wailing mostly as a defense against other, more 'primitive' or more 'advanced' conflicts. The latter tendency can lead to over-gratification of the patient and non-activation (hence, non-interpretation) of negative transference constellations. The former stance overlooks the patient's dependent strivings. The latter ignores the patient's resilience and creativity in face of the loss. The former type of countertransference leaning minimizes the patient's need for continuity and availability (e.g., for knowing where the analyst is going for vacation, for having some contact during long breaks in treatment). The latter type of counter-transference leaning minimizes the patient's developmental need for autonomy and to bear a modicum of pain at separations. Clearly, both extremes are to be avoided. A sustained, though benevolent, vigilance towards one's own emotional participation in the therapeutic process goes a long way in assuring a balanced stance.

Concluding remarks

In this chapter, I have surveyed the multilayered consequences of childhood parental loss. Employing the much avoided but direct and evocative designation 'orphan,' I have elucidated the life-long struggles and vulnerabilities of individuals whose parents have died early on in their lives. The realms in which long-term consequences of this trauma can be found include those of aggression, narcissism, love and sexuality, subjective experience of time, and attitudes toward one's own mortality. However, a more central issue is the intrapsychic relationship the 'orphan' maintains with his or her lost parent. Never fully relinquished, this internal object-representation exerts a powerful influence on the individual, an influence that can be pathogenic (e.g. life-long vulnerability to separation anxiety) or salutary (e.g. enhanced ambition and creativity). Clearly, the balance of outcome depends upon a large number of factors that include the age at which the loss occurred, the nature of relationship with the parent before he or she died, the constitutional talents of the child, the degree of love and reliability offered by the surviving parent and/or substitute parental figure(s), the availability of health-promoting role models, the monetary stability of the family and, the degree to which those around the child were willing and/or able to facilitate his mourning of the loss. This last mentioned factor can not be overemphasized since many adults feel uncomfortable in seeing a child sad and distract him from the work of mourning instead of helping him with it.

All this has consequences for the treatment of adults who have lost one or both parents during childhood. A greater degree of 'illusion' and 'holding', validation of the tragic nature of the loss, clarification and interpretation of defenses against mourning, unmasking of the defensive uses of the tragedy and of its consequences, and careful monitoring of the countertransference experience constitute the needed background for conducting psychotherapy and psychoanalysis with such patients.

While I have covered a fairly large territory of concerns, there still remain matters that need to be understood. Four unaddressed areas readily come to mind. *First*, and foremost, since childhood parental loss hardly ever occurs in isolation from other potentially pathogenic influences (e.g. destabilized family, compromised monetary situations, depressed caretakers), it is important that comparative long-term studies be made of 'real' versus 'psychic' orphans. The latter designation includes children abandoned by parents and raised in haphazard ways by this or that reluctant relative and children who were misinformed that their mother or father had died only to later find out the actual truth about the situation. Such comparative data might help distinguish the psychopathological impact of parental loss from other complicating factors that are often associated with it but are not specific to it. *Second*, while I have mentioned, in passing, the poignant depiction of orphans in literature, a thorough comparison of the personality characteristics attributed to them is still awaiting. Such pooling of the available 'data' might help in developing a finer and more sophisticated composite profile of the adult orphan's psychic functioning. *Third*, more knowledge is needed regarding whether the old style orphanages (or some contemporary reincarnation of them) are more ego-supportive of an orphan child or is it better that the child be shielded from orphanhood becoming a part of his identity? Investigations along this line might also yield strategies to help diminish what I call the 'shame of the motherless child' and to improve coping skills of the traumatized child. *Finally*, a critical revisiting of the psychoanalytic case reports dealing with orphaned children and adults – since it was last done over three decades ago (Furman, 1974) – is warranted in order to fine tune therapeutic strategies that best serve this clinical population. The technical guidelines I have offered in this chapter need to be examined, supported or refuted, and further elaborated upon by others.

As work along the lines suggested above evolves, the answer to the most frequently asked question in this realm ("does one every fully get over an early childhood parental loss?") might find further refinement and nuance. Meanwhile, Erna Furman's (1974) observation remains valid: "Some may be better able to cope with this tragedy than others; for all, it becomes a lifelong burden" (p. 172). At the same time, how one carries this 'burden' and to what extent the subterranean anguish fuels creative efforts also remain important. Georges Braque's (1882–1963) following statement is good to keep in mind in this context: "art is a wound turned to light".

Notes

* This chapter appeared earlier in Salman Akhtar (2011). *Matters of Life and Death: Psychoanalytic Reflections*. London: Karnac, p. 147–180.

1   Freud's (Letter to Wilhelm Fleiss, October 3, 1897, cited in Masson, 1985, p. 268) lapsing into Latin, *matrem nudam*, while describing, at age 41, the childhood memory of having seen his mother naked attests to the power of certain words and the strenuous efforts we make to avoid using them.
2   The Web also contains the contents of 56 major psychoanalytic books and the entire 24 volume set of the Standard Edition of *The Complete Psychological Works of Sigmund Freud*.
3   Paradoxically, the aversion is diminished if the broader context of parental loss is even more horrifying. A dramatic illustration of this is constituted by the nearly 4,000 children orphaned as a result of the bombings of Hiroshima and Nagasaki towards the end of World War II. They continue to be called the 'A-bomb orphans'.
4   Prominent among their list are *The Adventures of Augie March* (Bellow, 1953), *Great Expectations* (Dickens, 1860), *Tom Jones* (Fielding, 1749), *The Vicar of Wakefield* (Goldsmith, 1766), *Demian* (Hess, 1919), and *Of Human Bondage* (Maugham, 1915).
5   The award-winning French movie, *Ponette* (Les Films Alain Sarde, 1996) poignantly depicts a four-year old girl's anguish upon losing her mother as well as her desperate measures to bring her back to life.
6   The findings of the Harvard Childhood Bereavement Study (Silverman and Worden, 1993) confirm this. The investigation was based upon contacting families seen by funeral directors in the Boston, MA, area where a parent had died leaving behind a child between the ages of 6 and 17. Approximately half of the eligible families agreed to participate in the study; this included 125 children whose average age was 12. When interviewed, 81% felt that the deceased parent was watching over them and 57% reported speaking to him or her.
7   For a thoughtful discourse on the normal and pathological forms of altruism, see Seelig and Rosof (2001).
8   Few, if any, psychoanalytic texts describe 'mental health' explicitly, though implications about it are scattered throughout the corpus of our literature. Over three decades of absorption in this literature has led me to conclude that the following ten developmental achievements and ego capacities, if mostly intact most of the times, are sufficient to constitute mental health: (i) intact reality testing, (ii) capacity to experience and tolerate ambivalence, (iii) capacity for separateness, genuine attachment, and a mournful reaction upon separation, (iv) muted affects and reasonable degree of impulse control, (v) establishment of incest barrier, (vi) acceptance of generational boundaries, (vii) a well-internalized sense of morality, (viii) capacity to play, (ix) fusion of affection and erotic desire giving rise to a capacity for mature romantic love, and (x) a coherent sense of identity.
9   An admittedly incomplete list of renowned orphans in the course of man's history includes *prophets* (e.g. Mohammad), *great philosophers* (e.g. Aristotle), *kings and conquistadors* (e.g. Julius Caesar), *musicians and singers* (e.g. Louis Armstrong, Johannes Sebastian Bach, and John Lennon), *writers and poets* (e.g. John Keats, Rudyard Kipling, and Leo Tolstoy), *political leaders* (e.g. Bill Clinton, Nelson Mandela, and Malcolm X), and *film personalities* (e.g. Ingrid Bergman and Marilyn Monroe). The positive traits of courage, resilience, perseverance, imaginativeness, and creativity displayed by these individuals, though multiply-determined, might have been fueled by the trauma of childhood parental loss. A far less celebrated and yet profoundly impressive individual who could be added to this list was Korczak Ziolkowski (1908–1982), the Polish-American orphan from Boston who grew up to undertake the carving of the world's largest statue (in honor of the Native American chief, Crazy Horse) in South Dakota.

References

Akhtar, S. (1994). Object constancy and adult psychopathology. *International Journal of Psycho-Analysis* 75: 441–455.

_____ (1999). *Immigration and Identity: Turmoil, Treatment, and Transformation.* Northvale, NJ: Jason Aronson.

_____ (2007B). From unmentalized xenophobia to messianic sadism: some reflections on the phenomenology of prejudice. In: *The Future of Prejudice: Psychoanalysis and the Prevention of Prejudice*, eds. H. Parens, A. Mahfouz, S. Twemlow, and D. Scharff, pp. 7–19. Lanham, MD: Jason Aronson.

Bahn, P. (1996). ed. *Tombs, Graves, and Mummies.* New York, NY: Barnes and Noble

Bion, W.R. (1967). Notes on memory and desire. *Psychoanalytic Forum* 2: 272–273.

Blos, P. (1967). The second individuation process of adolescence. *Psychoanalytic Study of the Child* 22: 162–186.

_____ (1985). *Son and Father.* New York, NY: Free Press.

Breuer, J., and Freud, S. (1893–1895). Studies on hysteria. *Standard Edition* 2: 1–17.

Bronte, Emily (1847). *Wuthering Heights.* New York, NY: Kaplan, 2006.

Campbell, J. (1991). *The Masks of God, Vol. I: Primitive Mythology.* New York, NY: Penguin Books.

Cath, S. (1997). Loss and restitution in late life. In: *The Seasons of Life: Separation-Individuation Perspectives*, pp. 127–156. Northvale, NJ: Jason Aronson.

Colarusso, C.A. (1990). The third individuation: the effect of biological parenthood on separation-individuation processes in adulthood. *Psychoanalytic Study of the Child* 45: 179–194.

Erikson, E.H. (1959) *Identity and the Life Cycle: Selected Papers.* New York, NY: International Universities Press.

Escoll, P. (1991). Treatment implications of separation-individuation theory in the analysis of young adults. In: *Beyond the Symbiotic Orbit: Advances in Separation-Individuation Theory. Essays in Honor of Selma Kramer, M.D.* ed. S. Akhtar and H. Parens, pp. 369–388. Hillsdale, NJ: Analytic Press.

Fazli, N. (1980). On Father's Death. In: *Khoya Hua Sa Kuchh*, pp. 77–78. New Delhi, India: Aiwaan-e-Ghalib, 1998.

Fichtner, G. (2003). ed. *The Freud-Binswanger Correspondence: 1908–1938.* London: Open Gate Press.

Freud, S. (1912). Recommendations to physicians practising psycho-analysis. *Standard Edition* 12: 109–120.

_____ (1919). The uncanny. *Standard Edition* 17: 219–252.

Gabbard, G. (1982). The exit line: heightened transference-countertransference manifestations at the end of the hour. *Journal of the American Psychoanalytic Association* 30: 579–598.

Guthke, K. (2009). *Epitaph Culture in the West Variations on a Theme in Cultural History.* London, UK: Edwin Mellen Press.

Hilgard, J. (1953). Anniversary reactions in parents precipitated by children. *Psychiatry* 16: 73–80.

James, H. (1903). The Beast in the Jungle. In: *Short Stories by Henry James.* New York, NY: Signet Classics, 2003.

Kernberg, O.F. (1980). *Internal World and External Reality: Object Relations Theory Applied*. New York, NY: Jason Aronson.

Levy, S.T. (1987). Therapeutic strategy and psychoanalytic technique. *Journal of the American Psychoanalytic Association* 35: 447–466.

Mistral, G. (1914). Sonnets of death. In: *Selected Poems of Gabriela Mistral*, ed. V.B. Price, transl. U.K. LeGuin, pp. 144–162. Albuquerque, NM: University of New Mexico Press.

Newstock, S. (2009). *Quoting Death in Early Modern England: The Poetics of Epitaphs Beyond the Tomb*. New York, NY: Palgrave Macmillan

Parker-Pearson, M. (2001). *The Archeology of Death and Burial*. College Station, TX: Texas A&M University Press.

Poe, E.A. (1846). The Cask of Amontillado. In: *Collected Works of Edgar Allan Poe*, pp. 150–159. New York, NY: Vintage Books, 1975.

_____ (1850). The Premature Burial. In: *Collected Works of Edgar Allan Poe*, pp. 210–263. New York, NY: Vintage Books, 1975.

Renik, O. (1996). The perils of neutrality. *Psychoanalytic Quarterly* 65: 495–517.

Sloan, C. (2002). *Bury the Dead: Tombs, Corpses, Mummies, Skeletons, and Rituals*. New York, NY: Scholastic Inc.

Volkan, V.D. (1983). *Linking Objects and Linking Phenomena: A Study of the Forms, Symptoms, Metapsychology, and Therapy of Complicated Mourning*. New York, NY: International Universities Press.

Wheelis, A. (1975). *On Not Knowing How to Live*. New York, NY: Harper and Row.

Yevtushenko, Y. (1960). Pasternak's grave. In: *Collected Poems of Yevgeny Yevtuskenko, 1939–1990*, pp. 83–84. New York, NY: Henry Holt and Company.

Chapter 4

Mortality – the inevitable challenge
The development of the acceptance of one's mortality

Henri Parens

>Mortality.
>What mortality! Whose mortality?
>My . . . my mortality?
>No such thing.
>I had a life to save, a world to save,
>The world of my family.
>I was the only one left to stand.
>My family now numbers sixteen:
>My wife of sixty-one years and me,
>Our three sons and their wives,
>And our eight grandchildren.
>What a glorious family-world.
>For several decades now I am able to accept my mortality.

I was twelve when I first came face to face with it. I remember the moment: when I dropped to the ground—and "officially" started my escape from Rivesaltes. I'll briefly review this experience here as I recorded it in my Holocaust memoirs—which I wrote in 2002–03, starting on the sixtieth anniversary of the day my mother was sent to Auschwitz on convoy 19, August 14, 1942.

I wrote (Parens, 2004), "As I think of it now, my mother knew something very bad about our fate. I was not looking ahead; she was . . . She presented . . . I guess one of the biggest questions in my life. She told me that she wanted me to escape from Rivesaltes?! She made it a statement of her wish, but she did pose it as a question. She conveyed its seriousness and risk. She was telling me and she was asking me if I would escape without her; she really did want to know my response. Without her, that was the big part. I saw her wish on her face. "Yoh, Ma, ch'vet teen vus du zugst" ("Yes, Ma, I'll do what you say"), is most likely what I would have said to her in Bruxellois Yiddish.

>Our life together had made me fairly self-reliant, within limits of my age. She knew I could do things on my own, some things. I trusted her; and

she could count on me to do what she wanted me to do. That was our history, my mother and me. (p. 52)

1 May, 1941. I think I slept well-enough, the night into May 1. We were up fairly early. We waited till after we were regaled with our morning piece of bread. I absolutely do not remember our good-byes. I probably could not bear it. I . . . rejected its imprinting in my memory. Knowing my mother and me, we no doubt hugged and held one another somewhat longer than usual. I was to be inconspicuous from beginning to end. I felt odd and somewhat uncomfortable, with double layers of underclothes, socks, shirts and pants. I was already very skinny by then, so I probably did not look over-dressed . . . I left, armed with the small potato sack I had used for prior expeditions in our limited environs, on duty to collect wood for our still occasionally needed source of heat.

I walked to the specified outer area of the camp, in the direction that would head me toward the highway to Perpignan, as close as possible to the camp-adjacent elevated twin railroad tracks. I played the part well, I think, of taking seriously the task of bending down to pick up dead bits of wood among the briar. Casually I looked around to see where the guards were located. I was in luck; I didn't see any guards at all—maybe they were all in the latrine at once; who knows. I bent down, and still seeing no one, I dropped to the ground. With that, I could feel my whole body racing, no doubt my heart bounding. I know how I react when I get a sudden scare. Dropping to the ground frightened me. I now guess that I felt my escape set in motion just by this act. I had not felt any fear before that moment. (pp. 56–57)

Looking back, I managed to protect myself from considering what might have followed from my being caught trying to escape from this French concentration camp.[1] While Rivesaltes was not a death camp, that is, there were no programmed massacres there, the conditions, mass incarceration, starvation diet, bitter cold in winter, negligible health care were such that vulnerable elderly, adult, and children inmates with chronic illnesses died in much greater number than before the war. Nonetheless, the French camps were not as rigorously regimented as the camps directly governed by Germans, nor were punishments for trying to escape as deadly. While the potential consequences of being caught were not known to me or, I presume, to my mother, clearly, they did not deter my mother from wanting me to take the chance to free myself from the risk that in fact, one year later led to her murder in Auschwitz.

I had responded to my mother's "plea" which I saw more in her facial expression, in her eyes, than in her words, "I want you to escape from here" (in Yiddish), without even thinking that I might get caught and who knows what they would do to me, and to my mother! It was at the moment when I dropped to the ground to set my escape in motion that the dread of what might happen to me came into my head. But I quickly repressed it, got up, and started to run like hell with only one thought in mind: get out of here! As Walter B. Cannon (1915) described it: my "flight" from life-threatening danger.

This was no moment for reflection. But I think of it now: I was then twelve years old. As a child analyst I have on many occasions considered the question, at what age can one expect a child to become aware of his own mortality? Parents have asked me, for instance, how traumatized might their five or seven year old be by losing a much loved pet? While the child is very upset at the pet being taken away from him (because it had died) after several days or weeks, the latency age child, or the younger one, seems to no longer expect the pet to return. An acute loss reaction does occur but I could not by definition speak of the child's having a mourning reaction due to the loss. I will say that I am not on absolutely certain ground on this point; we can't escape the fact that children vary widely in how they experience and how they deal with very challenging events that befall them. Erna Furman's findings are most relevant here.

Acknowledgement of death and personal mortality in young children

In *A Child's Parent Dies*, Erna Furman (1974) tells us of a one-year-old toddler whose older brother had died. The toddler persisted in searching for his brother around the house. At one point his older sister went to dinner at a neighbor's. He was most upset and refused to eat. His mother, guessing that he feared his sister had also disappeared, took him to the neighbor's to see the sister and at once the toddler calmed down (p. 42).

From my own longitudinal mother-infant project (Parens, 1979, 1993, 2008), one child lost his father and we had an opportunity to see his complex reaction to it (Parens, 2001). Bernie was just past three years old when his father sustained a serious work-related injury and was hospitalized for ten months (see Parens, 2010, pp. 39–41). Unfortunately complicating the picture, his mother was thus compelled to work outside the home. When we saw them—though less regularly than usual—Bernie, his sister, and mother, all were subdued. Eventually his father returned home for several months, terribly debilitated. Then when Bernie was four years old his father was again hospitalized.

Bernie was four and a half years old when his father died. When we saw Bernie one week later, he was terribly sad; he stayed very close to his mother who was depressed and spoke very little. Since father died, mother said softly, Bernie has been very upset and wetting his bed. Mrs. Z. said that Bernie talked about his father having died. As was our strategy in this parenting-optimizing project we talked openly, though obviously thoughtfully, about these parents' child rearing challenges. I was well aware that Bernie was listening—as the kids commonly did. We talked about how angry we become when someone we love gets sick, because we're afraid we may lose them, and then when that person dies, we feel even angrier. As I wrote elsewhere, "Then, because we have been angry with Daddy, sometimes a child feels that his anger is what made Daddy sick and die." Of course that's not true, I said. And we need to explain, even many times, that being angry with Daddy is not what makes Daddy become sick and die.

The next session, Mrs. Z. said that she didn't understand some things Bernie was saying, that they made no sense. How should she deal with that? For instance, she said that Bernie had said to her that maybe they could bring Daddy out of the ground, take him to the hospital and Dr. Parens could make him better again. What could she say to that?" (Parens, 2010, p. 40). I explained to the mothers that the child's cognitive development is such that the four year old's mind cannot yet discern what is possible and what is not. This case helped us talk with the mothers about how they can help their children deal with sad, painful experiences.

> Nearly four months after father's death, he tells his mother from time to time that he is feeling sad that Daddy is not here. Both mother and Bernie do look sad at times alternately, at times simultaneously. I learned that in his therapy sessions with Dr. B., Bernie was also able to talk about his father's death, and to play at crashes and accidents, and attach them to his father's death. Gradually his phallic aggression returned, and his mood returned to its usual pre-loss state. (Parens, 2010, p. 41)

Bernie was four and a half years of age, not yet able to conceptualize the permanence of death. As such, he wanted his mother to take his father to the doctor in order to bring his father back to life. The developmental leap in brain function from pre-latency to early adolescence is large. Reality testing and cognitive functioning bring with them the recognition that life is finite and that death cannot be reversed.

Acknowledgement of death and personal mortality in young teenagers

Guy was a brilliant thirteen-year-old boy riddled with anxiety which, his associations suggested, seemed predominantly attached to his sadistic fantasies toward his parents (Parens, 2010, pp. 41–42). His anger toward them seemed to me clearly more intense than warranted by what I knew of them and their behavior toward him. He unquestionably loved them and his hefty guilt manifested in his being very troubled by his sadistic fantasies toward them. He started having difficulty falling asleep because he dreaded that he would "die in his sleep." He became increasingly preoccupied with thoughts of his own death and experienced intense fear of it at night.

His transference compelled him both to try to control me and sadistically manipulate me, this being driven by the sadism he felt toward his parents. In treatment, he cleverly managed to fail in his efforts to cause me injury, physical and/or narcissistic. The intrapsychic conflict caused by his intense ambivalence was palpable: his sadistic feelings as well as his warmth and concerns about me were easily evident. He was positively responsive to my interpretations, which was evident in that they helped him contain his occasionally mounting sadism toward me. Gradually and progressively his sadistic fantasies decreased, he became less provocative at home and in the transference, and his school work improved as did his peer relations. He also seemed less conflicted over masturbation.

From time to time Guy's associations turned to the threat of nuclear disaster and he twice enacted such scenarios in the office, mostly in narrations, and twice dreamt of a nuclear disaster (see Parens, 1988). He dreaded that he would die in his sleep. Yet in neither dream was he personally threatened. Gradually he was able to talk about his becoming aware of, and became preoccupied with, the thought that being dead really meant that this would be the end of his life. "I postulated that the dread that he might die in his sleep was contributed to by, at the aegis of his rather harsh conscience, his turning some of the rage he had long felt toward his parents against himself. Over the more than four years of analysis his harsh conscience seemed most resistant to analysis and were it not to modify over time, might well over the years continue to be a significant contributor to his fear of dying" (Parens, 2010, p. 42).

Over many years of clinical work from the age of thirteen, Guy was the patient who most clearly contributed to my grasp of the timetable for the development of the "psycho-cognitive" ability to conceptualize one's own mortality, the finiteness of one's own life. That one's pet or one's grandparent dies is grasped before this developmental era; it does not, however, bring with it conscious awareness that the self will also some day be subject to the same fate. The delinking of the application of this knowledge about the finiteness of life to another, from applying it to the self, seems to me difficult to explain on the basis of cognition alone; it may be that psychic self-protective defense plays a part in this delinkage.

I do not doubt that my initiation to and cognitive awareness of my own mortality was triggered, at twelve years of age, when I put my escape from Rivesaltes into action. My fear of being caught and punished, be it by isolation or whip-lashing or who knows what, would not have created in me the kind of dread I remember experiencing. It would not have led me to feel that, as I wrote in 2002–03, "I was never this close to filling my pants with the contents of my nearly empty gut" (Parens, 2004, p. 60). A more serious dread lay beneath this feeling.

Thirteen-year-old Guy had panic attacks triggered by his fear that he would die in his sleep. I take note of his fearing that it would happen in his sleep. Like every child analyst, I enormously value what I have learned about psychic life from what child patients have said to me over the years.[2] Guy's noting that he feared it would happen in his sleep leads me to think at this writing that in one's sleep, specifically in REM sleep (which is when we dream), one's ego is half asleep too. Impulses that press for expression are not as readily defended against; our system of adaptive functions (our ego) is not sufficiently alert to erect adequate defense mechanisms to prevent whatever mortifying fantasies we harbor from surfacing to consciousness. Given my understanding of Guy's dynamics, I cannot but wonder if when his ego was not fully alert, his guilt-driven harsh superego's demand for expression had the upper hand and compelled in him the now cognitively conceptualized knowledge that someday he would die. Two thoughts follow: (1) the fact that we do not commonly encounter young teenagers having panic attacks driven by the emerging awareness of their own mortality. Might this be due to their superego's not being as harsh as was Guy's, not as vigorously pressing from expression, and as a result, they are able to defend, that is, to protect themselves from being conscious of their mortality? (2) I think the same applies to me during my escape; I was able to protect myself from outright thinking: if I get caught they'll kill me. This line of thought brings yet another which I'll address below. For now, let me pick up the thread of my first self-protectively denied personal encounter with mortality.

Continuing my escape narrative,

> Determined now, I started to crawl toward the elevated train track. I soon found that what I knew before of the briar was so: the live bushes had big spines that hurt when, I hit them head on. I used the potato sack to shield my hands and forearms as I crawled more carefully, but just as quickly as I could. Within some twenty or thirty feet from the train-track-mound I stopped, raised my head slowly as little as I needed to again see if there were any sentinels, and saw none. The mound rose about five feet high. Bracing myself for it, I quickly bounded up and started to run. I cleared the mound, the tracks and landed on the other side. Shielded now from direct view from camp-side, . . . semi-crouched I continued to run, more scared than before. I ran like hell. I was running scared shitless through a still barren vineyard, the ground was sandy, I tripped on something, crashed to the ground, immediately got myself back up and continued to run as if I hadn't stopped. Beyond the vineyard I continued my course through more vision-protective shrubs and trees. Once in those, feeling less visible, I slowed my pace some; I didn't stop. Unexpectedly, I had reached the highway. Good fortune had it that the highway was sided by three or so feet ditches, all the way from where

> I met the highway to Perpignan. This, I guess my mother didn't know, that there was a protective ditch I could use for as long as it went and as I needed. Also fortunate, there was no water in the long ditch, nearly a trench, along the road. (pp. 57–58)

In my narrative I see my use of humor, an adaptive defense—one of what I have called the "sublime defenses" such as empathy, altruism, and sublimation (Parens, Scattergood, Duff, & Singletary, 1997)—I have long used, I would think most likely to mitigate and cope with my Holocaust experience. I continue:

> The macadam paved road, a two-lane, unmarked affair—of course this is 1941—ran to Perpignan, some 10 kilometers into the city. I marched as best and as fast as I could in the ditch. 1 May; no farmers in the fields; I doubt anyone saw me during those kilometers into Perpignan. My guess is that I got there at about two or three in the afternoon. Once into the small city—Perpignan was still small when we revisited in 1997—I had no difficulty finding the railroad station. I made a point of not looking into anyone's face, as we do when we hope no one will see us. I can't tell if I looked unusual. Skinny kids I guess were not a novelty then, anywhere. I worried most about my cloth shoes, that they might give me away as a penniless, homeless waif and who knows where I might've come from. Perpignan was not a war devastated zone; to the best of my knowledge, the Germans had not dropped bombs on Vichy-France. There were no signs of bombs anywhere; it's not as though I could have been taken for some poor orphaned kid whose parents got killed when their house was blown to bits by some bomb. To be as invisible as possible was one of my prime tasks. But I had to buy a train ticket ... (p. 58)

Again, reality broke in, disrupting my efforts to not look scared.

> I got to the train station, had no difficulty seeing the ticket counter; as casually as I could I asked for a ticket for the next train to Marseilles and its cost. The next train was at about 11 p.m. that evening. I had the money needed, handed it over; I think the clerk didn't even look at me. To my relief, the clerk just handed me the ticket and some change.
>   Once I got my ticket, I realized to my distress that I had hours to wait. It was about mid-afternoon and the train left late that night. I could not stay in the station. I needed a secluded place where I could hide until nightfall at least. What in the world led me to decide on one of those everywhere-in-France enclosed public toilets as a hiding place? Not difficult to figure out: find a toilet with cubicles with doors and I had it made. Not a savory place, but it would keep me hidden. (p. 58)

As I wrote my Holocaust memoirs, it was clear to me that I used humor throughout my writing of the experience, sometimes to my own surprise, often not, realizing that I did so to mitigate the pain and rage that came with remembering, with the reliving as I reflected and wrote. I know that I did not experience humor as my escape progressed. I go on:

> Hiding from early afternoon until an 11 p.m. train departure time in a toilet stall I can see to this day is not one of my favorite memories. I don't see the inside of the stall, I see the view of the stalls one gets on entering the toilet. I was not bored in that stall. I was out of Rivesaltes even if only for a few hours, with the promise of more. But I hated being where I was. To this day I feel rage at having been forced to hide in a toilet stall. And on top of it, I was scared . . .
>
> Night finally came. I came out of hiding and went directly to the train station. There were more people in the train station than I had anticipated, not a crowd, but at least there were not just a few of us which might have subjected me to closer scrutiny by some people looking for trouble. I may have waited half an hour within the station waiting room before we moved onto the platform to wait for the train. The wait then was not long; I liked the darker platform better than the more lighted station. I climbed onto the train. Quite soon we were off . . .
>
> The train to Marseilles . . . was packed; standing room only! Where in the world was everyone going during this war? I actually preferred the fact that the train was crowded and I among others had to stand in the aisle. This was one of those passenger trains that have small compartments for about six people each, with an aisle outside of these compartments on my left when I climbed in. I notched another step in my venture when the train took off. Now the trick again and still so far was to be as invisible as I could.
>
> In a way it was easy because, even in the aisle we were standing quite in close proximity of one another and no one seemed to stand out to be looked at. I don't know how long we had traveled so far, one hour, two, more? We traveled surrounded by a muffled sound of people in dialogue, over-ridden by the louder sound of the train running at a moderate clip . . . I felt an odd feeling of near-peace, maybe it was sleepiness; I had been on my feet, had run like hell and walked a good number of kilometers and had not slept since many hours now. I had not dared fall asleep in the Perpignan public toilets. Nor had I eaten since my piece of bread in the morning. I really don't remember being hungry; I guess that without being conscious of it, I was set to not eat till I got to Marseilles the next morning. It was no problem; I was not thinking of sleep nor of food as I am now that I write about it. I was rather in a state of alertness somewhat dulled by the train's moving rhythm; you know how trains in transit feel. There was more space between my standing-

room-only-neighbor on my right than on my left. In fact the one on my left was within two feet from me. He may have even been closer or moved closer because he quietly said to me, "Je sais d'ou tu viens" ("I know where you're coming from.")

I was scared to death. I had been running like hell, I was scared shitless much of the time up to now; this time I was petrified. I had not gone that far on my journey. To be sure, this was the end of me. I was never this close to filling my pants with the contents of my nearly empty gut ... (pp. 58–60). I see the moment now. I know the tenacity of powerful moments in one's life. It was a moment of naked helplessness and dread; a long moment. I often remember the sudden panic and seeming self-controlled. Perhaps I felt paralyzed.

He must have sensed or seen it because he said, "N'aies pas peur, n'aies pas peur." ("Don't be frightened.") He was reassuring. His tone gave me the courage to hesitantly look at him. "T'as faim?" ("Are you hungry?") Dramatically relieved by his look and tone, I nodded my head. He must have looked me over well and for some time to so sharply get to the core of my problems: I know where you're coming from and are you hungry? He was, I would guess from his observations and his approach to me, a fairly well-schooled man. He knew, I did not, that we would soon be making a stop of substantial duration. Looking back on my journey, on a map, it is clear that our stop was in either Montpellier or Nimes, another of the facts I can't remember. One fact I remember with distinction is that he provided me with my first meal in nine months—in the train station restaurant. Like in train stations of years ago, the restaurant was in a rather large open gray hangar-like space. I felt uncertain still of my newly-met traveling companion, but his demeanor and what he did, in the end made me feel more than grateful to him. I ate—a whole meal. He didn't eat; he may have gotten a coffee. I don't remember what I ate; I know there was meat and vegetables. Rabbit or horse, I would guess. It was war. I was surprised when he pulled out his food ration book—first time I learned that food was being rationed in France—and the waiter tore out pieces of it as part payment for what I had consumed. Even then I realized that he had given me some of his monthly allotment of food. He did not look starved, but still, even people who weren't skinny like I was got hungry. He did not have to do this or anything; he could have just turned away and looked elsewhere. What I best remember is his sympathetic reach toward me, and what the man did. Other than that, a big "that", there was nothing remarkable about him, an average enough office employee or businessman or who knows what. I also remember that he did seem to know what I was about, and that I felt protected with him in the station. He also helped me understand at least what some of the many travelers might be doing on this train. He was going to Grenoble to ski! While we were in concentration camps, some were skiing! Of course in the Alps you can ski in May; you can pretty well ski anytime. Not all evil people, either. Life just went on, even while so many of us were imprisoned and starving in camps! I suppose that a number of the passengers were going to Grenoble too, because when I re-embarked on our train Perpignan-to-Marseilles, many seats were now available; many had transferred to trains going elsewhere . . . From Nimes railways fan out, going further East-slightly-bearing-south along the Méditerranée coast to Marseille, or fully North toward Paris and midway a twist East to Grenoble, or West toward Toulouse and Bordeaux . . .

I was unpleasantly made aware of my arrival in Marseille by the train ticket collector's not so gently waking me. I am not surprised that I had fallen asleep. To this day I don't know what went through his mind. I can't be sure whether he looked annoyed or just surprised. I guess, it was a night train and he was just going through the wagons looking for passengers who like me had fallen asleep and had to get out. He might have wondered what hole did I come out of in such a state of dress. But scowling some, I thought, he just wakened me and seemed ready to move on. I quickly got out of the train; I didn't look back.

I had arrived in Marseille, yet another successful large step in my plan. It must have been past 9 in the morning, as what followed would indicate. Even now I wonder why it took so long to get from Perpignan to Marseille, from 11 or so p.m. to about 9 a.m. Except for the German army then, we did not travel then as fast as we do today. In any case, thank heaven, I got there. I knew the address I was looking for since I had left Rivesaltes, though I did search my pocket for the piece of paper on which I had written it. I asked someone, no doubt I selected a kindly disposed face, I didn't ask a gendarme or such figure, if he or she knew—can't remember if it was a man or a woman, I probably would have selected a woman—for the whereabouts and directions to my destination. My destination . . . the OSE Bureau in Marseille, was on rue de l'Italie. Another piece of luck, the OSE Bureau was quite close to the train station and easily accessible. I'm pretty good with directions, so that was no problem. The problem, as it had been since I left Rivesaltes, was to get to the OSE Bureau without running into a life-spoiler. I got there. (pp. 60–62)

Recognition and awareness of one's mortality in adolescence

Thirteen-year-old Guy rather suddenly became consciously aware of his mortality; he verbalized it with visible anxiety. How did this come about? Why do we not see more young adolescent patients with the kind of specific panic attacks he experienced? Why did my mortality, which I believe made itself felt several times during my escape, not declare itself in my conscious awareness? I felt terrified; for me, as I believe for many young teenagers, this feeling of terror seemed to only have meant that I might suffer serious painful consequences if I were caught. Why did I not consciously think, "They'll kill me! And, my life will be over"? Self protectively, I could not allow this potential "knowledge" to overtake me; I had to escape—and survive. Relevant is that Kestenberg and Brenner (1996) noted that among Holocaust child survivors, a number of teenagers, even some pre-teens, carried out risk-laden activities to survive that one would not have expected them capable of at their age. I postulated that Guy's conscience broke through whatever defenses his ego put up to protect him from panic reactions. I believe I was able to defend against thinking, "I am putting myself in danger of being killed" even though I felt an intense threat to me. I will attest to the fact that, unlike Guy, I do not recall ever wanting to destroy my mother[3]; I was angry with her at times, to be sure; but I just don't recall hating her and believe I did not suffer the severe guilt Guy suffered, no guilt being as harsh as that which follows the wish to destroy one's own mother. It might follow then that not suffering such intense guilt, my superego did not override my setting up self-protective defenses to prevent my having panic attacks during my escape.

Bearing in mind that in the normal course of psychic development, adolescence is the decade when the child transitions the center of his universe from his family of childhood to that of his chosen peer group, a process that will take the child into adulthood, several lines of psychic development undergo substantial modification, including especially the adolescent's superego.

From its emergence the young child's superego is the heir of his "crime and punishment." Freud (1923b) said this much when he held that the superego is the heir of the Oedipus complex. The superego additionally develops under the impetus of the child's own (side by side with the parent's) punitive reaction to the child's hate toward the love-object, that is, under the impetus of the child's ambivalence. In this, the child's judgment function plays its part in the structuring of his superego in that (1) it does not measure, that is, judge, whether or not the child will act on the fantasy of harming the now hated loved-parent and equates the wish with the deed; and (2) the young child himself evaluates the wish to harm the parent to be "bad", that is, "Nice kids don't hate or hurt their parents!" In this then, the young child's immature judgment function can be unduly harsh and unreasonable.

Considering the adolescent, what is interesting and we might say paradoxical, adolescent superego modifications occur at a time when the brain development-dependent function of "judgment" continues its development independently from and lags well behind the marvelous leap we observe in cognitive function—for example, when adolescents virtually overnight give evidence of thinking, in discussing life issues for example, that are breathtaking. This discrepancy in brain development that serves cognitive function on the one hand and the judgment function on the other, makes for many parents' hair-pulling (their own) at the bizarre behavior of their bright adolescent who also indulges in risky activities.

Consider those smart-enough mid- to late adolescents who engage in the life-risking challenge of "Chicken". Why do they play this insane, high-entertainment challenge at the edge of a cliff? Two adolescents omnipotently emboldened by having recently acquired their own cars—that singular adolescent male symbol of power—drive at full speed toward the edge of the cliff where they and their cohorts have gathered, and the one who first stops is "Chicken!", a label weighted with humiliation. They do not see the insanity of the act by virtue of the failure of their still much-underdeveloped judgment function. As I wrote elsewhere, "In a recent piece, journalist Elizabeth Cooney[4] reported on findings on the adolescent brain, which she garnered from an interview with Dr. Frances Jensen, a neurologist at Harvard Medical School and Children's Hospital Boston. Cooney wrote that Dr. Jensen pointed out, 'We all know what the frontal lobe does: ... its insight, judgment, inhibition, self-awareness, ... acknowledgment of cause and effect. And big surprise: [Its development is] not done in [the] teen years. Hence [teens'] impulsiveness, their unpredictable behavior, their lack of ability to acknowledge cause and effect, despite the fact they are getting 800s on the SATs and can be cognitively highly functional and memorize at a much more impressive rate that we as adults do later!'" (Parens, 2011, pp. 160–161). There's more.

As colleges know only too well, the same lack of judgment development leads many a freshman and even sophomore, finally emancipated from home, intrapsychically compelled to individuate, and free(?) to do whatever he or she chooses to do, not uncommonly to recklessly imbibe alcohol and social drugs that have at times led to very serious consequences, including acute alcohol poisoning—and every year, virtually wherever one lives in the US, there is a report of a college freshman who died due to alcohol poisoning. While no doubt a number of factors may lead them to so behave, ultimately their underdeveloped judgment conspires to insufficiently protect them against death. We may blame their seeming indifference to toxicity warnings to a denial of their potential mortality, but their lack of judgment certainly plays a key role in this behavior.

And there is another challenge to their sense of mortality of much consequence that late adolescents have on occasion even happily ventured into. Why does the threat or start of war always draw many eighteen to twenty year olds to volunteer for military service? This is a very real dilemma. Of course any nation needs to defend itself. Of course, it is most reasonable that the young—really late adolescents—take on this enormous challenge for the nation. It is fortunate that each person's threat to limb and life is quieted by the idea of serving the nation, of being patriotic, even heroic. And for many an eighteen year old who volunteers to go to battle to save his or her country, as Chris Hedges (2002) has most cogently elaborated in his *War Is a Force that Gives Us Meaning*, doing so gives them a sense—which many have not felt before—of being valuable, of serving family and country. But we have to wonder, how many among them truly experience and weigh the challenge to mortality which such volunteering brings with it? Most likely many among them do not even think of what they may face—until they get there, and in the face of the dangers to which they are subjected, come to truly realize the risks that come with having volunteered. Yes, other factors play their part, such as for instance, being jobless at home and here, in the military, being offered a salary and benefits. But should we not be concerned about the denial by the young and the romanticizing by the nations' elders?

Koenigsberg (1975, 2009) has amply documented how Hitler was fixated on dedicating the life of Germany's youth to die heroically for the sake of his One-Thousand-Year-Reich, which fortunately lasted just twelve years, but not before it took the life, as best as I can estimate from readily available internet sources[5], of about four million German soldiers (Overmans, 2000)—and we can guess from filmed evidence (Rees, 1997) that near the end of the war, even sixteen year olds (and possibly younger boys) participated as soldiers.

Awareness of one's mortality in adulthood

The judgment function progressively matures during the third decade of life. Awareness of one's mortality may be most acutely experienced from young adulthood on, say from one's early twenties:

1. In the dread of one's own mortality not allowing one to achieve the fulfillment of one's self-development plans, be it to become a professional of some kind, or an artist, or a successful business man/woman, or auto mechanic, or whatever one prizes becoming; and
2. When having come to the point of launching oneself into "Mother Nature's mandate" to preserve the species, one ventures into generating a family of one's own. At perhaps no time is one's mortality more suddenly consciously perceived and potentially more anxiety producing than when one has one's first child.

In both cases one becomes conscious of the need to be able to sustain one's commitment to be there, with the sense of responsibility to fulfill these goals. Both goals require the promise of being able to continue on these paths. But when due to some event or otherwise-driven reflection one runs into the possibility of one's own mortality, existential anxiety may make itself acutely felt.

1. For many a mid-teenager the thought, "I'm gonna be a lawyer, or a doctor, or an engineer . . ." more or less begins to organize. But the commitment is projected into the future and the process of organizing receives only a relative load of psychic energy; it commonly has an element of tentativeness and is not a "sworn commitment." Once into the third decade of life—interestingly, it's in the junior year that most colleges require students to declare their "major"—a commitment must be made as to what work-life track one will pursue. The declaration now becomes invested with a great deal more psychic energy, taken much more seriously, and generally draws from the twenty-plus year old a greater work ethic than might have been developed to date. The commitment now attains a central potential element of one's continually developing sense of self. The concept of one's self-representation now acquires the critical dimension: "I am a lawyer (in the making)" or "I am a doctor (in the making)" or "I am an engineer (in the making)"; "I have a specific purpose," first to become who I want my "self" to be, and then to be that "self." This specified commitment now becomes a first-order goal for oneself. It becomes invested with much meaning, much psychic energy, and becomes a "must achieve" part of one's identity. Now any threat to achieving the goal leads to a generalized existential anxiety, a reaction to the possibility that the meaning I gave to my life in declaring "I am a lawyer (in the making)" or "I am a doctor (in the making)" will not materialize. Now, the threat to life, the awareness of one's mortality may emerge at a level denied until this time of life.
2. With regard to one's family formation, awareness of the possibility of falling ill or one's life being in jeopardy also rouses a great deal of existential anxiety given that it carries much meaning for who one is. Whatever event or spontaneous reflection raises awareness of one's mortality, the thought of not being able to fulfill one's promise to love and cherish one's mate, or even more so, of not being there for one's child(ren) is likely in most of us to create intense anxiety: What happens to them if I die? At the very least, unless one comes from a wealthy family, life insurance is purchased hoping against hope that there will be sufficient funds to help the family left behind to continue life in a reasonably favorable economic state. This step though, however adequate economically, does not secure a substantial reduction in existential anxiety and quite understandably further requires some complementary rationalization and denial.

Considering for a moment the advent of an actual threat to life in mid-adulthood, of a possibly physical life-threatening crisis, the sweep of actual death-anxiety and its unavoidable anticipatory depression are of a most challenging dimension, given that one then faces the possibly most painful threat to life one will ever experience—rendered so by virtue of the fact that one leaves a child without a mother/father!

I would add another somewhat equivalently dreadful condition for many a parent, one I have personally thought about again and again. What courage it must have taken, what fortitude, for my mother (my father no longer being in our daily life) to pleadingly tell me that she wanted me, her twelve year old son, to escape from Rivesaltes. This camp was the ultimately notorious southern France concentration camp from which, one year after my escape, detainees were sent (via Drancy) to the death camps in Poland—including my mother! What dread must she have suffered wondering if I would succeed in the challenge she put before me – the dread of her child's possible death. I am not alone in thinking this. For the German edition of my Holocaust memoirs, the German publisher—who became a personal friend—had first sympathetically proposed the title *"Healing after the Holocaust: What Courage of His Mother to Let Him Go!"*

Late adulthood, old age

Erik Erikson (1959) proposed that when one has lived a sufficiently gratified life one tends to develop an acceptance of one's mortality without experiencing undue pain and distress. Surely one has come to the philosophical reflection that "Every plant or animal that lives will die." The life of every living thing comes to an end, be it by illness or by natural wear and tear of living tissues and/or organ systems. We know that Freud ascribed this phenomenon to a self-destructive death instinct; that is, to an instinct that compels a living organism to return to its original inorganic state (1920g, pp. 37–38). I have argued against the death instinct theory because it has never been proven that an internal force or instinct actively compels any organism's death; I believe such a force or instinct cannot be proven, and looking at the question through the prism of the Multi-Trends Theory of Aggression which our research findings compelled me to propose (Parens, 1979, 2014, chs. 1 and 2), I ascribe the death of living things ultimately to the breakdown, be it by an act of violence against the living thing, or due to the wear and tear of the organ systems that maintain life. Even inanimate things seem subject to such wear and tear and ultimate breakdown; for example, the sculptures in Venice have caused the city's monument keepers no end of dismay at their ongoing weather-beaten deterioration; toward a decade's use of my cars I invariably come to find it more psychologically and monetarily economical to replace them than to keep worrying that my car will breakdown at a most undesirable moment, besides increasingly paying for their repairs; all things, animate and inanimate seem to so breakdown.

To a degree, the converse of Erikson's proposal that having lived a sufficiently gratified life leads one to accept one's mortality without experiencing undue pain and regret seems to hold as well. Insufficient gratification in what one has achieved and experienced in life is likely to lead the individual to feel bitter about the unavoidable loss of function and the pain caused by disorders and disease that come with aging. Bitterness may set in; one's mortality may be seen as the rotten end to a rotten life. For individuals who have lived a painful life the awareness of one's mortality may of itself become overly distressing. Continuing lifelong reverberations of early life trauma, even a life laden with later years' trauma may lead to paradoxical reactions: (1) bitterness that hopes for a change for the better is fading; one will never get the gratification one yearns for; and/or (2) one may wish to already be dead!

In my wish to support and further affirm Erikson's sound 1959 epigenetic developmental postulation on how humans experience their approaching mortality, let me elaborate a bit on this latter point. A magnificent human being with whom I have long been in frequent contact, a highly achieved ninety-plus-year-old woman, suffers much agony at her declining cognitive, memory, and various physical system functions. A lifelong vigorous and successfully productive worker, driven obsessively to become such by a very demanding father, continues to feel inner driven demands that she continue to perform even in the face of her age-appropriately lessening capability. Despite her father's obsessive demands that she perform and achieve, I have over time come to find, however, by her own repeated documentation, that her present agony is not what her father imposed on her, but rather is the product of having suffered what I consider to be the ultimate trauma: to be rejected from infancy on, which leads to being emotionally neglected and maltreated, that is, emotionally abused, by one's own mother. I have found this to be so with a number of patients I have treated in more than five decades. To be so rejected and maltreated by one's father does not seem to cause an equivalent degree of traumatization. Paraphrasing what Freud wrote in the next to last paragraph of his paper on Some Psychical Consequences of the Anatomical Distinction between the Sexes (1925j, p. 258), I want to put forward an hypothesis that may not hold up as a generalization, but I am here positing that if it cannot be generalized, I have no doubt that it will certainly be applicable in many instances.

There is an element of uniqueness in the mother-child relationship that may well contribute to its causing the ultimate trauma. As I wrote elsewhere, the only relationship in which humans are likely to experience unconditional love is in the love the parent experiences for her or his own child. No other relationship—apart from the short-lived idealized romantic love of adolescence Shakespeare immortalized in his *Romeo and Juliet*—including the child's being biologically primed to attach to his or her mother and father—will not guarantee unconditional love by the child toward the parent, nor certainly will the husband's love toward his wife and the wife's toward her husband, or that between siblings, or the reciprocal relationships between grandparents and their grandchildren, none of these is unconditional. A significant injury by one member of these dyads toward the other will more or less diminish, and even disrupt or even destroy the love that was there between them. When the parent-child relationship is stable, consistently and sufficiently positive, with evidence of sufficient gratification of the child's basic emotional needs, etc., then the child's love for the parents is likely to obtain unconditional status. But when the parent neglects, abuses, and maltreats the child, the child's love for the parent will not become unconditional; it will wax and wane.

In the course of my clinical work, as with my dear ninety-one-year-old friend's trauma experienced at the hands of the mother from nine decades earlier on, I have found that the decline of bodily functions and the pain this adds to an already traumatized psyche can lead to a genuine yearning to have it all over and done with! I find Erikson's position to have much merit. The ultimate trauma can destroy the ability or opportunity to structure and internalize a representation of the loving parent which can then provide the older individual with an "inner sustainment" that, in my friend's case, was structured nine decades before and could survive unmodified to the end of life (Parens, 1970). In short, to be traumatized by one's own mother—I will not try to explain here why the same seems to not hold up with one's father—may be generalized to be the ultimate trauma. To be sure, the level of traumatization can vary along a wide range, depending on the qualitative parameters of the injury and complementarily, the inborn vulnerabilities versus resilience in the young child.

One more word on my speaking of this as the "ultimate trauma": Once I had written my memoirs, several of my patients who had long suffered in consequence of their subjection to the "ultimate trauma" at one point or another said to me, "How can I tell you of my suffering with what you went through [during the Holocaust]?" I tell them, just as Holocaust survivors Henry Krystal said at a Margaret Mahler Symposium years ago, and Anna Ornstein said in public at a national meeting, each of us independently of one another, "My mother loved me!" Each of us therewith declared that it was our internalizing such a representation into our psyches that gave us the strength to withstand what we did. And ultimately, to not dread, fear, or yearn for our ever nearing mortality. The true love of one's mother is a balm to the existential anxiety of mortality.

Of course, in old age as well as earlier in life, intense, consistent pain may lead to rumination about and wish for an end to one's unbearable life. Many such individuals have chosen, impulsively or calculatedly to facilitate the hand of their mortality, bringing it about by suicide.

How the threat to my life at age twelve impacted my clinical handling of patients' death anxiety

Given that I cannot know how I would have dealt with existential anxiety or death anxiety (fear of their own death) in others had I not experienced exposure to grave danger and fear of my own death at age twelve,

I cannot say that my experience at that young age is the prime or principal determinant of how I have dealt with my patients' fears of death. Like so much else we deal with in our analytic work, analyzing and helping a patient cope with death anxiety is not a simple matter. That I experienced life-threatening dread decades ago cannot have the equivalent effect that a recent or currently ongoing threat to life might have on my reactivity to such dread in a current patient. Surely, a recent or even actively ongoing threat to a clinician's life would idiosyncratically impact the clinician's here and now reactivity to a patient's overt existential anxiety and/or death anxiety.

Of course, whether or not we have actually faced the threat of our own death, in the clinical situation we each bring our variable inborn and experience-dependent sensitivities to addressing our patient's death anxiety experience. But focusing on the effects of our own threat to life experience, several factors will affect the impact our individual experience has on how we handle our patient's death anxiety clinically. The threat to my life coming from an outside danger posed a very different challenge than would a danger by a near-catastrophic dysfunction occurring within my own body. Critical here is that in many cases, threat to life coming from the outside is time-limited. In my case, for example, it was World War II's Holocaust which, for those of us who survived this shameful era, no longer actively threatens us. Its reverberations have lasted a lifetime, but its threat to life has not.

When the traumatizing threat to life has occurred decades ago, it leads to a very different experience in the clinician who in the present encounters death anxiety in the patient than when the clinician's threat to life has been recent (see Masur, Introduction to this volume, Garfield, this volume, Schwartz, this volume), and surely when it is ongoing. In contrast to the clinician whose encounter with the threat to life came from an outside danger and was time-limited, when the threat to life has occurred recently, its impact on the clinician's handling of death anxiety in the patient is likely to become quite challenging. Intrapsychic work will have to be done, episodically and even continually; the clinician will very likely need to self-analytically address her countertransference as her work with the patient progresses.

The burden for the clinician whose threat to life is due to a pathological bodily process from which the clinician will from hereon never be fully free, no doubt leaves a painful challenge for that clinician. Adaptive ego strength, psychic strength, resilience, self-supportive self-analysis, and strong love ties are powerful advantages to being able to continue analytic clinical work with and certainly to analyze a patient's death anxiety. A return to analysis to foster the working through of stress-induced ego vulnerability would very likely be helpful.

I would like to briefly consider some of my handling of several patients' death anxiety and how my own early experience with danger and threat to my ongoing being affected my later clinical work. That thirteen-year-old Guy's acute death anxiety occurred when he was about as old as I was when I encountered the very real possibility that I might get caught and it would be the end of me, I believe heightened my empathy to the point of sympathy. I identified with his plight and I undertook to help him to address his death anxiety head on. It was essential that I not ignore, deny, or try to divert him from the recognition that he, and I, like all living creatures, will eventually die. He dreaded that an atomic bomb might be launched and he would die during the night. While his dread occurred at a time when the threat of a nuclear catastrophe that had worried many among us during the height of the US and Soviet Union "cold war" was now in the past, his dread, while fantasy-driven, felt real in the present. But he was not in actual danger; he was not threatened in actual reality. This allowed me to reason with him that, yes, human life ends in time, but average life expectancy at this time was between seventy and seventy-five years, and thirteen year olds today, like him, would in all likelihood live on for some sixty more years. I said to him, "Just look around; how many people much older than you do you see around you, including your parents and even your grandparents—and me?"

Some of his then recurring associations led me to wonder with him if being angry with his mother at this time might be making him feel that he should really be punished for it! We had been working on this issue for some time. We looked at his anger with her again; and it would not be the last time. But given the harsh dread he experienced that he might die in his sleep, I stressed the reality was that there was no threat to his life coming from the outside, that this was a fact, and that except in times of war, most people live for a very long time beyond age thirteen. I relied on heightening his perception of reality, allocating the dread that he might die in his sleep as perhaps arising from guilt but also trying to help him to neutralize his intelligent but nonetheless unrealistic and unpredictable fantasy life. I worked at both levels, the intrapsychic conflict produced in him by his anger toward his quite genteel and intelligent mother, but also recognizing the early adolescent's coming to understand that some day he in fact will die—a difficult milestone. I tried to sharpen this bright young adolescent's reality testing and age-appropriate immature judgment. While of course guilt in a thirteen-year-old intelligent, reflective boy will rouse the dread of punishment, in Guy's case, the punishment he somehow unconsciously selected took the shape of this age-appropriate, realistic but usually very quickly repressed recognition of the reality of his own death. It was good to see that in time, while his anger toward his mother unavoidably cropped up from time to time, it decreasingly stirred up his existential anxiety and ultimate fear of his own death.

Quite differently than thirteen-year-old Guy, two late middle-age patients who within the past several years were diagnosed with stage-2 cancers and have undergone rigorous chemical and radiological treatments were—and still are—sharply subjected to the reality of their mortality. For both, the threat to their lives has been real, coming from internal bodily sources and is a painful part of their current everyday life. While it is not in constant conscious awareness, it is never far from it. Most consciously worrisome for the younger of these two patients is that, being divorced (and her former mate's not inspiring her with confidence that he would perform the necessary parental tasks that would befall him) she most dreads dying before her young teenage offspring reach adulthood and the capability for self-sustainment. As I noted earlier in this text, it is reasonable that the dread of one's death would be heightened in most adults who have children. With this patient, in fact with both these adult cancer victim patients, I have supported their reality-testing, have listened empathically—and sympathetically—to their pained associations about the threat under which they have been living and to a degree currently still do, taking note of their regaining strength, their bodies seeming to be healing well given their appearing in a healthier state than a few months, and then even a year, ago; as well as being attentive to their parental concerns and addressing the successes and setbacks their children were sustaining. These interventions necessitated my stepping out of my analytic stance including my checking on their routine self-care and especially their diet, exercise, and sleep-wake patterns.

One of these patients, a very capable self-employed professional, woke up terrified, she told me, and started her session by bursting out: "I hope you don't die . . . and I don't either!" Given that I am well older than she, her anxiety about my dying was not outrageous. Nor, given her cancer history was her own death anxiety. Well engaged in her analytic treatment, her reliance on my being there to continue to help her work through the impact on her of her early childhood and subsequent traumas and her resolving masochistic adaptation, speaks to her positive transference and productive working relationship. I was and am very sympathetic with her plight but, retaining my analytic position and reality orientation, in essence I said to her that "Much as I have tried to become a therapeutic magician I have never succeeded in getting there." But with her I have held the view that no one can predict the future and, given the evidence of her healing well and reconstituting her strength, chances are good that she may well live for some three more decades and who knows what time might bring? The fact is that she is working through past maladaptations and masochistic tendencies and, while we can't be absolute about her continued recovery from cancer, given the rigorous treatment she got for it, there is reason to assume that she may go on for some years to come. To her occasionally challenging my "optimism," I told her as Abraham Lincoln had retorted long ago to the same accusation, that "It is better than the alternative."

Mortality and religion

As time has passed, I have experienced, as a physician, awe at the marvel that is the human body. It is a complex entity of various types of tissues constructed to make these tissues do what they do, and by the remarkable "engineering" of these tissues into organs and systems it functions to sustain the state of living. I have been given to reflect along these lines especially in times when this living marvel reacts to maintain its life under most challenging conditions. And further fueling this awe is the fact that homo sapiens is just one among many species of animals and an entire kingdom of plants also constituted of many species, large and microscopic. It defies comprehension how these multiple marvels came to be. No doubt, I am the zillionth human who has had such moments of awe and reflected on this question. It certainly was not homo sapiens itself who "engineered" all this.

Let me venture further on this path where it might be wiser for me to not tread. The only thing I risk is being ridiculed for putting such thoughts on paper. Considering one's mortality, one cannot escape the probability that it gave rise within homo sapiens to the belief that there is an Almighty Power to whom one can turn for protection, for comforting, for one's self-perpetuation beyond one's life as we know it. Of course, this thought then gave rise to religion; each subculture generating its own version of it. To be sure, there are many among us who do not believe that an Almighty Power figured all this out and made it happen. "How did it come to be?": these nonbelievers postulate that a chain of events from the beginnings of time brought about life on Earth. Some assume that long, long ago, among the numerous atoms in the universe some found affinity for one another, starting with, say, negative ions coupling with positive ones to combine various atoms; which then spontaneously and fortuitously further combined and organized into organic molecules that again, spontaneously and fortuitously combined and organized into compounds, which in turn eventually further combined into a collection of reciprocally interactive compounds; then surrounding themselves with a containing-shielding membrane and ultimately finding that most mysterious self-generating impetus to maintain its own existence: "life" was born. Furthermore, living things became compelled to reproduce themselves, first simply by parthenogenesis and then, miracle of miracles, they fortuitously divided the challenge of reproduction into a dualistic gender-based regenerative arrangement. And to secure that this reproduction be perpetuated, chance brilliantly saw to it that reproduction would require activity the members of the species would not want to forego! Survival achieved primacy.

However it came about, those who came to accept/believe in the Almighty Power hypothesis found a much easier explanation and avoided having to deal with the imponderables with which atheists and agnostics have burdened themselves. "God created man in his own image!" If the reader has not yet abandoned me, let me follow further down this path.

Whichever explanation of life-generation one accepts, we living animals have come to value our existence. But it did not take long in our efforts to maintain life to recognize our individual mortality. This fostered in us an inner-driven assignment not only to survive and to perpetuate ourselves, but foremost, to find meaning and value in all this, in our individual existence during our brief stay on Earth. But the challenges of making our being and life meaningful sometimes, perhaps often, bring with them "existential anxiety," and retreating in the face of these and insecure in our search for meaning, the awareness of our own mortality compelled many among us to creatively generate religions. Would religions have come about without "existential anxiety" that culminates in the recognition of one's own mortality?

One more thought on the possible role of one's mortality and religion. Countering Freud's declared atheistic position, Romain Rolland challenged him to explain the worldwide experience humans have, the "oceanic feeling," Rolland taking this to best represent for him a basic religious feeling of being one with the universe. My sense is that Freud (1927c) addressed Rolland's question of feeling one with the world exceedingly well, ascribing this feeling to originate in the infant's sense of feeling one with his mother, a concept that was later postulated by Winnicott in his well-known principle that, "There is no such thing as an infant, there is only an infant and its mother" (1960, p. 39); as well as, of course, by Margaret Mahler, who went quite a lot farther than Winnicott by proposing the "separation-individuation theory" which at its start holds that the neonate, once he perceives the steadfastness of his surround (from about six to twelve weeks), perceives himself as one with mother, as if in a symbiotic membrane (Mahler, 1968; Mahler, Pine, & Bergman, 1975).

It is not reported whether Rolland objected to Freud's speaking of religion as the "neurosis of society"; however, I have questioned Freud regarding this phrase. Freud was not an observant Jew. Nor am I an observant Jew. But as I noted above, as a physician, in awe of the complex magnificence of the human mind and body—and other living things—there is much to wonder about in Rolland's question, and otherwise. But my question lies more with Freud's view that religion is a neurosis. Rather than a neurosis, it seems to me that religion is a reaction creatively invented by humans to protect themselves against "existential anxiety," the anxiety produced in the course of humans' struggle to find meaning in life over which, from about ten years of age on, hangs the recognition of their own mortality. I say "creatively invented" in the sense that (1) we erect defenses to protect us from anxiety, which when intense enough threatens to overwhelm our ego rendering it dysfunctional; and (2) I see religion as the product of a defense that ranks alongside altruism, humor (both of which to a degree commonly are positive reaction formations), and sublimation, all in essence being defenses which by virtue of our variably noteworthy creativity yield a positive character trait or a product as a work of art, a piece of music or literature, defenses I have in fact spoken of as "sublime defenses" (Parens, Scattergood, Duff, & Singletary, 1997).

And how regrettable that if religion is a sublime defense, that each one can become so reified and so violently held to by some of its adherents, that so much conflict in our world has been created and for so many millennia. The insistence that all humans should adhere to the same religious ideology can never be achieved given that every large group has its own variable individual historical narrative (Akhtar, 2007) which, over time, has given rise to their variable religious ideologies. Can we ever hope to become accepting of each other, accepting of our differences?

Notes

1. None of the French concentration camps were death camps—as they were in Poland and eventually in Germany itself. (The deadliest were in Poland. We may presume that the Germans were not eager to have death camps on their soil. In fact, Dachau, near Munich installed one crematorium chamber, but according to its brief information-descriptive note, it was rarely used.) While during the World War II Vichy France era, these camps were called "*camp de concentration*" (Marrus & Paxton, 1983), they subsequently were re-labeled "Detention camps" (Peschanski, 2002; and personal communication which revealed to me that many wartime documents were no longer available; and I venture to presume, the name change may have been motivated by the French effort to distance itself from its complicit past, a history many French denied—"Tout le monde était dans la Résistance!" [Everyone was in the Resistance]).
2. I recall with much pleasure the times when Selma Kramer, Joe Rudolph, and I, close friends and colleagues, used to now and then tell one another of the incredible things kids say in analysis. I recall the time Joe told us that a twelve-year-old patient was home ill and for a few days could not come to her appointments. Her mother had called Joe to let him know she was ill. Joe asked to talk with her briefly. After a few inquiries Joe asked her what she was doing at the moment. She was in bed, she said, stroking her pussy! She really meant her cat; but you know the minds of analysts!
3. My parents had separated many years before. When I was about three, my mother and I left our family in Poland and moved to Brussels, Belgium where we were when World War II erupted. To escape the German invasion we left, as did many, to seek asylum in France. After four months, the asylum turned into concentration camps (see Parens, 2004).
4. Cooney wrote this article for the *Globe*, which via the Internet was distributed to its members by the Regional Council of Child and Adolescent Psychiatry of the Greater Philadelphia Region. Cooney can be reached at ecooney@globe.com.
5. https://en.wikipedia.org/wiki/World_War_II_casualties#Nazi_Germany

References

Akhtar, S. (2007). From unmentalized xenophobia to messianic sadism: Some reflections on the phenomenology of prejudice. In: H. Parens, A. Mahfouz, S. W. Twemlow, & D. E. Scharff (Eds.), *The Future of Prejudice – Psychoanalysis and the Prevention of Prejudice* (pp. 7–19). Lanham, MD: Jason Aronson.

Cannon, W. B. (1915). *Bodily Changes in Pain, Hunger, Fear, and Rage*. New York: Appleton.
Erikson, E. H. (1959). *Identity and the Life Cycle. Psychological Issues Monograph No. 1*. New York: International Universities Press.
Freud, S. (1920). *Beyond the Pleasure Principle. S. E., 18*: 1–64. London: Hogarth.
Freud, S. (1923). *The Ego and the Id. S. E., 19*: 3–66. London: Hogarth.
Freud, S. (1925). Some psychical consequences of the anatomical distinction between the sexes. *S. E., 19*: 248–258. London: Hogarth.
Freud, S. (1927c). *The Future of an Illusion. S. E., 21*: 1–56. London: Hogarth.
Furman, E. (1974). *A Child's Parent Dies*. New Haven, CT: Yale University Press.
Hedges, C. (2002). *War Is a Force that Gives Us Meaning*. New York: Anchor.
Kestenberg, J., & Brenner, I. (1996). *The Last Witness: The Child Survivor of the Holocaust*. Washington, DC: American Psychiatric Press.
Koenigsberg, R. A. (1975). *Hitler's Ideology: A Study in Psychoanalytic Sociology*. New York: Library of Social Science.
Koenigsberg, R. A. (2009). *Nations Have the Right to Kill—Hitler, The Holocaust and War*. New York: Library of Science.
Mahler, M. S. (1968). *On Human Symbiosis and the Vicissitudes of Individuation*. With M. Furer. New York: International Universities Press.
Mahler, M. S., Pine, F., & Bergman, A. (1975). *The Psychological Birth of the Human Infant*. New York: Basic Books.
Marrus, M. R., & Paxton, R. O. (1983). *Vichy France and the Jews*. New York: Schocken.
Overmans, R. (2000). *Deutsche militärische Verluste im Zweiten Weltkrieg* (pp. 228–232). Oldenbourg, Germany.
Parens, H. (1970). "Inner-sustainment": metapsychological considerations. *Psychoanalytic Quarterly, 39*: 223–239.
Parens, H. (1979). *The Development of Aggression in Early Childhood*. Revised edition. Lanham, MD: Jason Aronson/Rowman & Littlefield, 2008.
Parens, H. (1988). Psychoanalytic explorations of the nuclear threat: three notes. In: H. B. Levine, D. Jacobs, & L. Rubin (Eds.), *Psychoanalytic Explorations of the Nuclear Threat: Aggression, Projection and Identification* (pp. 223–243). Hillsdale, NJ: Analytic Press.
Parens, H. (1993). Toward preventing experience-derived emotional disorders: education for parenting. In: H. Parens & S. Kramer (Eds.), *Prevention in Mental Health* (pp. 121–148). Northvale, NJ: Jason Aronson.
Parens, H. (2003). Mothers' emotional investment in their children. In: P. Turrini & D. Mendell (Eds.), *The Inner World of the Mother* (pp. 43–70). Madison, CT: Psychosocial Press.
Parens, H. (2004). *Renewal of Life – Healing from the Holocaust*. Rockville, MD: Schreiber.
Parens, H. (2008). *The Urgent Need for Universal Parenting Education – a Documentary*. A DVD produced by Parens, H. & Gilligan, P., director. Philadelphia, PA: Thomas Jefferson University, Medical School Media Division.
Parens, H. (2010). Children's understanding of death. In: S. Akhtar (Ed.), *The Wound of Mortality* (pp. 37–50). Lanham, MD: Jason Aronson/Rowman & Littlefield.
Parens, H. (2011). *Handling Children's Aggression Constructively—Toward Taming Human Destructiveness*. Lanham, MD: Jason Aronson.

Parens, H. (2014). *War is Not Inevitable: On the Psychology of War and Aggression.* Lanham, MD: Lexington.

Parens, H., Scattergood, E., Duff, S., & Singletary, W. (1997). In: Parens, H. (2010). CD: *Parenting for Emotional Growth: A Textbook, Two Series of Workshops, & A Curriculum for Students in Grades K Thru 12*(c). ISBN 0-9726910-0-6. L. Mikita (production manager). Philadelphia, PA: Thomas Jefferson University, Media Division.

Peschanski, D. (2002). *La France des camps—L'internement 1938–1946.* Paris: Edition Gallimard.

Rees, L. (1997). *The Nazis—A Warning from History.* DVD. L. Rees (writer & producer), Prof. I. Kershaw (supervising historian). London: BBC TV production in association with BBC Worldwide and the Arts and Entertainment Network.

Winnicott, D. W. (1960). The theory of the parent-infant relationship. In: *The Maturational Process and the Facilitating Environment* (pp. 37–55). New York: International Universities Press, 1965.

Illness

Chapter 5

Psychotherapy – a life's work

Ruth Garfield

Everyone ages or gets hurt or sick – and then we die. When illness and the specter of death invade the clinical space, they have potent effects on the therapist and the patient. In this essay I hope to describe the impact of illness on me as a person and on me as a psychoanalytic therapist and how the two intertwine. I will discuss how being seriously ill has challenged my zeal for my work and confronted me with the need for better self-care. I also include clinical vignettes to describe some of the many ways the issues of my vulnerability and mortality have affected my patients.

Background

The work we do as psychotherapists and psychoanalysts is very difficult. The therapist is usually in the position of caregiver or provider. This isn't to say that we don't receive or learn from our patients, but largely they look toward us to "use" us, in a Winnicottian sense, to receive insight, support, suggestion, and/or medicine, and to enact their most fundamental unconscious conflicts with us. As I approached my early sixties and many years of practice, I was becoming more aware of the pull within me to give to others in my work, and of the paucity of time I spent making sure my being and soul were protected. I was just starting to think about future years of less work, at some point retirement, and about what other adventures would interest and perhaps even satisfy me. At about that time I heard Adrienne Harris Ph.D. give a talk about the need for the therapist to take care of herself. How that resonated with me!

A few months later in July of 2012, routine labs found that I had significant and alarming abnormalities in my blood counts. My regular doctor didn't even want to see me but over the phone directed me to a hematologist whom she had already contacted. It was midday and I was at my office. (I'll get to how I carried on that day.) I phoned my husband and my sister to tell them something was wrong. Fortunately for me, my two physician nephews quickly mobilized and got me in touch with the hematology departments at each of the two leading hospitals in the city near my practice. I was seen within a few days.

I was immediately told that I had leukemia. For a short while it appeared that I had acute leukemia, which would have necessitated immediate long-term hospitalization and treatment. On review of my pathology labs, subsequent tests and bone marrow aspiration, my diagnosis turned out to be a rare form of leukemia that was to be treated by bone marrow transplant.

I have had a strong work ethic. My ethos has been characterized by pushing myself and pushing on. And that I mostly did during this initial time. I shared the diagnosis with my closest friends, most of whom were colleagues, but asked them to keep this news confidential until the time when I would inform my patients.

The aging process definitely had something to do with how I then metabolized this new information including the new question regarding my future. It also affected how I considered my life and work. I had experience with serious medical situations in the past. I had been diagnosed with breast cancer in my early thirties, and then with a recurrence nine years later. Each of these times I took only the necessary time off for surgery and only the medically necessary (very little) time off for additional treatments; I was of course very anxious but I was also very young. I had a sense of robustness and not fragility, and of life as ongoing and not as time limited.

I believe I used my clinical work to distract myself. There were many times when I was scared especially when getting repeated scans and tests, but in my thirties I felt a strong determination to go on, to achieve some of the goals I had hoped for both personally and professionally. It was around the time of my first cancer diagnosis that I decided to go to a post baccalaureate pre-med program that would clear the way to go to medical school. I knew that I could die from breast cancer; my denial was not so huge that this was far from my mind; I had read about people who had died from metastatic disease. I was scared, but how I lived my life was largely my focus and I felt impelled to persevere.

I think there is something very life focused about psychoanalytic thinking. At the time of my first cancer, I was taking a three year program in psychoanalytic psychotherapy as a psychiatric social worker and getting supervision from psychoanalysts. They knew of my diagnosis and treatment. They encouraged me to be optimistic and to continue with my goals for medical school. I think there was some denial in their attitudes and my affirmation about life, but at that time it was helpful. I have a vivid memory of receiving a gift when I was diagnosed from a social work colleague entitled "Living Well on Borrowed Time." I was frightened and horrified at this grim view of my illness and prognosis. Now of course I live with the awareness that we are all on borrowed time. Though young, I wasn't avoidant about death thoughts.

I grew up surrounded by and close to my extended family, which included grandparents and elderly aunts and uncles. I had experienced many deaths. I was especially close to an aunt who was more the age of a grandmother.

She was philosophical and cynical and talked a great deal about death. As a young practitioner, I was also quite taken with Carl Whitaker's advice in his "set of rules that will keep the therapist alive" to "practice dying" (from Plato). Thoughts about death had been close by growing up. This time round, however, in my early sixties, I have been more consumed with how my thoughts about death influence how I live my life. This is where I was just prior to my leukemia diagnosis and where I continue to be as I live with the illness and the effects of my treatments.

Early impact of my illness

In this chapter I hope to demonstrate how the latest life threatening illness has affected my work and my life. With over thirty years of cancer I have had much time to practice life in the shadow of death. This latest time has been different, and I will focus on that.

Following that first phone call from my internist regarding my lab work, before I had a definitive diagnosis, I met with my scheduled patients. That day I finished out the afternoon and I believe I saw most patients for the remainder of the week. As I said, this was my way of living, pushing through, trying to focus on my patients and my work, and thus getting away for periods of time from my anxiety. I realize now that I could not do this completely (perhaps at all?), and I wonder if my patients sensed my preoccupation or emotional absences. In any event, no one said anything. Over the next weeks I canceled patients, traveled to get consultations in other cities, and also arranged to take a week away with my family and dear friends.

Once it was clear that I would have a bone marrow transplant, and needed one as soon as possible, I knew that I would begin to talk to my patients. Andrew Morrison, in his paper, "Trauma and Disruption in the Life of the Analyst" (1996) calls this "enforced disclosure." At this time in my career, I believe that many situations demand honesty over abstinence and nondisclosure. Our patients know much about us and don't know much about us. When we are tired and weak, pale or bald, they have questions about our physical well-being. At such times, I feel that they have a right to know the truth. In my situation I did not feel that there was a choice. I had decided that I would answer questions as truthfully as I could. I continue to take this stance now that I'm back in practice.

I had been working a full schedule seeing adults, children, and adolescents. There were so many people to tell, and most were people with whom I had had years of treatment relationship. I was informing my patients not only of my illness, but of the need to be away from practice and from them for at least fifteen months. They therefore knew of the seriousness of my condition and the uncertainty of whether I would return. The period of my absence had to include periods of isolation, without visits, and without phone contact.

It was interesting to me that my oncologists specified "no phone sessions." They'd clearly had other therapists who underwent the bone marrow transplant, and they knew that many of us prioritize taking care of others over caring for ourselves.

With children and adolescent patients, I called the parents first and discussed the situation with them. I am glad that when I work with children, I try to include the parents, and I consider my relationship with them extremely important. I asked each set of parents if they wanted to meet with me first, and then talk to their child themselves, if they wanted us to all meet together, or if they wanted me to meet with the child myself. I met with some parents first, but each set said they would talk with their child themselves. In each case, they then set up a meeting for me to also meet with the child or teenager. It is touching that although I was very scared and uncertain, and at times internally bleak and pessimistic, so many parents knew people who had had bone marrow transplants and wanted me to know how well these people were doing. I was encouraged and very moved by this.

My practice has been analytically oriented, with patients either in psychoanalysis or psychotherapy. This means that I have known most of my patients for years. My diagnosis was ominous and the procedure I was to have was often as unknown to them as it was to me, and it sounded frightening. I knew that I could not hide my sadness and fear, as much as I tried. I had two weeks to terminate with my patients, to tell them I would find other therapists to continue with them and if they did not want this, who to contact if they changed their minds, if something came up, or they wanted to know about my progress.

We tried to hold/contain our feelings for each other. Most were alarmed for me and sad with me (and themselves). I shed tears with them during those weeks. Most of my patients returned for the second session before I left. They had questions they wanted to ask and they wanted to have more time with me as I did with them. There were also hugs of goodbye and good wishes.

Two of my patients were not able to be with me once they heard what would be happening, and left the session early. As I look back, what these patients had in common was a history of early abandonment or extreme neglect. This history made their feelings about my illness and departure intolerable and they had to flee. I had worked with each of these people for less than two years. One returned the next week with a gift and we were able to talk briefly about what my news had stirred up for her and who she could see for therapy at this time. The other found someone else to work with immediately. I think it demonstrates something about my state of mind that I did not anticipate these reactions despite knowing these patients well and trying to focus on taking care of their needs. I think this is just one illustration, understandable and unavoidable, of how much I was concerned, anxious, and preoccupied about my own condition and prognosis.

Following my bone marrow transplant, during the time of my "recovery" I heard occasionally from patients with notes and cards. I tried to respond to each of these with a brief note. The psychiatrists covering for me also let me know if someone called to ask about me.

My interest in psychoanalytic work reaches back to my social work education, in the late 1970s. There has been much psychoanalytic training and treatment in my adult life. Many times I have asked myself if my personal analysis helped me to deal with the renewed issue of mortality. By the time I began my analysis more than thirty years ago, I had had one brush with cancer, and during the analysis, another. My analyst encouraged me to have hope and face life rather than death. I do think this is the bias of psychoanalysis. Suffering is frequently seen as neurotic and to be cured, more than to be known and accepted as a condition of life. Traditional, earlier psychoanalysts even had postulated that the roots of illness lie in one's personal neuroses. Death and my fears of it – I didn't hear too much about in the course of my analysis. From another perspective, I believe that the depth of the work I did in analysis helped me become more stable and able to tolerate and manage my anxiety. With the latest diagnosis of leukemia, though anxious, I had some inner calm and strength. I credit my analysis with much of this.

When I was diagnosed, a friend, also an analyst, gave me a book, *Being Well (Even When You're Sick)* by Elana Rosenbaum. The author writes about mindfulness in the context of cancer and serious illness. My friend had suggested other meditation or Buddhist oriented books over the years, but I was probably more cynical at that time about anything other than psychoanalysis helping the mind. Following my diagnosis I found this particular book and the mindfulness techniques it discusses extremely helpful. At this time in my life, I was open to and seeking additional help with the life threatening events that were cast upon me. I have continued a mindfulness practice and have found it helpful in dealing with the stressful periods of my illness and life.

Return to work

As I approached the end of the fifteen month mandated hiatus from work, I spoke with my doctors about my return. They were clear that I needed to monitor my stress levels and not take on too much either in my work or my personal life. I decided that I would start with about ten hours per week, and then work no more than half time. This was also necessary because of the many medical appointments that I had to fit into the schedule. Following this long break, I was increasingly aware of changes in my priorities, my approaches to life and work, and more acutely conscious of the limitations of time. I wanted to continue to have time to read, meditate, watch a movie, do yoga, exercise, all things that I had done during the break.

I prepared a letter that would go to my patients, advising them that I would be returning to practice in several months. I was explicit about not wanting to disrupt a treatment that they had begun with someone else. I consulted closely with several colleagues and had them review the letter. I also discussed with them the need to restrict the types of patients I would take on. I knew I could not see patients with deep character problems, narcissistic vulnerabilities or rage, or about whom I would worry too much. I knew that I would find this too burdensome and stressful at this time.

I was torn about the return of one such patient, since I had treated her for a long time. During my absence she had seen another psychiatrist/psychoanalyst, although I wasn't clear how she found him. The patient let me know in a note that she did not like this psychiatrist. While I was in the early isolation recovery period, I received an email from this psychiatrist who sharply wanted to know if I was planning to see the patient again, since he didn't want to continue with her. I was surprised to find this in my email, and was reminded how difficult this patient was. I wrote to tell the psychiatrist that at this early stage of recuperation I did not know how I would be doing and if I'd return. (This was an early example of how anxious colleagues could be by the threat of illness and mortality, and how denial could be so strong that it could block empathy or even sympathy about my medical condition.) When I returned to practice, I decided to treat this patient but also decided that I would not treat anyone else with that type of deeply traumatic history and character pathology for the time being.

A surprising number of "former" patients called and gradually I had a small practice again. In one of the papers she wrote following her treatment for ovarian cancer, Ann-Louise Silver (2001) comments on this "phenomenon" of patients staying with an ill therapist. She writes:

> And why did my patients choose to stay with me? Do our patients stay out of loyalty or to avoid beginning with someone new? Do they dread magical retaliation for abandoning someone in distress? Perhaps our patients stay because they think, "Good. Now she is no longer just the doctor, the one with authority. Now we both are sick together. It isn't just me putting anxiety into the atmosphere. Maybe finally we can help each other . . ."

Silver is correct in her observation that we all have fears of mortality and death, and that, at the least, it is a mutually held issue.

I had relinquished my previous office location at the time of the procedure and thus I had to find a different space. This was also disruptive and evocative for my patients; it was a concrete declaration that our work, though renewed was different.

Questions and issues have arisen with each patient as I have returned to clinical work. For some patients there has been deep denial, based, I believe, on their need to see me as whole and available to them. Perhaps their denial of mortality persuades them to see me as robust enough to conquer not just this illness but my mortality. A forty-two-year-old unmarried lonely man, who had suffered severe early parental neglect, became angry with me shortly after returning. He made it clear that he knew that I was now fully recovered (he didn't ask). During my absence, he had sent me occasional notes with good wishes. I knew how difficult this break was for him and I wrote brief notes back. He especially focused on having been deprived of being in personal touch with me. He assumed that colleagues or friends were able to visit me, and he was angry that he could not. There had been occasions prior to my illness when he was very angry at me for slights he perceived, but his anger had an intensified edge to it at this time. I tried to listen and tolerate, understand and contain his feelings, but he eventually broke treatment. I have to admit that his anger at me at this time was hard for me to bear, and perhaps he unconsciously perceived this also.

EL is a woman in her early forties with whom I worked in analysis for many years and in psychotherapy following the analysis. She very rarely brings up our hiatus or my health. She also has a history of early parental neglect and spent much of her life waiting and hoping to be seen by her highly visible parents. As she has worked so deeply on this feeling of invisibility, I think the idea of losing me as someone who has tried to see and know her over twenty years may be too difficult to acknowledge. When I left, she was in a new relationship. She, in fact, had emailed me early in my absence (I was in the hospital and I recall that there was a sense of relief not to have lost all clinical contact) with a request for help in finding a couples therapist. She did this despite having heard from me that I would not be reachable. Later when I sent my letter about returning, she contacted me and said that although she had tried a couple of other therapists, they hadn't worked out. We continued our work, but as if we hadn't skipped a beat. She (like the above-mentioned patient), seemed to assume that I was fine and didn't entertain the thought that I wouldn't be fine. In the long time we had been working together she had experienced significant family losses, one of a parent toward whom she was highly ambivalent. Her emotional response was complex and muted. She includes me as one of the few people she can be close with, and her relative silence about my illness and absence reflected her fear and denial about the possible loss of me.

Another patient, also with a trauma history, became sick with several sequential ailments or debilitating conditions shortly after my return. I listened to him and was empathic, but I did not interpret what I believed was his wish to endure illness as I had, either in an identifying or competitive way. He is someone for whom the work had progressed and still progresses very slowly. I continue to have concerns about how much I have been able to help him and how treatable through insight or interpretation he is; however, I think the relationship with me has been very important and my absence was extremely difficult for him. He allows himself only to perceive me as healthy. In this way he can continue to feel hope for me and therefore, for himself, and he continues to hold on to our work together.

As I write, I reflect on the question for myself of how difficult it is for me to both sit with someone and be aware of the possibility again of loss. At moments with the above three patients, I was aware early in my return of still feeling hobbled and weak, not yet myself. I wanted to protest, "Don't you see that I'm still recovering?" At other times I wondered if, through my own denial, I missed openings or opportunities to raise issues because of my concern about loss and mortality.

With other patients, there is often, maybe always, a sense of awareness that I have been sick and away from them. A patient who had been in intensive psychotherapy waited through my fifteen month absence to resume the treatment. He soon expressed his anger that I didn't get back to him in six months as I had promised I would. I had no memory of this promise, but I don't doubt that I made it. He was also upset that he couldn't get information about my return from sources he thought he could. His anger came out in various ways. He told me about his friends, physicians and a nurse on oncology units who saw numerous patients relapse and die after having a bone marrow transplant. This was hard for me to hear, but I also felt that I needed to accept and help process his anger with me. He ended the analysis early, at least earlier than I thought was good for him. I am left to wonder if this was his way of making sure he left me before I left him again. I did not process this with him at the time. Again I think that the denial I struggle with may have prevented this.

At the time of my return to clinical practice, I was in frequent contact with two colleagues with whom I could review and process clinical issues that newly arose. I knew they were pained and protective when they heard about such angry interactions. I felt that if I was returning to the work, I had to be able to tolerate some amount of questioning and anger. Some patients expressed their thoughts and feelings about my illness indirectly. However, not only was it necessary for me to contain their feelings but also to make them conscious so that we could talk about them.

One patient, a forty-nine-year-old woman, had been seeing me for several years following a traumatic life event. Very verbal and psychological, she had found the treatment extremely useful in helping to deal with the trauma, and at the same time carry on with her family and professional life. She decided to see another psychiatrist at some point early in my absence. When I returned she was at first undecided, but made the decision to return to treatment with me. What followed were a couple of meetings with me, at which time she asked, and I answered, questions about my current health and prognosis. By this point, my hair had in part grown back, and I looked fairly healthy. She knows that my future is uncertain but that right now it looks good, and she wants to continue her work with me. Death is in her mind at times. When I was able to move back to my original office space, I had decided not to continue to see young children. The small room that had been my playroom still housed my toy cabinet and a couple of chairs, but there was a lot missing. There was no doll's house, small play table, or comfortable small sofa where there had been before. As she was leaving, after the first session there she turned around and said that the room felt like "a room of death." When I raised this with her at our next session, she had no memory of having said this. She could, I believe, momentarily confront the possibility of my death, but couldn't hold onto it. At other times, she talks about books she has read about a physician's death or the deaths of physician friends. There are times when she will comment on my appearance, whether tired or moon-faced from prednisone, and with some anxiety ask directly how I am. I tell her that I would let her know if my situation changed, but also inquire about her anxiety about my health and availablity to her.

Another patient with a history of early traumatic loss decided not to see a different therapist in my absence. She has dealt with the deaths of several people in her life with whom she was very close. One of these was her dearest friend. She also lives in utter fear that something catastrophic will happen to her children. Whenever I went on vacation in the past, she would question me about whether I was flying, and worry about my safety. She still does this. She also "looks me over" to see if I'm OK. Often she'll stop herself and say something like, "How can I talk about myself? My problems seem trivial compared to what you've been through." She wants my permission to go on and continue to "use" me as she had, but she wants also to make certain that I am strong enough to bear her pain.

SF is a forty-three-year-old man who has had trouble in relationships with women. During the time of our analytic work together some of the themes that emerged were his wish to both take care of me and to want more from me. He saw me as both strong and able to give him more than I did, and fragile, someone to be taken care of. At the time our work had to stop, he had been in a relationship that although problematic looked more promising than previous relationships. This new woman was more independent but also could only indirectly express her wish to be taken care of. During the time I was out, they became engaged and married. He sent me an announcement and a photograph. Since I've returned, we have revisited these themes. At times he expresses concern about my health directly. He also has talked at length about a female friend who is sickly, and whom he cares about. I have raised with him how this mirrors his concern about me and his thoughts about taking care of me and he agrees. Prior to my illness, he expressed thoughts and anxieties about his mortality and the meaning of his life. He had a very close colleague die recently which was very difficult and frightening for him. He talks at times about people with celebrity who have died, and their legacies. I don't always draw the comparison to questions about me. Sometimes I do not think these thoughts are related to me but rather reflect his singular reverie about mortality. However, I think he has a certain freedom in knowing that we can talk about my illness and about mortality in general.

Of course not every patient returned to treatment with me. A few found other therapists they wanted to continue with and some ended treatment (as far as I know). One of the unsatisfying aspects of this work is that we often don't know how our patients are faring after they leave us. For the few patients that I no longer have contact with, I feel this curiosity and lack of resolution acutely. Often it is with the knowledge that our work together (even though I know it is never done) is not "complete."

Some patients came back to treatment more slowly. Last year I received a call from a patient who I had been treating when I was diagnosed. I had heard from her once during my illness and time away. She called to ask if I could see her again. Her husband had been recently diagnosed with a blood cancer, related to mine. He was doing well but she was struggling with issues of being the spouse of someone with this diagnosis. I was glad that she had conveyed the gist of this information on voicemail. It gave me some time to consider if I felt I could treat her. I worried about how well I could listen and be with her as I might hear about anxieties that echoed mine, or, perhaps worse, push me to confront my fears of renewed illness or death. What if her husband relapsed; how would I deal with both the exacerbation of my patient's fears about his illness and the exacerbation of my own anxieties? She had questions for me about my health and whether I felt I could deal with her life-changing concerns as the spouse of a cancer patient. I answered directly. I have always felt that we learn so much from our patients, but EB pushed me to think more deeply about the impact of my illness on family and friends, and about what they were suffering and fearing, feelings they had largely spared me; embedded in their suffusion of support and care for me was their sadness and fear.

Another patient, EN, returned to treatment with me just a few months ago. She had immediately begun to see someone else, whom I had recommended. I did not hear from her during my time away from work and I hoped she was finding treatment with her new therapist helpful. She explained that she had left the other therapist months before and had felt that the connection was not as deep as that with me. Pressing concerns brought her back into treatment with me. She has not yet brought up directly the impact of my illness on her and her treatment. Worries about how she uses the time left to her in her life also brought her back into treatment with me. While she did not express this directly, I believe that she intuits that I ponder this question all the time myself. I believe that in the coming weeks this will be something we discuss together more explicitly.

Another clinical question I ponder is that of whether to disclose to a new patient that I have had this life-threatening and life-changing illness. I had two patients return to me after a three-year break which spanned the time I'd been out. I have not disclosed my illness to them, or to new patients. I wonder if the returning patients sense me as different. I know that I am different in many ways: I look somewhat different, my hair is shorter, my body is fuller, and during the time of high dose prednisone, my face and body clearly were changed. I even may be more attuned to my patients' internal affects than before, less distracted by what's external. They have not brought up these differences in appearance or focus, however. Perhaps they are following "the rules" for good patients – or they may not want to know.

Colleagues' responses to illness and mortality

During the time of my recovery I heard from many friends and colleagues expressing support and good wishes which I very much appreciated. My close friends and some new friends supported me. They phoned or visited often or came to cook for me. I have always valued friendships and felt that psychoanalysis didn't do justice to the importance of our relationships with friends in our lives. I have come to believe that developing dear friendships is part of taking care of oneself.

When I returned to work, it was with the imprimatur of my physicians, but also with the anxiety and question within me of how well and capable I was. Should I begin to work with patients when I could not guarantee that long-term work was possible? Of course I could rationalize that no one could truly make that promise, but my history skewed that implicit if unrealistic contract. I had concerns about my anxiety level on days when I had doctors' appointments, and when any medical complications arose. Could I listen adequately when I also was dealing with personal anxiety? Would this interfere too much? I have used my closest colleagues as consultants regarding these questions and hope that their wish to protect me includes the wish to protect my patients.

Once I returned to work, I soon became aware that other than my former patients I was not getting new referrals from clinicians who had referred previously. I was in three study groups and once I could leave my house I attended them again, even before I resumed practice. For well over a year after I was back practicing, I got very few new referrals unless it was for a rare low fee patient, which was difficult now that my practice was so reduced. I could understand that colleagues were concerned that I wouldn't be able to continue the work. At one study group, the one that I felt closest to, I raised the issue. People were very quiet and it seemed clear to me that they were not comfortable discussing this. Again, it is possible that the choice of this work, so multi-determined by our psychological histories, may also relate to its focus on life, and not the inevitability of death.

I had been elected to the board of a professional organization shortly after my return to practice. Several months later I was questioned about my "many absences" and asked if I would consider resigning. This did not seem accurate to me, and I asked to review the attendance records. At several meetings, I was not noted as being either present or absent. I believe I became somewhat invisible as a reminder of the fragility of life for all of us.

From some more distant colleagues, I had a different response. I received a call from a psychiatrist I was only acquainted with, who had obviously heard about my illness. She left me a message saying that she heard that I had been sick. She wanted to know how I was doing, and if I'd take referrals. I appreciated her candor. We spoke, I told her about my medical status, and I have received several referrals from her.

Another friend and colleague with whom I hadn't been in touch for a while made contact soon after she heard I was ill. She became a friend again and upon my return sent me two referrals for long-term therapy. A colleague from my analytic group called to see if I'd take a position which would give me visibility. I was so grateful to these people. I know them well enough to know that illness and death has touched them very closely. Perhaps their capacity to face such loss enabled them to be more available and empathic than others were able to be.

I imagine that by my age, my cohorts would have had this experience, but some have been spared. Still it's clear for therapists as well as for patients that death, illness, and mortality are very hard to discuss and hold in one's mind without a great deal of anxiety. As Ann Louise Silver writes, "All defenses against anxiety ultimately develop to distract us from our knowledge that we each will die" (2001, p.54). In the silence, there is an unconscious fear of seeing the possibility of one's own vulnerability and mortality. The longer I have practiced, my referrals from former sources have increased, although with little or no conversation.

Amy Morrison, an analytically oriented social worker wrote two moving papers about disclosure and practicing psychotherapy with a life-threatening illness. She writes, "Another kind of ramification for the therapist is in the effect of knowledge of one's illness on the attitudes of colleagues, and the loss of control over rumor and misconception" (1997, p.238). She heard from a patient that her couples therapist advised her to terminate the individual therapy because of her illness. It was reported to her that another colleague/therapist said, "Oh, she's dying," when her name came up. I have felt a sensitivity to being seen as sick and, even more difficult, that this perception is out of my control. And that this occurs without active, conscious, acknowledgement or questioning of my condition is a further frustration.

In summary

Because of my early history of cancer, knowledge of my mortality has been a fairly present companion. I have wanted to live fully, to accomplish personal and professional goals and at the same time continue to face the inevitability of death. With the onset of this latest illness, my professional goals have receded as I focus more on life with my family and friends.

Most of my patients want to be thinking about their lives, living more fully, with less angst and conflict, and are not death focused. I consider this the kind of existential denial that we all usually live with. For my patients who know about my leukemia diagnosis, I believe there is an implicit understanding that if my condition changes we will talk about it and process it emotionally and practically. I would like to think that my honesty about my medical condition enables them to go on with their work on their life concerns. I attempt, not always successfully, to stay attuned to my patients' concerns about my health. I think it is probable that my illness and treatment have raised awareness of their own mortality. Perhaps it has also sensitized them more to issues about relationship loss which would eventually be a part of any treatment or relationship. I know that I carry the existential mantle of mortality into our space together; although it is now not frequently brought up, it is necessarily with us. Once a therapist has experienced serious illness, the practicing of living and dying are more patently in the clinical setting.

The focus upon living a fuller life, with less anxiety, depression, and conflict can be present for older or younger patients. Our work in therapy or analysis is usually about living a fuller life. Although the aging process with its losses, and incapacity may prod an older person to think more about her own death, living well in the time left is often the reason she may seek therapy. My oldest patient is someone who is very psychologically minded, thoughtful, and anxious, with whom I began treatment after my return. I did not disclose my illness to her. After seeing her for about a year, she told me that she had heard that I had had cancer. She asked how I was now, and later remarked on my weight gain (from medication). I answered her questions directly and honestly, and then each time she continued with her own life work, some of which included worries about her death or that of others close to her. Although they were caringly concerned at the time of my illness, my younger patients, adolescents or young adults, clearly want to focus on their own lives.

I try to deeply respect my patients' wishes to focus on their lives, and I feel a greater capacity following my most recent illness to be attuned to the inner life of my patients. Perhaps this is because I carry the awareness of the limits of time. I'm more able than before to accompany my patients who fear death or who want to talk about their own death or that of a spouse. My anxiety about my death is less than before, and I think that must make me a calmer and stronger therapist. When patients want to go there, I willingly and more calmly go there. When they want to discuss their success or failure in love or work, I listen. It is rare that I will think that's someone's life struggles are trivial compared to mine. I can't say that that has never happened, but it is rare.

My awareness of mortality is not only about time left, but also about how and with whom I want to spend my time in the present. This awareness has deeply sharpened since my illness. Appreciation for my own needs and wishes, taking care of myself emotionally and physically are much more important than I allowed them to be before. Carl Whitaker, in his paper, "The Hindrance of Theory in Clinical Work" about the benign absurdity of life, ends with the advice, "If we can abandon our missionary zeal we have less chance of being eaten by cannibals."

If I have learned one thing that is worth sharing from this experience, it is the necessity for a therapist to care for herself. Often what draws us to our work is a need to take care of or be responsible for others even to the point of heroics. We can get lost in this propensity through our own goodwill or narcissism, or a fear of mortality. Through all of my training in social work school, psychiatry residency, or analytic training, I don't recall any teacher advising us to be evaluating frequently how we're doing with self-care, to question how many and what types of patients we take on, and to take stock of our deepest wishes and priorities. We are advised to get supervision or consultation but I fear largely from a group which may not acknowledge their own mortality and vulnerability. I attend to these things now and I think that I am a better, more attuned therapist for it.

> We are here for what amounts to a few hours, a day at most.
> We feel around making sense of the terrain, our own new limbs, bumping up against a herd of bodies until one becomes home.
> Moments sweep past.
> The grass bends and then learns again to stand.

This poem by Tracy Smith (2011) expresses feelings about our finite time in a way I could not. In a beautiful way, she expresses my own sentiments. This latest encounter with the limits of time has changed me personally. I'm more connected to my priorities and my values. I am, or at least try to be, a more grateful, compassionate, and kind person. These aren't attributes that we hear much about in psychoanalytic circles, but I think we would do well to take stock of this.

References

Morrison, A. L. (1990). Doing psychotherapy while living with a life-threatening illness. In: H. J. Schwartz & A.-L. S. Silver (Eds.), *Illness in the Analyst: Implications for the Treatment Relationship* (pp. 227–250). New York: International Universities Press.

Morrison, A. L. (1997). Ten years of doing psychotherapy while living with a life-threatening illness: self-disclosure and other ramifications. *Psychoanalytic Dialogues*, 7(2): 225–241.

Morrison, A. (1996). Trauma and disruption in the life of the analyst: enforced disclosure and disequilibrium in "the analytic instrument." In: B. Gerson (Ed.), *The Therapist as a Person: Life Crises, Life Choices, Life Experiences, and their Effects on Treatment* (pp. 41–54). New York: Analytic Press.

Silver, A.-L. S. (1990). Resuming the work with a life-threatening illness—and further reflections. In: H. J. Schwartz & A.-L. S. Silver (Eds.), *Illness in the Analyst: Implications for the Treatment Relationship* (pp. 151–176). New York: International Universities Press.

Silver, A.-L. S. (2001). Facing mortality while treating patients: a plea for a measure of authenticity. *Journal of the American Academy of Psychoanalysis and Dynamic Psychiatry*, *29*(1): 43–56.

Smith, T. K. (2011). *Life on Mars*. Minneapolis, MN: Graywolf Press.

Whitaker, C. (1976). The hindrance of theory in clinical wok. In: P. J. Guerin (Ed.), *Family Therapy: Theory and Practice* (pp. 154–164). New York: Gardner.

Chapter 6

Illness in the analyst – thirty years later

Harvey Schwartz

On a Friday afternoon in April 1985, after a full morning of patients and administrative activities as psychiatric residency director, I went to my internist at my old medical school because of worsening pain of five days' duration on my right side. Radiologic examination revealed a large mass of unknown origin in my right chest cavity. I knew I was in for something when the radiologist put me in front of a fluoroscope machine and called in the fellows: "Hey, come take a look at this thing." His initial (and perhaps intended for reassurance) impression was that it was "probably benign," but he recommended an immediate thoracotomy. My hospitalization was scheduled for that Monday. It was estimated that with chest surgery and convalescence I would be able to return to work in six to eight weeks. I called my wife and returned to my office to close down my practice and delegate my administrative responsibilities. I called all my patients and told them that a medical problem had arisen that I must attend to and that I expected to be fine. I said that I anticipated returning to my office in approximately two months and that I would call them some time before to schedule appointments. Patients were variously shocked, did not ask the details of my problem, and wished me well. I made arrangements with a colleague for coverage of my patients and in case I would not be able to return to work.

As the implications of what was happening to me grew more apparent I became terrified for myself and my family. Closely parallel to my personal fears, I developed a concern of panic proportions that was focused on my patients. Under the traumatic impact of these events, my initial realistic concerns for their well-being mushroomed into my projecting upon them my own distress as well as reliving through them a painful event from my past.

Some years earlier in my own experience as analysand I had felt abandoned and profoundly shaken by my analyst's repeated hospitalizations and ultimately his sudden death. This perceived new version of an old trauma reawakened my grief and my sense of loss and guilt.

This history as well as the earlier sudden death of my father remained encapsulated within me and emerged in my overidentification with my patients. I experienced again an overwhelming sense of loss that transcended my self-observing capacity. As a projection, my patients' perceived abandonment temporarily became my near exclusive focus of pain. A potential empathic link with my patients became instead a regressive identification in service of my own repetition compulsion and need to avoid facing the real dangers that lay before me.

By the next day my emotional investment in my patients' presumed fears waned as I left the past behind to face my frightening future. While I looked and generally felt healthy I began to enter the regressive role of the self-involved medically ill. I started to measure all personal relations by the degree to which they attended to me and found myself inclined to mentally turn to others, including patients, in search of objects who would be concerned for me. As a result of this deepening narcissistic functioning, "as if" relationships lost their traction and latent and not ordinarily pressing countertransference fantasies emerged. Just as the day before I had reduced awareness of patients' complex individual reactions to my illness, I now was losing meaningful awareness of the metaphorical aspect of the relationships – it all seemed "real." Now I wished for their feelings of abandonment.

After a prolonged but inconclusive diagnostic workup and mental preparation for the surgery, most all relationships other than those immediately involved in my care fell away in importance. My attention was focused exclusively on my body and my future.

One week after what turned out to be successful surgery for a noninvasive tumor, I returned home for recuperation.

In *The Interpretation of Dreams*, Freud comments, "Unconscious wishes are always on the alert, ready at any time to find their expression when an opportunity arises." He goes on to say that these wishes are "as ghosts in the underworld of the Odyssey – ghosts which awake to new life as soon as they tasted blood" (1900a, p. 553).

In his 1990 paper on psychoanalytic process, Boesky writes, "It is not enough to say that lapses in technique are unavoidable. These lapses are highly valuable glimpses into the nature of the psychoanalytic process itself" (p. 573). And later,

> If we as analysts ignore these inevitable failures of our own, we do so at our own peril, because it is at the point of failure in our effort to remain objective that we will be able to make valuable new discoveries about the patient and sometimes about ourselves. The true success is the understanding of the interaction between the failures, the patient's and our own. (p. 574)

I bring these two sets of ideas forward as they inform for me the clinical challenges I faced when I became ill and when I returned to work. Freud's quote poses the question of how we can best be available to our patients in order to awaken their ghosts for analysis. What blood is best offered to bring to analyzable life patient's unconscious wishes? What does it mean when our blood is not simply a metaphor and how does that literalness impact on our efforts to touch our patients' inner lives? Boesky's notion has to do with how we experience what might be called errors. This question taps into the heart of how we observe our interactions with our patients, not to mention how we relate to our own consciences. What does it mean to both parties if retrospectively viewed errors, not of the malignant sort, are not critiqued but embraced for what they have to teach us? Perhaps this is the essence of post-oedipal functioning. This issue raises for our consideration what the interpretive impact is on our patients if we view our "errors" as opportunities for growth, not as occasions for the narcissism of self-abuse. After all, after being ill, many of us are focused on how we can best reengage with patients and minimize what might be "errors" in our approach.

In this chapter I will comment on my thinking on this issue at the time of my original illness, my current reflections of the subject, and some thoughts on the meaning of an analyst being ill for our professional community.

Some years ago I received a call from a colleague in another city asking if I would be a discussant for her paper on her own experience of having been ill. While I was in the midst of feeling pleased by her request she went on to tell me how much she enjoyed my 1987 paper on the subject and how thoroughly she agreed with my thinking. With some humor and awkwardness I told her of my pleasure in both her invitation and appreciation. However, I also told her that I no longer believe in, that is, no longer find clinically optimal, much of what I then wrote. I briefly explained, we laughed at the oddness of the exchange, and went on to present what we both felt was a thought-provoking panel on the topic.

It is in the area of my two opening quotes that I feel that my thinking at the time was limited. Despite my best efforts to finesse the question, I did at that time fall into the dichotomous position of asking, "Do you tell or not tell patients about your illness?" In 1987 I wrote,

> Given my understanding of the clinical importance of my being able to recreate an analytic condition, I set aside the question of what I would tell patients and instead focused on rediscovering that psychic space in myself. Sometime later, in so doing, it emerged there was no need to discuss the details of my illness with my patients. Indeed it seemed quite beside the point. The issue was, given the reality of my physical well-being of which I reassured patients, to resume an analyzing relationship. In that capacity, the fact of my illness was as irrelevant as any other

personal information. The real question of consequence was whether I could re-provide an uncontaminated analytic space in the present within which they could continue to affectively encounter their past. The answer to this lay outside the issue of the details of my illness. (Schwartz, 1987, p. 673)

On the one hand this sounds good. However, many years later I can state with some assurance, though not as much as I had thirty years ago, that this point of view is not correct. By that I mean that while sounding theoretically solid, the position of an "uncontaminated analytic space" is not in fact the position that offers the greatest analytic usefulness to many patients at many times. It does not best further many treatments. Simply, what I was confusing at that time was that what was important to me was what was important to my patients. I myself needed to feel firmly organized around an agreed-upon standard theory and technique. This is quite comforting after having been immersed in the frightening regression of illness. Patients, and this is key, obligingly complied with the false self I was promulgating for both of us as they for the most part did not want to nor were they able to challenge my seemingly necessary self-comforting. Patients of course vary in their defensive complicity based on their history of childhood honesties and the confidence they have in their underlying libidinal ties to us. Most patients though will seal over their losses, imaginings, and terrors in the face of their analyst's withdrawal into illness and then into anonymity. Withdrawal begets withdrawal. It is easy at such times to confuse abstinence with neutrality. Abstinence is the behavior of anonymity. Neutrality is the analytic state of mind that allows us to float equidistant between the past/present, fantasy/reality, I/thou. It is our mentalization of the analytic third.

The problem with my thinking at that time was that I misunderstood the power of transference. As is commonly and I believe mistakenly taught, the tradition-weighted notion is that "answers provided are fantasies lost." The fact is that one cannot close down a patient's transference-driven perceptions of his analyst with mere information. The analyst's ambiguity, which is that which elicits transference, is easily maintained alongside the providing of some factual information. Answers provided simply offer a nidus around which transference fantasies coalesce. Often, though of course not always, a patient's character will wrap itself around provided factual information more analyzably then it will around a vacuum. In addition, there are occasions when answering offers the advantage of being more experience-near for both parties. As such, fantasies that are built around a kernel of fact allow the entire exchange to be more than an intellectual exercise. That is, answering questions allows the subsequently stimulated fantasies to take on a more personal feel and hence carry more affect for both parties of the dyad. If you will, self-revelation can function as an interpretation precursor. If one appreciates that vital meanings can be generated and subsequently analyzed by staying alert to their presence after answering questions then both parties can be spared the obsessional question of: "Should I tell or shouldn't I tell?" My answer is: Do either, for experience teaches us that there are times when not answering stimulates productive imaginativeness and there are times when answering does the same. More important is the imperative to listen to the impact of both. Or, said more succinctly, it is useful to feel free to act interpersonally while always thinking intrapsychically.

We must, however, strive to be honest, sometimes painfully so. Our illnesses, like our mortality, mark us all in common as human. Greater than the individuality of one's fantasies, and this is the essential point, our fragility before fate must be honored as the overarching essential meaning of the illness experience. Psychoanalysis uniquely appreciates the representational aspects of such events. Nevertheless we must be humble in privileging the fundamental fears at such times that we and our patients have in common. Only in the face of that frightening truth does the elaboration of the secondary fantasies then become more than protective storytelling.

My attention is focused on how best to enlarge our patients' freedom to experience the post illness analyst. This includes considering the question of how much to answer questions about our illness. As Boesky recognizes, if one maintains one's analytic functioning, errors can be opportunities, not simply a source of worry or self-preoccupied regret. Optimally, one's intimacy should be with the contours of our patients' unconscious life, not with our relationship with our conscience. Accordingly, in lieu of attending to formulas concerning what is called "self-revelation" we can instead attend to our own inclination to reveal or not reveal and try to remain aware of what it means to both parties. It's the "try to remain aware" that is the analytic model that we demonstrate to patients and that contributes to their learning to cathect process over content. That is why I was mistaken in 1987 when I wrote, "Assuming one's health is actually no longer in jeopardy, one's illness and absence should be used strictly transferentially as an opportunity to uncover and rework the past." The error in this statement is again built upon the certainty of my conclusion. I was deciding a priori what one's stance should be with all patients at all times – and that can't be optimal. For example, in the different phases of an analysis and certainly in different patients' analyses the workable ratio of literalness to metaphor is always evolving and does so in individualized trajectories. My early mistake took me years to recognize. Perhaps aging itself is useful as part of our analytic maturation. But whether one uses the "mistakes are bad" model or "mistakes are opportunities" model, it is a mistake to think that either model will spare us the confusion and uncertainty that comes from dealing with our own morbidity and mortality. Whether we focus on our patients' genetic meanings of our illness or on the here and now dimensions, we are necessarily inexact. Neither position is capable of capturing the fullness of our patients' or of our own experience at such times. One is well advised to include at these moments the fundamental notion that "shit happens." Correct technique cannot spare any of us the terrors of our vulnerabilities.

The challenge the dyad faces post-illness is to assist patients to affectively recognize the meaning to them of their analyst's illness even in the face of their analyst's own necessarily incomplete acknowledgements. At such times, patients often react to the terrifying vulnerability of loss with varying degrees of a defensive "sealing over" process. The notion of sealing over is a shorthand. It is in fact a process born from a complex series of compromise formations that carry a long history that course through an individual's development. Nevertheless, such an affective withdrawal is experienced, often by both parties, as a monolithic unavailability as if it lacks the very nuances that we know are its constituents. As a consequence of this sealing over, the patient's affect may flatten, his relating narrows, somatic reactions may take center stage, and survival mechanisms may trump creative adaptations. In the best circumstances an analysand will be able to use this experience as yet another opportunity to recognize his characterologic fingerprint and will be able to reemerge into healthier, if not humbler, functioning. That depends of course on a host of factors including constitutional ones, history of trauma, phase of analysis, and the capacities of either the ill or the subsequent analyst.

We must return though to Freud's challenge of finding the blood to awaken the ghosts. Patients' ghosts live in their syntonic disguises which we call character. Our work is to help reconfigure these ghosts into conflictual entities so that, as felicitously described by Loewald (1960), they may be analytically reincarnated into ancestors newly worthy of identification. A question faced by the ill analyst is, how does our personalness aid in these ghosts becoming recognizably dystonic to our patients? We all approach this hinge point, between what the physician/writer Jerome Groopman (2007) calls the interface between science and soul, in our individual ways and we teach it accordingly. We teach the basic structure of how the mind works and how we become part of our patients' minds. Some of us will take these basic scales and develop them into exquisite classical orchestrations where the effort to be technically precise becomes the vehicle of our affectionate wish to heal our patients. Others of us will take our knowledge of these scales and find clinical utility in object-attentive improvisation. In that form we find our own idiosyncratic voice which reflects our technical proficiency and our best efforts to reach our patients' hidden meanings and shameful self-representations. This technical relativism I am suggesting might sound reasonable if we were simply musicians. Then, whatever style moved us personally would be an adequate justification for its utilization. But we are clinicians, devoted to a different purpose and a different ideal. What we personally find pleasing is perhaps irrelevant to the clinical task at hand – helping the patient heal. This raises the question for me of what we can mine from our analytic technique that reflects our individuality apart from the reductionistic aspects of abstinence.

It turns out that we have data on this question. Not quantitative data but data nonetheless. Lora Tessman in her book *The Analyst's Analyst Within* (2003) describes asking graduate psychoanalysts about their own analyses. She specifically asked about the presence and role of their analyst's self-revelation and how they felt that it did or did not impact on the overall quality of their analytic experience. Her findings are telling. It turns out that to these graduate analysts whether their analysts were self-revealing or not had no correlation with whether these analysands found their analytic experience to be a positive one in their lives. In and of itself, self-revelation was not a meaningful variable in their treatment's outcome. Judy Kantrowitz in her book *Myths of Termination* (2015) similarly interviewed former analysands about their analyses. When faced by their analysts' illnesses and what they felt was their analysts' denial of the gravity of their condition they "experienced disappointment, a loss of trust in their analyst [as they] expected that their analyst's emotional capacities to share and not deny would be greater." While disillusionment with one's analyst is ubiquitous and human limitations in the face of mortality are not surprising, Kantrowitz concludes that "The anxiety and loss of trust that may follow being told nothing [about the illness] will surely do far more damage to the analytic relationship than providing factual information" (p. 75).

Do these findings answer the question about what one should tell patients about one's illness? Certainly not. There are many ways one can understand these findings. To me they are suggestive, not proscriptive. What is more telling for me personally is my experience with one of the patients I reported on in my original paper and my follow-up with her post publication.

This was a woman in her late twenties who responded to my sudden illness and absence with a constellation of actions designed to both represent and avoid its meaning to her in the context of her childhood abandonments, overstimulation, and her father's prostate cancer. I wrote then that when I returned to my office she commented about her thoughts of my illness, "I have no idea and I hadn't thought about it since I don't know about medical things." The next day she revealed that she thought I had prostate cancer like her father did and had to undergo the same procedure. Alternatively, she imagined that I suffered from infertility. She had the further fantasy that she had caused my illness because of her hostile wishes. The following day she recognized the childhood fantasy that she had caused her father's illness from her rage at him for his damaging her as an infant by dropping her and leaving her as a mere female all her life. I used this material in my paper to explain my stance of not telling patients the details of my illness. Follow-up revealed something less categorical. After the publishing of my paper and a few years after my illness, but during the same month of its occurrence, I noticed a rather sudden regression in this patient's material that included concerns for my well-being. This led me to recognize its juxtaposition with the time of year. I asked her if she was aware of this being the anniversary of my having been ill. This then led to a flood of feelings, fears, and at this point in her treatment the freedom to think about and directly ask me what had happened. We both recognized that this had been missing and with it was missing a deeper degree of honesty between us about this major event in our life together. I had originally not addressed as fully as I might her resistances to acknowledging her curiosity. Now, I simply told her what had occurred and with that something changed between us. I had been keeping an unnecessary secret which served to help her keep a secret from herself. I used my allegiance to what I had construed as correct technique as a justification for my countertransference which at the time led me to feel safer with more distance. This character trait led me at the time to misunderstand the powerful role that the analyst's affective availability plays in helping to evoke patients' histories of pains and passions. In retrospect, perhaps I was ready when she was ready. But this consideration spared me from learning as much as I could from this experience. It also spared me from recognizing the possibility that had I felt less constrained when I had first returned to work, I could have helped her more deeply and more expeditiously. Said differently, in retrospect it appeared that my countertransference withdrawal was internally driven, not in correspondence with an unconscious aspect of the patient. My answering her question became a piece of our story in understanding the childhood basis of her long secreted curiosity. Given the fullness with which the patient eventually experienced her oedipal desires in the transference as well as rages and sorrows during termination I am left to conclude that my freedom to answer her question helped engage her curiosity and not only did not limit our work together but arguably was a component of its depth.

I have learned that the obsessional question of "Do I tell or do I not tell?" is beside the point. Similarly, the limitations of such ruminations also apply to our attention to the relative roles of patients' aggressive vs. libidinal transference fantasies at such times. When the analyst has been ill the balance between the two is more delicate than ever. As always but more so, we see that loving feelings can defend against frightening angry ones and angry feelings can defend against frightening loving ones. The analyst's tolerance for both without prejudice is key and always imperfect. Many factors impact upon our inclination towards one or the other of these affects. More about this in a bit.

> My illness occurred while I was an analysand. I can share an aspect of what it was like to be on the couch and be suddenly and frighteningly ill. In fact I can report on a sort of imperfect experiment on the topic for I had to suddenly return for surgery seven years later related to the first condition. As life would have it I was on a different couch when

I went through my second surgery and experienced two very different analytic approaches to being so vulnerable. The first experience was handled from a distance by both parties. I informed my analyst of the sudden circumstances with all the insight and protectiveness that I had available to me at the time. We left things that I would call him some time after the surgery and let him know how I was and when I would be able to return. I did that and when I returned we analyzed the various infantile fantasies I had about the origin of my illness with masturbatory guilt being prominent. I found this experience to be helpful and interesting.

In the later analysis I again learned that I would be hospitalized for surgery and was unsure of my return. Having been through this before and being more clear about the medical issue I was less terrified as well as more alive to my fears. This time, my analyst called me after my surgery to check in with me and see how I was. We had not discussed this and I was surprised and touched. In fact, this gesture and my reaction to it opened up a piece of my character that had been syntonically untouched in prior extensive treatment. The meaning to me of this simple act in the context of my particular background made available for our work a rawness and authenticity that was vital in my growth.

Upon reflection, I realized that the light I have attempted to shine on this issue of "telling or not telling" is a bit brighter than I wished it to be. This has alerted me to its defensive aspects. We know from clinical work, and this has been beautifully described in our literature, that excessive brightness in remembered images is due to their function as screen images – that is, an image which is overly vivid in memory functions to withdraw attention from a more deeply conflicted arena. When this occurred to me it provided a relief of tension that I am familiar with from work with patients. I pursued it further. It then seemed to me that what the authentic difficulty is is not what we do or don't tell our patients – likely we will handle that as we do other delicate matters, more or less satisfactorily. The more latent question seems to be, what do we tell our colleagues?

I learned from speaking on this subject throughout the time around my paper being published that in many institutes there are analysts who have been ill and have chosen to not share this information with their colleagues. I certainly am not questioning such a decision. Groups, as we well know from the history of the American Psychoanalytic Association, can be malicious and not at all trustworthy places. One's personal health is a deeply private matter and reasonably one would not want to subject oneself to the often mean-spirited gossip attendant upon personal revelations. The usual explanation for such silence is that it might negatively impact referrals. I don't think, however, that that explanation acknowledges the full truth of one's gut-driven caution.

I am aware that with this notion I am touching upon an additional aspect regarding the ill analyst. That is, what is the impact of an individual's illness on his or her relation to the group at large? Included in this question is how the group encounters one of its members who becomes ill. Again, every institute has its own painful history of ill and demented analysts. Groups struggle, often unsatisfactorily from the point of view of analysands, with this not uncommon challenge. This is a crucial subject mostly to be addressed in the realm of institutional recommendations, obligations, and protections. Though related, this is not where I would like to draw attention at this time. Instead I would like to emphasize a matter that is delicate in another way. I am referring here to the meaning that we all carry inside us of the question, are our colleagues and is our group a trustworthy place within which I can expose vulnerability?

I take this question further and wonder if it has something to do with what I mentioned as the imbalance in the literature on the ill analyst. What has been mostly emphasized is the conflict of patients at those times over their aggressive wishes towards their analysts almost to the exclusion of their conflicts over their libidinal ones. That is, we seem to easily fall prey to our temptation to obscure for all concerned the painful helplessness of our vulnerability. Instead, we focus almost exclusively on patients' guilt over their aggressive imaginings. For me this raises a question to be considered. As mentioned, groups can be cruel places. It is possible that if we took more caring interest in our members in need then maybe we would not be hyper-attuned to the centrality of our patients' aggressive fantasies. Stated differently, if we as analysts felt reasonably cared for by our analyst colleagues when we were most vulnerable then perhaps our clinical ear would in turn better register patients' conflicts over their sorrows. Addressing patients' resistance to their libidinal attachments in a more balanced fashion can be a powerful tool in softening their need to seal over. Feeling cared for begets feeling cared for – a necessary foundation for the subsequent and important analysis of conflicts over aggressive fantasy. Stated differently, one's capacity to love contextualizes destructiveness.

One may reasonably raise the question whether the focus I'm suggesting on the post illness role of the group's kindness towards its members serves as a turning outward, an externalization, of one's conflicts with one's own illness reinforced harsh conscience. Searching for kindness outside instead of inside. In part that is true. But only in part. Groups functioning at their best should serve as affectionate foils for an individual's temporarily regressed conscience. After all, if the group can't help you when you're down, why bother being a part of it, much less giving it your heart?

A final point. If truth be told, as analysts we deal very poorly with our analyst colleagues when they become terminally ill. And when we ourselves become terminally ill (it has often been noted anecdotally) we work very poorly in the clinical situation. There is a startling degree of consistency in the stories one hears about analysts who are dying. This is true for the many personal stories I have heard over the years as well as in the literature on the subject. This is a finding that is so painfully obvious as to require collective denial. Analysts cannot work analytically with their own fatal illness with the minimal regard for the patient's welfare that they would demand of themselves in all other circumstances. We cannot, nor should we expect ourselves to, be able to help our patients mourn us while we are struggling to mourn the loss of our own well-being and indeed, our life. And this in the face of our best intentions.

Freedman described such a situation in "Death of the Psychoanalyst as a Form of Termination of Psychoanalysis" (1990). He reported in intimate detail the blinders we have when faced with our own dying. He had a close analyst friend who learned that he had a terminal illness. Freedman spoke to him straightforwardly about the importance of discussing this clearly with his patients and supervisees. His friend assured him that he was completely transparent about his situation. After his friend's death, he interviewed those patients and supervisees and learned something entirely different. Even though the topic had been honestly taken up between two analyst friends, the dying analyst failed to do what he said. His patients and supervisees were taken completely by surprise.

We analysts always say that we need data from which to draw conclusions. The data on our ability to conduct ourselves analytically when faced with our own dying is quite conclusive. We have no need for additional data. We need to act on the basis of the data we have accumulated. I have in the past recommended that each institute establish a "buddy system" – a program where each analyst confidentially informs the institute office of a chosen colleague with whom he has agreed they will keep an eye on each other's health. It is the responsibility of this "buddy" to be in conversation with the analyst if there is any reason to suspect that he is not up to the clinical task of engaging with patients. It is the responsibility of the buddy to work with his colleague if he should develop a terminal illness.

To conclude, despite the evolution of my thinking as an analyst I don't want to suggest that I have neither regard for nor pride in my earlier writing on this subject. Accordingly, I would like to close with a quote from my introduction to the book, *Illness in the Analyst – Implications for the Treatment Relationship*:

> We have compiled this book with the intention of stimulating individual and collective attention to the understudied though common phenomenon of the ill and dying analyst. This topic is a rich source of subtle data on the very essence of what makes a relationship psychoanalytic. It is also an area requiring institutional consideration and recommendations for practice. We hope this work is of assistance to those who have been afflicted with illness and are engaged in the clinical challenges of psychoanalytic work. (Schwartz & Silver, 1990, p. 3)

References

Boesky, D. (1990). The psychoanalytic process and its components. *Psychoanalytic Quarterly, 59*: 550–584.
Freedman, A. (1990). Death of the psychoanalyst as a form of termination of psychoanalysis. In: H. J. Schwartz & A.-L. S. Silver (Eds.), *Illness in the Analyst – Implications for the Treatment Relationship*. New Haven, CT: International Universities Press.
Freud, S. (1900a). *The Interpretation of Dreams. S. E., 4–5*: 553. London: Hogarth.
Groopman, J. (2007). *How Doctors Think*. New York: Houghton Mifflin.
Kantrowitz, J. (2015). *Myths of Termination*. New York: Routledge.
Loewald, H. (1960). On the therapeutic action of psychoanalysis. *International Journal of Psychoanalysis, 41*: 16–33.
Schwartz, H. J. (1987). Illness in the doctor: Implications for the psychoanalytic process. *Journal of the American Psychoanalytic Association, 35*: 657–692.
Schwartz, H. J., & Silver, A.-L. S. (Eds.) (1990). *Illness in the Analyst – Implications for the Treatment Relationship*. New Haven, CT: International Universities Press.
Tessman, L. (2003). *The Analyst's Analyst Within*. Hillsdale, NJ: Analytic Press.

When a patient dies

Chapter 7

When a patient dies
Reflections on the death of three patients*

Sybil Houlding

Our profession elevates the status of what we – somewhat brutally – designate the "termination phase of analysis." A terminated case – one in which both parties agree to conclude their relationship at some specified date in the future – is often a requirement for graduation. We recognize the demands on both analysand and analyst during this anticipated ending of a long and intense relationship. The unexpected death of a patient short-circuits this process for the analyst and highlights the special difficulties of mourning this unique relationship.

Within a five-year period, three patients in three different forms of treatment with me died unexpectedly. The differences among the three situations – the timing within the treatment, the transference/countertransference matrix at the time, and events in my own life – all profoundly influenced my response to each death. They led me, in retrospect, to consider the developmental aspects of this unexpected event in the life of a working analyst. It is a situation that is not addressed in our training, and it is one for which we are quite unprepared. A patient's death leaves the analyst struggling to find her way, usually alone.

I was not eager to write this chapter. I did not want to revisit the losses that had caused so much disruption in my internal life and that were now sealed over and behind me. But after considering how much a book such as this would have helped me to locate myself at the time of these deaths, I realized that this would be a unique opportunity to think more carefully and, perhaps, to a larger purpose than my own recovery.

Julie

Julie was in analysis – first at four and later at five times per week – from May 2003 through August 2004. In her early fifties, Julie was petite, lively, and attractive, a married mother of three. She had been in several relatively brief treatments with a colleague who had seen her in weekly sessions for depression. It was after this final episode of treatment for depression that my colleague recommended analysis and referred Julie to me. Julie seemed eager to understand and change her chronic unhappiness but also reluctant to acknowledge the seriousness of her difficulties. Although often filled with despair, Julie tried to present a happy and successful face to the world. "All my life I've been a really good girl," she reported in our first interview.

Julie was raised in a wealthy family, surrounded by a successful brother and many wealthy and accomplished cousins. Julie's mother was a narcissistic and mentally ill woman. Her primary mode of relating to the world was to maintain a privileged social position and to "look good." These were the values she instilled in Julie, without providing her with the means to succeed.

Julie continued to be preoccupied with trying to emulate and please her mother while also rejecting what she perceived as superficial and unattainable. Her brother was the recipient of the family's largesse. It was he who was given the opportunity for private schooling and the financial means for social success. When Julie met her first husband at the age of twenty, she felt she had found a place for herself. But after a year of marriage, her husband committed suicide. Her husband's parents were nurturing – that perhaps had been part of her attraction to him – and continued to be so after their son's death. After her husband's suicide, her brother wrote, "Don't come back [to the family home] – there's nothing for you here."

Her second marriage, to Jack, her modest, intelligent, gentle husband, was a safe haven for her, and motherhood provided satisfaction. At the time that we began our treatment, Julie's children were in college, and she was working at a job well below her abilities, but one in which she still felt inadequate. She was envious of the people with whom she worked who had more education, confidence, and success. Julie's pattern had been to flee treatment when she began to feel better; part of her motivation for analysis was her worry that with her children launched, she could not live without her husband if he died. Jack was older than Julie and had had a serious illness several years before she began the analysis. Julie realized that she needed to become more internally self-sufficient.

An early note from the analysis reads, "Activity, frantic activity, has been her defense against chronic sad feelings but in the analysis J. has begun to be able to tolerate them. Central themes are her feeling of estrangement, chronic feelings of outsider status, envy of others who have close family bonds, and constant preoccupation with social status."

I liked Julie and responded to her eagerness and her capacity for hope. She had an entertaining way of presenting herself. But after a few months, she allowed herself to show me the envy, rage, and deep despair hidden beneath her bright surface.

About one year after we began our work, Julie and I had reached a new phase of treatment. In the transference, I became the close female confidante she longed for. "You remember Jan," she would say, telling me the latest installation in her complicated relationship with a friend. Or, "my mother called again . . ." The comfort of our relationship in the transference allowed her to make tentative contact with the more disturbed parts of her inner world. This new feeling of connection was also used to disguise and avoid her growing dependence on me, one that felt deeply threatening to Julie's conscious ideal of complete self-sufficiency. I was able to interpret her difficulty with our weekend interruptions and her difficulty letting herself acknowledge this. She then accepted my recommendation that she come five times a week.

This period of the analysis also coincided with intermittent comments from Julie about difficulty swallowing and pain in her esophagus while eating. On some level, Julie welcomed this symptom. It helped her to control her appetite and maintain her ideal of slimness, and also supported her fantasy that she was without need – of food or nurturance. But as the discomfort persisted, she did call her doctor, who suggested an over-the-counter remedy for gastric reflux. When this did not alleviate her distress, tests were ordered. Ultimately, a full workup led to the shocking diagnosis of esophageal cancer.

"I did this to myself," Julie wept as she lay on my couch. Julie now threw herself into getting well with all the ferocity she had previously brought to other important challenges. For example, she had become a marathon runner and had pushed herself to learn to ski, despite her terror, because it was important to her husband. Her treatment involved chemotherapy and radiation, to be followed by surgery, but first she needed to gain weight. This required her to have a feeding tube inserted directly into her stomach, a daily procedure that lasted for a month.

A note from this period reads, "I have been working supportively with J. by phone these last two weeks after an interruption for chemo and radiation ... slowly I see a glimmer of a fuller analytic process." I look back on this note with amazement at my capacity for denial, my wish to preserve the analytic process in the face of such a serious, life-threatening situation. Julie, too, needed the idea that she was "in analysis" and that the surgery would lead to recovery and a resumption of our former relationship. A feeding tube to the stomach is a metaphor for an umbilical cord. So, too, a telephone line. Julie's deep regressive wishes were being met in the context of a life-threatening illness, one that also served her need for punishment for her rageful and envious feelings. While these thoughts are available to me now, they are useless. At the time, I felt like her lifeline.

Julie's surgery was scheduled for early August and coincided with my planned three-week break. "Oh good!" she said. "I'll be out of the hospital and ready to see you right when you return!" Those were her last words to me.

I thought about Julie during my time off. I returned to the office on the day of Julie's first appointment with great anticipation. When she did not show up or call, I became alarmed. I called her home and left a message, which was not returned. I want to write "weeks went by," but probably it was only days. This time is still a blur in my mind. I called the hospital but they would tell me nothing except that she was still a patient. When Jack did call, he informed me that the surgery had been successful but that Julie's lungs had collapsed afterward and that she was being kept alive by an artificial respirator.

After a number of agonizing weeks, Julie died. I remember those weeks as a time of waiting with very little access to news about Julie's situation. I don't remember whether it was Jack or a member of his office staff who called me. And there is no one to ask, no family or friend to whom I can turn and ask, "How do *you* remember this?" Bereft, lonely, isolated, I searched the literature on PEP-Web for reports of others who had endured this experience, but I found nothing.

I went to Julie's memorial service with two colleagues who knew her husband and thus, tangentially, knew Julie. They were caring and aware of my situation, but they were not grieving as I was grieving. Sitting at the service, I struggled with the feeling that most analysands express at some point in their treatment: *Who am I – really – to you?*

Listening to Julie's children, her friends, and her husband, I thought, *Oh, I know you!* This helped me feel connected to Julie, as if later – after it was over – we could discuss it. As her community mourned Julie, I was invisible. I knew Julie as no one there knew her, but only she and I knew that. I was in that strange state where the mourner both knows her object has died but has not fully accepted this knowledge. Julie had often talked of feeling outside the bonds of the human community, very much alone. I felt outside the bonds of the mourning community, unable to participate in the comforting ritual of talk with others who knew and loved her. It was clear to me that as important as I was to Julie, I was totally irrelevant to her family. Several months later, I did receive a kind letter from Jack, when he paid the final bill, telling me how grateful he was for the work with Julie and how much it meant to her. The letter was meaningful to me in part because I felt acknowledged as someone who had sustained a loss.

For months, I walked around with Julie in my mind, hearing her chattering voice, imagining what story she might bring to a session, thinking of all the promise this analysis had held.

There were two important factors in my own life that had special resonance for me and made this loss unusually powerful. Nine years earlier, my mother had also died in August, also of cancer, also unexpectedly, during a reunion after a long and difficult estrangement, which left me hopeful that we were on the verge of a new and different relationship. The wound was not fresh and analysis had helped me to mourn her but there was a powerful resonance about lost opportunities when Julie died. The loss of a compelling patient in a shocking way at a time of hope was very difficult, but in time I experienced this loss as part of my professional identity, something I understood and had integrated, rather than as a personal loss.

Ralph

Ralph and Lucy were referred to me by Dr. Jones, a clinician in the community who I knew by name and reputation. I met with the couple for seven sessions over the course of several months. Ralph was a highly successful professional; Lucy had decided to stay home with their two children after the birth of her second child. Much of the tension in the marriage revolved around Ralph's parents' opposition to his marriage to Lucy. The second source of tension was Ralph's obsession with work and his unavailability to Lucy and his children. Lucy had filed for divorce the previous year but agreed to reconcile after three months.

During the period after Lucy had filed for divorce, Ralph moved into the garage, drinking heavily and threatening suicide if Lucy went through with her plan. Lucy withdrew her motion for divorce. Suicide was thus in the air from the first session.

Ralph was a large, aggressive man. It was clear that his only reason for participating in the sessions was to persuade Lucy to stay in the marriage. Alternately pleading and bullying, Ralph was unreachable. While he continued to insist that suicide would be his response to a separation or divorce, he was equally convincing that he could not be committed because he knew what to say to avoid this outcome.

Ralph rejected any interpretation I attempted to make about his extreme reaction to the possibility of separation; Lucy wavered between trying to persuade Ralph that she was no longer attracted to him and wanted to separate, while still wanting to maintain a good working relationship with him on behalf of the children. She hoped I could help them find a way to stay together for the sake of the children.

I too felt alternately hopeful – when Lucy suggested she might want to stay – and despairing and trapped by Ralph's intransigence, when Lucy expressed her wish to leave. The sessions were often stormy, and I worried about Ralph's stability. He categorically refused any treatment for himself.

My note for our last session reads as follows: "During this session spelled out rationale for continued therapy: to work out a companionate marriage on behalf of the children." This was the couple's new goal, and I felt some relief that we had seemed to settle on a plan, one that I could help them with. I was to be away from the office for a week, and we were to resume when I returned. While I wasn't sure my feeling of relief would last for long, I imagined it would last at least until we met again the following Wednesday. On Tuesday, I received a telephone message from Lucy. In it, she told me that on the prior Sunday she had requested a divorce and that Ralph had agreed. He went to work the next day but that night completed his suicide. In this message, Lucy also indicated that her individual therapist had "told" her she must tell Ralph she wanted a divorce. It is hard to believe that Lucy really conveyed such a significant piece of information to me over the telephone. But such is the nature of shock. I just can't recall.

Shortly after I heard the news, I ran into a senior colleague on the street, a friend who saw that I was distraught. We retreated to his office, where he listened, empathized, and helped me to regain my balance. He was pointed in his comments about the therapist who had encouraged Lucy to confront Ralph in my absence. I worried that if I had not been actively complicit in this *folie a deux*, I had, at the very least, been incompetent. I felt angry with Lucy for her timing and angry with Ralph for his belligerence and hate. I felt sorrow for the tragic outcome. I felt grief only in the grand sense: that the human condition is ultimately tragic. I felt profound concern for the children. But personal grief requires personal connection.

In the aftermath, I received a call from Dr. Jones, who wanted to talk about what had happened, and we found solace in our conversation. We were comrades in arms in a battle we had lost. I learned that Lucy had terminated her treatment with Dr. Jones shortly after the couple had begun to see me and had begun to see a different therapist, the woman who (perhaps) had encouraged her to leave Ralph. I felt like I had been dealt a bad hand from an incomplete deck of cards. I had a final session with Lucy several weeks later. My memories of what we talked about are vague and blurry. Lucy was still in shock, and probably I was too. I have no notes from that session. I was grateful to learn that clinical interventions had been initiated on behalf of the children and Lucy.

This death was very disturbing in a way markedly different from the death of Julie. In the immediate aftermath, I felt manipulated and used by this couple, an unwilling witness to their game of Russian roulette. This characterization is harsh – they were in pain, floundering. I felt the assault on my competence, and it stung. I had consciously felt that the only way for this couple to separate would be through death – Ralph's suicide – but I had also hoped, perhaps expected, that I could help prevent this. I think about this couple from time to time, mostly trying to find the intervention that could have changed things.

Another significant difference was that I now had a context in my mind: a category marked "when a patient dies." I had moved – without my consent – from innocence to experience, and I knew that, however disturbed I felt, I would recover. With Julie, I did not have to question my implication in her death. With Ralph and Lucy, I felt different things.

Peter

Peter too died in August, also during my summer break. At the time, I had been experiencing some medical worries. I left the doctor's office with good news, feeling elated. Sitting in my car in the warm sunshine, I was relaxed and happy. I picked up my cell phone to check my messages and found one from a former patient who had referred Peter, asking me to call her. Alarmed, I phoned her and learned that Peter had died that week. While on vacation, he had fallen down a flight of stairs. My mood also plummeted. The transition from elation to shock and horror was swift and in itself disorganizing. Slowly, I absorbed the few details that my former patient knew. I called the psychiatrist who had been medicating Peter, and she was able to gather more details. We learned that he had fallen, hit his head, and died instantly. As it turned out, the stairs in his rented house were not up to code. Somehow this tiny nugget of information provided solace of a kind, perhaps a *cause*.

I had been seeing Peter for about fifteen months in weekly psychotherapy. In his first session, he announced he had become depressed when he received the papers from his second wife, who was suing for divorce. Although the couple had been separated, and in fact it was Peter who had moved out, he was still troubled enough for his friend, my former patient, to refer him for treatment. Usually, although I take notes after an initial session, I have no trouble remembering what was said when the patient returns for the second session. But with Peter, I found myself struggling to remember him more clearly, and I checked my notes, which still did not bring him into focus. When he arrived for his second session with a large bandage on his head, he said, "Now let me tell you why I'm really here." Peter had struggled with alcoholism in the past, but after a long period of being sober, he found himself drinking heavily during this separation, even prior to receiving the divorce papers. The bandage covered a wound incurred when he fell and hit his head on a coffee table in the living room, having drunk an entire bottle of scotch.

The beginning of treatment was marked by a detoxification program, followed by Peter's voluntary participation in AA and in an outpatient treatment program for substance abuse. He also accepted my referral for a medication consultation. Peter was a talented and valued teacher, and the university where he taught gave him some time off to recover. He was also a successful artist and a musician who had toured Europe after college, supporting himself playing music. He had been married to his first wife for twenty years and had been very involved in raising his daughter. Even with all these talents, however, he was a very lonely man. Peter had sought therapy once in the past for help with his drinking, which had led to the twelve-year period of sobriety prior to his current lapse. His working-class background and his deep identification with his family left him feeling shame at the prospect of needing therapeutic help. Like Julie, he presented a happy face to the world, and although his inner world was richer, deeper, he often felt very alone. Slowly, over the course of the year, Peter began to open himself to the process, and I was more aware of his dependent longings. He recognized that our relationship was becoming much more important to him.

In the weeks before the August break, Peter was in good spirits. He was going to a place he loved, the island to which he returned each summer, and he was feeling hopeful about a new relationship. He appeared healthy and sober. I was feeling much more deeply involved in the treatment – a very different state of mind from my initial difficulty forming an image of Peter. I was looking forward to continuing our work together after the August interruption.

I went to the memorial service with my colleague and friend who had been medicating Peter, and we cried quietly together. It was a small gathering, but the eulogies were eloquent and heartfelt. Peter had touched people very deeply. There was an image of him on the podium, smiling and radiant.

In addition to my grief about Peter, I was struggling with the parallels with Julie: August, vacation, a time of hope followed by death. That was the third time in five years that I had experienced the death of a patient, and I wondered if I had the psychic energy to do the work of mourning. But what choice did I have? I felt tired and on some level resentful that this had happened again. I was also in a vulnerable place because of the recent concern about my own health. Looking back, I think that in addition to the real grief over the loss of someone I had come to care deeply about, I also knew about the toll and trajectory of mourning a patient one has lost to death.

Conclusion

The termination phase of an analysis will revive, for the analyst and her patient, previous experiences of loss and mourning. These feelings will be encountered within the frame that the analytic pair has agreed upon, in the service of the analysand's development.

The death of a patient – a person with whom one has been involved at the complicated intersection of professional obligation fueled by personal involvement – truncates the development of the treatment and deprives the analyst of the opportunity to anticipate and process the ending to an important relationship, one in which the sadness of the ending is accompanied by feelings of accomplishment and satisfaction.

The sudden and unexpected deaths of my three patients suggest to me that how one experiences the death of the patient is closely linked to a number of factors. These include the timing of the death in relation to the development of the treatment and the particular moment when the death occurs in relation to the analyst's personal and professional life. When Julie died, I was three years post-graduation from my psychoanalytic training. Five years later, Peter died. Ralph's death occurred in the interim. I suspect that these deaths affected my analytic identity in ways that I cannot articulate, although I now have a hard-won inner knowledge of this particular terrain.

My experience of Julie's death was heightened by the revived memories of my mother's death and the long mourning it initiated. I felt much more keenly the loneliness and isolation that accompanies mourning a significant loss without a context or community. The intensity of my involvement with

Julie, which was invisible to people who mourned her, coupled with the newness of the experience, made this death particularly difficult.

Ralph's death was disturbing in a very different way. While I was deeply upset about his tragic suicide, my grief was mixed with anger. The feelings were more short-lived and less painful. After Peter's death, I grieved for him and our process, but with an element of fatigue. I deeply regretted that a vital life and process had been cut short. But I was also somewhat preoccupied with my own resolving health crisis. Mourning was something to be endured, and I was weary. And while I was emotionally involved with Peter, the rhythm of psychotherapy is necessarily different from an analysis conducted five times per week and the involvement less intense.

The cumulative but varied experience of these three deaths led me to consider developmental aspects of the unwanted experience of the sudden death of a patient. The phase of the treatment, the state of the transference, the status of the analyst's professional development at the time the patient dies, as well as the proximity – both in timing and content – to resonant issues in the analyst's psyche at the time of a patient's sudden death will have a profound effect on her experience. As our field becomes more prepared to discuss this aspect of our professional work, perhaps these reflections will help to chart the territory.

Note

* This chapter was published previously in Anne Adelman and Kerry Malawista (2013) *The Therapist in Mourning: From the Faraway Nearby*. New York: Columbia University Press, p. 107–117.

When an analyst dies

Chapter 8

Mortality, integrity and psychoanalysis

(Who are you to me? Who am I to you?)*

Ellen Pinsky

Here is a fact: We all know that we'll die—intellectually, anyway, we know it; it's the definition of being "a mortal." And the corollary is that at any moment we *might* die. Most of the time we don't think about these facts: a necessary, protective forgetting. Forgetting—or in Freud's term, repression—can be on the side of life, just as the River Lethe has two banks, one demarking the realm of the dead, the other that of the living.

Here are some questions that, to my mind, follow from what I've just said. If we analysts accept that we are mortal, our patients, then, are vulnerable—at all times vulnerable—to losing us, whether we're thirty or sixty or ninety. Do we hold any responsibility to provide for them in that event? If we don't hold a responsibility—and maybe we don't—why not? And if we *do* have a responsibility, what constitutes reasonable provision? Finally, if we think there should be provision yet tend to neglect it, why is that?

This last question may be the most interesting and the most analytical: *If we think there should be provision yet tend to neglect it, why is that?* I think we'd all agree that analysts have an unusual, even extraordinary kind of power in their professional role. The way our work *works* is by our becoming important to people, in whatever individual ways they will make us important: we aim to matter. And we could say further that the psychoanalytic situation is purposefully configured to intensify our mattering. We call that process the transference. Ours is a professional encounter structured to invite intense transference reactions, at times in both people, with the purpose of understanding those reactions for the benefit of the patient.

If our aim, then, is to *matter*, and if we set out to court that condition, what is it for us to be lost? There has been relatively little written about such loss or its meaning. How are we to understand such absence? In the spring of 1994 my therapist, an analyst with whom I'd been working two and three times a week for over four years, suddenly died. In the face of that stunning event, I was fortunate—not only personally fortunate, in terms of friends and family, but professionally fortunate: My therapist's colleagues provided me a strong safety net in the wake of his death. I emphasize my good fortune and good treatment here because much of what I have to say in this essay will be critical of psychoanalysis—especially its literature, but also its professional organizations—and I'll even interrogate the psychoanalytic situation itself, asking whether it includes an element that is unsettling, dangerous, or even unsavory.

So it's important that I make clear a distinction between the reality of good practice—what many people actually do, and my own experience as beneficiary of good practice—and these other areas I mean to question. Others have been less fortunate than I was.

I was a beginning graduate student at the time my therapist died, and a beginning clinician as well, but I was already an avid reader of psychoanalytic literature. I turned to the papers on the therapist's illness and death—looking for understanding, for comfort—but instead found a body of work characterized by avoidance, confusion, sometimes even a condescending grandiosity.[1] The subject of the analyst's mortality itself seemed to inspire avoidance and disarray. But perhaps most remarkable to me was the near absence of the patient's voice or even the patient's perspective. Eventually I wrote my doctoral dissertation out of both experiences: that is, the loss itself, but also the dismay I felt at the inadequacy of psychoanalytic writing about such loss.

Subsequent to the loss, I've become an analyst, something that was not consciously in my mind at the time my therapist died. And, as here, I have written about the analyst's mortality (Pinsky, 2002, 2004, 2012). Both activities—the writing and the taking his seat—I now understand as personal means of mourning, aspects of an effort to understand what happened with that death. I believe it's a peculiar loss, like no other—here I echo notions of the analytic relationship as extraordinary or unique. As I've said, family and friends, and the profession, were generous; but my grief was amplified by confusion and isolation, and complicated by a sense of absurdity, too: no one close to me knew this person to whom I felt close and spoke to so freely and privately. What is it to lose someone who attends the way the analyst does? Who *was* this person to me? Who was I to him?

In melancholia, in contrast to mourning, writes Freud (1917e), the bereaved one "knows *whom* he has lost but not *what* he has lost in him" (p. 245, italics in original). However, even after dealing explicitly with object loss in "Mourning and Melancholia," Freud never referred in his writing to the loss of the analyst or the meaning of such loss for the patient and the analytic process (Blum, 1989). The loss of my therapist had to be mourned, and absence filled. But whom had I lost? *What* had I lost? To take its measure I also had to wonder, what had I been given? I found such questions remarkably hard to answer. The man mattered, he died, and I had to grieve. But how was I to do that? What form would it take? For starters, maybe something socially ordinary: I'd go to his funeral. On whose invitation? Who would I sit with? Who would I talk to? Would I sign a book? Who were his friends and family to me? Who was I to them? (In the shadows always: Who was I to him?)

Let me turn the subject around for a minute. There are two people in the consulting room, and the therapist isn't the only one who can die—a truism. Sybil Houlding (2013), in a moving essay, tells about her patient Julie dying, and her own struggle to grieve. (The essay in fact is about Houlding's loss of three patients, all within five years.) She writes: "Bereft, lonely, isolated, I searched the literature . . . for reports of others who had endured this experience, but I found nothing" (p. 110). Houlding attends the funeral: "I went to Julie's memorial service with two colleagues who knew her husband, and thus, tangentially, knew Julie. They were caring, aware of my situation, but they were not grieving as I was grieving. Sitting at the service," she continues, "I struggled with the feeling that most analysands express at some point in treatment: Who am I—*really*—to you?" (pp. 110–111).

I am speaking here from the other position, the other seat: who was he—*really*—to me? Whom had I lost? *What* had I lost? My search for answers to these questions, I now understand, was, and still is, the mourning process itself. I repeat again, I was the beneficiary of *good* practice—sound crisis intervention. Good practice not only facilitated my resumption of work with another therapist, but it also meant that I've approached writing about this subject from a position that includes gratitude. I was angry at the man for dying, and I was angry at the literature for its inadequacy, but not at the particular community that cared for me.

Writing these sentences, I hear my own repetitiveness. Whom do I reassure? Does the repetition speak to some sense of grievance, hard to shake? I'll add that my anger, intense at first, has shifted—a function of time but also, I believe, a function of writing—away from a merely dismissive feeling and toward a more sympathetic curiosity about the pure difficulty of the subject. It has become increasingly pertinent, and interesting to wonder: *What, exactly, is the difficulty?*

Here is the notable fact: since what brings many people to analysis is a difficulty with loss and grief, it's *remarkable* that analysts have given so little consideration to the implications of their own mortality. Nor have we (I mean our profession) adequately considered our responsibility to patients in the event of our dying. In my view, this extraordinary absence, which can be considered an abrogation of responsibility, deserves investigation.

Let me pause to pose a question: Is what I'm saying true? Are patients, in fact, ever abandoned this way? I'll offer two brief examples, one in the discipline's early years and one more recent.

Karl Abraham died suddenly in 1925, following many months of speculation about his delay in resuming his practice. His patient Alix Strachey writes to her husband, James, about the discontinuity: "Yesterday I telephoned . . . and was, as I expected, told to telephone again on Sunday morning. He *may* possibly, they say, start again on Monday, but they don't sound very convincing" (Meisel & Kendrick, 1985, p. 279, italics in original). According to Meisel and Kendrick, Abraham was "steadily growing worse, although the full extent of his illness was as yet unknown even to those closest to him" (p. 290). Further on they note: "[Abraham's] sudden and premature death (he was only forty-eight) came as a personal and professional shock to the whole psychoanalytic community" (p. 306). It is believed that Abraham died of lung cancer.

Leap ahead eighty years, to 2005, and another patient, whom I'll call B, also tells of his analyst's lung cancer. Unlike Abraham, B's sick analyst returns to work following medical treatment: "Dr. X seems fully recovered," writes B, "back to where he was a few months before he had to stop working. He said the radiation results were much faster than expected—'unprecedented' was the word he used" (private correspondence).

B tells that Dr. X continues to *seem* well, though his condition is in the room, with the oxygen tubing that trails from his face, back beyond his chair and out the interior office door. Nine months later Dr. X dies unexpectedly, as B experiences it, and, according to B:

> ... apparently without having made any arrangements for his patients—or at least without having made any arrangements for me ... I was literally left standing on the lawn when I showed up for my session ... informed by his wife, through the door, that he was not feeling well and was still in bed. Then when I left a message on his answering machine the following week to confirm my next appointment, she returned the call the next morning to let me know he had passed away the night before. "Oh, no, I'm so sorry," was all I could say, repeating it twice more with increasing emotion as I felt the loss, first for him, then for her, then for myself. "Thank you, take care, and goodbye," she said. And that was that.

B's account is remarkably forgiving and humane toward what is, after all, an abandonment.

In an earlier essay (Pinsky, 2002), I try to put the problematic literature on illness and death—that is, the literature on *catastrophic* ending—into context by taking one step back to look at the literature on ending itself: the psychoanalytic writing on termination. I propose that the absence of theoretical and clinical provision for the therapist's illness or death reflects underlying problems regarding termination—the "routine" ending foreshadowed in the first hour the patient and therapist meet: The work begins, the work will end, just as the hour begins and the hour ends.

Our customary word for this ritual of saying goodbye—*termination*—is an odd term to denote the natural ending of an analysis, but quite appropriate for what I'm talking about here. With the analyst's death, patient and therapist really face "termination"! But the therapist's death isn't supposed to precipitate the ending (nor is the patient's). The analyst isn't to be blamed for his human condition; but if he does "fail"—if he does die there's still been a catastrophic breach of the therapeutic contract. Without an implicit promise of constancy, who would ever embark? Robert Galatzer-Levy (2004) writes, "When the analyst dies at a time when the transference is still intense, analysands may feel they have lost the most important person in their life" (p. 1011).

A remarkable phrase: "the most important person in their life." Yet this intimate and private relationship exists all but outside the social realm; certainly, the bereaved patient finds no clear place within a social community of mourners. Ann-Louise Silver (1990) describes the literature on the subject as an "affect-filled silence" (p. 2). If we believe what Galatzer-Levy suggests even a little, the pointed question must follow: Is psychoanalysis reluctant to take responsibility for the tremendous power of its very method?

Why has the profession resisted addressing the analyst's mortality? I'm not persuaded by the most common retort to this question; it goes like this: "No one likes to think about death, the analyst is only human, why should we expect him to be any less reluctant than the rest of mankind?" Try putting words like those in the mouth of a father or mother with dependent children. How, then, to understand the resistance? Finally, my earlier essay takes the argument to a difficulty in the profession with grief and mourning. The "termination" that designates the end of an analysis is an extended process of mourning: in Loewald's (1962) terms, a "long-drawn-out leave-taking" (p. 259). It's through this ending process—painful work likely to include anger, disappointment, acknowledged limitation—that the patient takes leave well.

But there's a second person in the room, and that person also loses a partner. Though the analyst's role is different, the task is the same—leave-taking—and the analyst, at parting, is no more immune from a complexity of feeling than the patient is. In fact, Jack Novick (1982) suggests that "[I]t may often be ... that termination will be a greater real loss for the analyst than it is for the patient" (p. 356). That's because, while the patient has relinquished mainly the transference object of illusion, a shadow puppet, the analyst knows the patient more clearly, as well as intimately, and in Novick's view therefore loses a more real object. In a study exploring the impact of termination, Stephen Firestein (1978) writes that the analysts he interviewed "experienced not only varying degrees of anxiety over termination, but gradations of what, for want of a better description, could be called grief" (p. 214).

"For want of a better description"? We don't have to debate Novick's point or Firestein's distrust of plain English to agree that the analyst, too, experiences a loss, or that both people will mourn. John Klauber (1981), remarking on the strains inherent to being an analyst, writes that:

Practically no word ever appears in the literature about how the analyst manages to form relationship after relationship of the most intimate kind with patient after patient, of the mourning that he must feel for each one of them, and of how he discharges it. (p. 174)

Mourning is at the center of the termination process—for both people.

Am I reproachful? Whom would I reproach in matters so thoroughly human? In a passage paraphrasing Freud's "On Transience" (1916a), the essay in which Freud describes a walk in the mountains with the young poet who feels no pleasure in the beauty of nature, Franco De Masi (2004) writes:

Freud maintains that an inability to enjoy and appreciate the transience of beauty is due to an inability to mourn. The thought of transience puts the poet in touch with the pain of loss and interferes with his capacity to enjoy things. The inability to appreciate beauty comes from a rebellion against temporal boundaries. Those who cannot mourn unconsciously reproach their love object for not being perfect, but only finite as humans are. However, there is no love relation without loss; love is always faced by separation. (p. 32)

Here is the essential point: Underlying the problem of termination is the reality of loss on both sides. If termination theory is problematic—whether in regard to ordinary endings or disastrous ones—that problem reflects a difficulty with loss and grief. Further, this quite human difficulty of mourning is located just as much, and sometimes more, in the psychoanalysts as it is in the patients.

The psychoanalytic situation induces an extraordinary intimacy that is its reason to exist. Through this singular human connection—an intimacy that intends separation—the work is accomplished and the end-point reached. But the patient is in a quandary if the helper is shy of endings. The capacity to consider one's mortality, by which I mean human frailty and limitation in every sense, perhaps defines the capacity to be a good guardian of the therapeutic situation: a medium through which patient and analyst alike may discover, and discover again, how closely related are the workings of grief and love. How much more complex such matters are—matters of ending, of loss, of transience, of "goodbye," of grief—for the therapist who is sick or aging, and for the patient.

Let me be clear: I offer no directives here for "good practice," no rules for what the clinician "should" do—most of these are common-sensical enough;[2] rather, my effort is to find a vocabulary to make a difficult conversation within the profession possible. Does the conversation matter?

I return to the patient B for help with this question. B, as already noted, is remarkably generous in response to his therapist's human failure. Months after the death, B reflects that, when his therapist died, B himself was "in an emotional state capable of dealing with the loss." He wonders further about people who might have been more vulnerable than he was when Dr. X died: for an example, B asks, "What if someone were suicidal?" We of course may wonder, too, about the untold effect on B.

> I'll repeat the truism with which I began: No one likes to think about his own death. Now let me substitute for *death* in that truism the word *mortality*, and it becomes, *No one likes to think about his mortality*. What is our mortality? Our mortality is our human nature, and our mortal nature includes (who could doubt it?) our aggression, our destructiveness, our hatred, our envy, our . . . whatever else one might add. Is this what psychoanalysis would rather not think about? *Timor mortis*—fear of death disturbs me? What are we *timorous* about? Are we timorous to look at what motivates us? Do these not-so-benign, less conscious parts of ourselves underlie avoidance? We don't want to look because we prefer not to see? Winnicott can help here.

Winnicott's (1955) twelfth rule states: "The analyst survives" (p. 21). He means much more, of course, than that the analyst lives to see the treatment through. He means that the analyst survives the patient's attacks without retaliation, and, in not retaliating, maintains the *analytic function*; in holding his seat the analyst thereby accomplishes something. Most pertinent for my argument, Winnicott (1969) also writes that the analyst's retaliation may be worse during a treatment than his death: "Even the actual death of the analyst," he famously says, "is not as bad as the development in the analyst of a change of attitude toward retaliation" (p. 714).

Retaliation is worse than *death?* I return again to B and his analyst's narcissism: Does Dr. X, whose radiation results are "unprecedented," blind himself to the obvious—that he'll soon die and that his death affects his patients—as an act of retaliation? Is countertransference hatred (Winnicott again, 1949) at least a component? In not acknowledging his vulnerability (which B can *see* in the room), does Dr. X retaliate? Retaliate for *what*, you may ask? If Winnicott is right, that the analyst's retaliation can be worse than his death, then the analyst's infirmity or death, while a catastrophe, isn't necessarily the greatest problem the patient faces. Nor is it the greatest threat to the analytic process. The greater problem and threat would be the imbedded aggression: the analyst's failure and the profession's failure to think about, confront, and better provide for that eventuality. I'm suggesting a motivated neglect—a countertransference hatred—within the profession. Failure to protect the clinician means not protecting the patient—the two cannot be separated. Dr. X's neglect occurs under the umbrella of the profession's neglect.

These, then, are some of the things I considered early in my exploration.

A central link to my thinking as it has unfolded over time is a focus on the ethical: The abrogation of responsibility for the bereaved patient raises ethical issues. The analyst whose body fails doesn't will that failure or hold responsibility for it, although he may in some circumstances be held responsible for mismanaging it, and the profession for failing to shepherd and guide. It may be easier to forgive the therapist whose body fails than the professional community that surrounds him. I gradually began to think more about the other sense of *mortal*—one's humanness includes not only a frail body, but also one's fallibility. Man can die and he can also err in the words of Shakespeare's (1600) Puck, "What fools these mortals be!" (3.2.121). If that's true of mankind, it's also true of analysts.

Reflections like these took me to considering the character side of things—call it the matter of the analyst as person. As I learned more about clinical work, and myself experienced the extraordinary power of the transference and the strains that come with it, I began to wonder about the invitation imbedded in the psychoanalytic situation for the analyst, the purveyor of illusion, in his human capacity for self-deception and grandiosity, to believe he inhabits an enchanted kingdom, magical in his powers, an "exception" (Freud, 1916d).

And I couldn't *avoid* thinking about character, had I wanted to, because concurrent with my analytic training were three disturbing events, close up: the ethical misconduct of three highly esteemed senior analysts in my home city, Boston, two of them in my home institute. These were catastrophic losses, stunning for everyone. But for students, for those learning what it is to be an analyst, immersed in their own analyses and still holding some necessary healthy idealizations, it was a too-early shock and disillusionment. A supervisor put it to me this way:

> When our leaders commit sexual boundary violations, they place every analytic relationship at risk. Every patient wonders whether they may be hurt. Every analyst wonders whether they may slip into the role of an abuser. And many a patient who needs our help is advised to stay away from psychoanalysts because they are dangerous.

Far from being upset by my supervisor's words, I took comfort—he was not glossing over or turning away. He was talking turkey to me.

I began to wonder: How might Winnicott's (1949) countertransference hatred, as with the dying analyst, also underlie such destructiveness?

As the reader can see, I couldn't avoid thinking about the sexual exploitation of patients, and I became curious about the history of what we call, euphemistically, *boundary violations*. I began to think more about the structure of the psychoanalytic situation itself and the nature of the analyst's activity—the audacity of it, I would say. I can perhaps best capture that expanding interest with the opening sentences of my essay, "The Olympian Delusion":

> This is an essay on an unpleasant subject: a subject so painful that some within the discipline of psychoanalysis wince and turn away from it—the sexual exploitation of patients. The psychoanalytic situation is an audacious endeavor that purposely courts risk: for a time placing one human being *as if* at the center of another's emotional life. In that power-imbalanced relationship, behind closed doors, what is the patient's protection? (Pinsky, 2011, p. 351, italics in original)

In that paper, I explore particularly Freud's much misunderstood and caricatured notions of abstinence and neutrality, considering them fundamental guiding principles as well as ethical precepts. Perhaps most important is the paradox of abstinence: Abstinence itself is alluring—the principle protects but at the same time, by design, heats the treatment crucible, the abstinent analyst serving as a deliberately incendiary human lure in a process focusing and magnifying the patient's love cravings. The psychoanalytic setup is a structured invitation to fall in love, a form of seduction, courting the transgressive.

If one accepts these terms, that's quite a seat the human analyst occupies.

A human being is perfect neither in character nor body; rather, imperfection and limitation define us. The situation, then, is always under threat. But here's another paradox: This same limitation or humanness is also necessary to the work. The psychoanalytic situation itself is defined by carefully structured limitation that creates freedom, by restriction that creates range: It's a "No, we will not touch" that says "Yes, you may freely speak your desire." Taboo and transgression: don't touch, speak desire. Only an imperfect being—an ordinary person—can energize this extraordinary therapeutic offering, as no god or robot could do.

The analyst brings, along with technical skills, both body and character; just as the one is subject to idiosyncrasy and to frailty, so, too, is the other. The patient has the hopeful expectation that the analyst brings a good enough character, along with a healthy enough body so that he will survive in both the ordinary and the Winnicottian sense. The reader may see how my subject—the analyst's mortality—expands to include impaired character and the terrible ethical violations that can ensue. Here, too, are echoes of an earlier question: Is it an ethical violation not to provide for our patients' care should we be lost—whatever form that loss takes?

Whatever form that loss takes? I'll return to this question. Let me pause to summarize what I've done so far. I've said something about my particular experience of losing my therapist and how the loss took me to writing about it and to becoming an analyst myself. The exploration in writing became an investigation of the psychoanalytic situation itself, of the analyst's activity, and led to reflections on the humanness of the analyst, in both the sense of body frailty (he is mortal, he can die) and the character sense (he is mortal, he can err). As I see it, both endeavors (writing, becoming a clinician) are my efforts to understand the loss and to grieve it—call these forms of working through, if you like (I do). I've tried to make something out of the loss that takes me closer, in Loewald's (1960, p. 29) language, to laying the ghosts to rest as ancestors.

Loewald writes:

> In mourning, an object relationship is gradually given up, involving pain and suffering, and is substituted by a restructuring of the internal world which is in consonance with the relinquished relationship. In this way pain and suffering can eventually cease, even while the memories of the lost person do remain
> ... In this sense one can say that the individuation of the individual comes about by the losses of separation. (1978, pp. 559–560)

With my therapist's sudden death, there was no opportunity for the long drawn-out leave-taking that is the ritual of ending; and so it's been through these other means of mourning that I take leave—and, I'd like to believe, retrieve the person, locating him more securely inside.

Here is perhaps the most important point: There are many ways to lose the analyst, on a continuum from necessary and benign to destructive. All of these losses, in some sense, are inevitable. One loses the analyst at the end of the hour; one loses the analyst if he's distracted or sleepy; one loses the analyst if he doesn't understand; one loses the analyst when treatment ends. One may even lose the analyst retrospectively in learning of his ethical misconduct, however sound and ethical one's own treatment. Loss, functional loss, is structural; it's imbedded: The work begins, the work will end.

Even the analyst's ordinary intervention, a good interpretation, induces a kind of loss. Just so, the analyst's failure is imbedded: The interpretation may be really bad or tactless (reminding us again of Winnicott: "I think I interpret mainly to let the patient know the limits of my understanding" (1969, p. 711)). There are all kinds of ways for the analyst to fail, from benign to toxic. And it is the inevitability of failure—of disappointment, of loss—that gives the therapeutic gift value (similar, perhaps, to what makes the appreciation of beauty possible with the acceptance of temporal boundaries, of transience).

On these terms, do the ailing Dr. X and his patient B represent a relatively innocent instance of failure? Can we isolate principles, can we make useful distinctions?

So, to that end—and with the crucial caveat that such things are impossible to parse or measure neatly—I'll offer two more brief examples, very different from each other, to add to the collection.

First, the example of Pat and her analyst, Dr. D, an experienced, highly respected, gifted clinician. Early on in the treatment, Dr. D falls into subtle neurological decline—cognitive decay. Slowly, Pat realizes for herself that they are "hitting dead ends"; as she puts it, "I had to act as my own container, tamping down my enthusiasm so as not to inflict my own mind onto an un-accepting mind." In bewilderment and confusion, and alone, Pat leaves the analysis; Dr. D deteriorates, eventually closes his practice, and dies. Throughout, for Pat, there isn't much help from the community, though eventually she finds her way to a productive new analysis. A few years later, Pat likens the experience with Dr. D to her work with a patient of her own, a child with Asperger's syndrome with whom she struggles painfully to make contact. Pat grieves for the boy and for the limitations of treatment—she can't save him, any more than she could save Dr. D.

Here is another example, far more mundane. A patient, Leigh, has recently ended a productive five-year analysis with Dr. O. Three months after the ending, Leigh phones Dr. O and leaves a message with news about her child who had been sick, with cancer, and whose illness, treatment, and impending recovery coincide with the end of the analysis. Leigh calls to leave happy news, wanting the analyst to know that the child, in a follow-up medical exam, has been declared well. Dr. O doesn't return the call, nor does he respond to the patient's note expressing bewilderment and distress; it was as if the analyst had fallen off the face of the earth. Eventually, Dr. O explains his silence: he did not want to be intrusive.

What kinds of distinctions can we make here? In both instances, the analyst is lost. Which of these two is a more notable loss—how to think about it? The first is clearly more terrible: The patient has lost the analyst in some more absolute sense and in a particularly heartrending way. But in another sense, is Dr. D's loss of function, as his mind declines, less a failure? Though it fractures the analytic frame, it's not, after all, a failure of humanity. In the latter instance, trivial by comparison, has the analyst who does not want to be intrusive retaliated? Is Dr. O's rigidity an upside-down breach of the analytic frame—he is not too loose, but instead too tight and unbending? On a continuum of damaging behaviors, Dr. O's failure to respond is fairly mild, Dr. D's unresponsiveness extreme. But on a different continuum—call it the continuum of enactments, or of Winnicott's countertransference hatred, or, if you like, call it moral—Dr. D's failure, wholly unwilled, simply can't be placed, where Dr. O's silence, in contrast, can.

In other words, the virtual death (whatever its form, be it neglect, a noxious enactment, a misguided coolness, or distance), wherein the *analytic function* is lost, may be more destructive than the actual one.

Howard Shevrin (personal communication, 2012) considers the psychoanalytic situation as ceremonial form:

> Analysis as ritual is both real and imagined; in fact the genius of analysis (the "transference") is that it is reality that is imagined and lived, as in art. It has to be real or else it doesn't work; and it has to be imagined and lived or else it doesn't last. This I think is altogether new, *nothing like this has ever existed before.*

If Freud's creation offers a new form of human relationship, it's no wonder the matter of endings is puzzling to conceive. A hundred years ago, Freud speaks to this same remarkable newness: "The course the analyst must pursue," he writes, "is one for which there is *no model in real life*" (1915a, p. 166, italics added).[3]

I don't believe it's merely avoidance or grandiosity that explains the neglect of the subject of the analyst's mortality. If that were the case, there would be easier answers to questions hovering over my effort here, questions such as "What should analysts do (and what should the profession do) to address the problem—more accurately, the fact!—of the analyst's mortality?" But if we agree that what is lost is both real and imagined—both individual and also not specifiable—and that the psychoanalyst's activity can't be defined in everyday terms, must we conclude that the management of loss can neither be conceived nor prepared for? Are there no forms for conceptualizing conduct in a relationship in which the course the analyst pursues is quite new, having no model in "real life"?[4] If there are no rules (beyond the commonsensical, like the sealed list of names in the desk drawer), is nothing therefore mandated? More than sixty years ago, Ida Macalpine (1950) offered an incisive answer, locating "form" in the analyst's moral integrity—the necessary safeguard, by her understanding, that underlies every treatment; the analyst's moral integrity is "a technical device," she writes, "and not a moral precept" (p. 527).

Lawrence Friedman (personal communication, 2012) describes the analyst's struggle as requiring "an impossible balancing act." On one hand, the analyst has to keep in mind: "I know better than anyone else how much I mean to you and how much you will suffer by my loss," and on the other he must not forget, "I know better than most know that it isn't really me that means so much to you," while at the same time he must not lose hold of, "I know you will miss the real me personally after all this." The analytic stance requires all three internal visions—"It is a matter of spiritual positioning," notes Friedman. We might consider the analyst's work in safekeeping such a position to include an acceptance of his own transience, both as person and in the specialized role. That acceptance is perhaps another form of moral integrity.

The analytic situation tempts the analyst's grandiosity, constantly testing that integrity, no matter his age. Shelley Orgel (2013), working into his ninth decade, expresses with characteristic straightforwardness his view of the analyst's responsibility in the seat:

> A number of patients who have come to me in recent years were in treatment with analysts who became seriously ill and were functionally impaired. Some died. A major reproach these patients have brought in centered around their analysts' inability to help them speak about their

perceived sense of what the analyst was facing, and what it meant and would mean to the treatment and, overwhelmingly, to the relationship itself. They felt prohibited from connecting their sadness, anger, fear about these realities with the transference awareness they had thus far achieved. They guiltily reproached their analyst for being unable to remain analytically "neutral" in their interest in the face of the coming tragic loss to each of them, to confirm and clarify their observations and reactions when there was evident physical and/or mental deterioration. (p. 941)

Along with his patients, Orgel shares a belief that they "needed their analyst to break into these denials." While some therapists could do so, ". . . it was humanly impossible for others to affirm . . . such cruel realities to their patients." Orgel considers his work with these patients to include helping them find in him "someone who can enable them to continue the aborted work of mourning for their 'lost' analyst" (p. 941).

I've used a number of examples to suggest a continuum with degrees and kinds of mortality in both senses of *mortal*—integrity of body, integrity of character: vulnerable and fallible. The necessary source of the therapeutic gift is, put most simply, the quality of integrity: a condition attainable *only* as a mortal attribute. Integrity is a gift—like a talent—that can be achieved, or not, because and only because the therapist is human. At integrity's center—since every person is imperfectly whole—is a striving toward a consciously impossible ideal.

At this point, I'll offer a narrative of such striving and integrity.

When my therapist, Joseph Nemetz, suddenly died, I had been working with him in an intensive psychotherapy for more than four years. Nemetz's professional conduct, in retrospect, serves as an implicit critique of the inadequate professional literature regarding the central matter of the therapist's mortality.

I had asked several weeks earlier if we could talk about my beginning analysis.

Nemetz was surprised by my request, and I by his surprise; I thought I had made many less-than-subtle hints about analysis. I told him I thought I had been reasonably clear; he replied that he had not understood me. Possibly, both of us were right. I came to wonder later whether I had in fact been quite clear but that his usual capacity to hear me had in this particular matter broken down: Did he wish *not* to hear me? I've wondered whether his deafness to my hints came from his intuitive understanding that, if I were to ask, he would have to say no—the answer he'd be compelled, as I now understand, to give. With the refusal, I would, if I wanted analysis enough, move to another therapist. I believe that he cared very much about me, enjoyed his work with me, and preferred that I not leave him.

He didn't answer me right away. He told me that, because of his age (he was seventy-one), he was cautious about beginning new analyses; when I asked if our four years of work together made no difference, he answered that of course it did, and that he would need some time to think about it. Over the next ten days I argued my case, growing more excited and hopeful as the days passed and he did not refuse.

Several minutes into our fifth meeting after I had first asked to begin analysis, I was speaking with an animation, every minute moving closer to pleased assumption: I *would* have my wish. I remember that he lifted his hand lightly, several inches off his knee, in a gesture that stopped me dead—a "Whoa!" to a racing horse. The very long silence lasted perhaps five seconds, and then he spoke quietly: "*There's more than one person in this room to be considered*," he said.

I was speechless. At that moment and in that pause, I caught a clear glimpse of him, perhaps for the first time in ten days, so hard had I been working to obliterate him in order to have what I wanted. I saw something then about what he might feel, what he might wish, and what this decision might mean for him. I was able then to say, calmly and with tremendous sadness, "This must be hard for you, too." He nodded very slightly and said, "In many ways."

Although he didn't give me his answer until the next time we met, I knew then what he would likely say and began to prepare myself for it. Sometimes I think I'd really known the answer from the beginning, maybe even before he did, and my wish not to hear what I already knew explained my impetuous rush to fill with words any space for an honest exchange with him. My unconscious hope was to keep both of us from reflecting; but he didn't give up that responsibility.

Near the start of our next meeting, he said that, given the nature of my own losses and the power of analysis, and given the good possibility that he might die before the work was done, analysis with him was not a good idea; he said that, if I wanted analysis, he'd help me arrange it. I knew that, given his love for the work—and especially for that work from behind the couch—his decision was not easy. But I also knew in a hazy way that it was his commitment to the work, and to me, that guided his decision.

I asked him if he'd ever changed his mind about anything, and he replied, quickly and very gently, "I once decided not to be a cowboy." As was often true in my time with this man, my laughter was part of the power of the moment: Few people have ever looked *less* like a cowboy. My tears and rage followed.

But I didn't fully understand his words for a long time. Many months after his death, I did understand that Dr. Nemetz was telling me far more than "No, I can't be your analyst." He was telling me that, however much he might wish to give me what I wanted, he couldn't change his mind because any other decision, *by his lights*, would be wild and incautious; his refusal was dictated by his understanding of and respect for the power of the analytic process, for his own human limitations, and for me.

With that decision, I think he looked squarely at the ending of his lifework, and of his life. At some point, I also understood it—"I once decided not to be a cowboy"—I understood it as a rejection of the charismatic style of certain analysts (I use the word here in the pejorative sense). Nemetz had the capacity to bear the responsibility of "No," and at the moment he spoke, it was to remind me that there are *always* two individual, mortal people in the consulting room. And in that quiet reminder is located the most essential principle guarding the patient's safety.

A few weeks later, on a Wednesday in mid-May, the hour came to a close. I remained angry at him. He was going away for the weekend to a conference in Philadelphia. He often ended an hour with something intended to leave me thinking. This time it was a question. His last words to me were: "What have I done to make you think I don't understand how disappointed you are?"

I paused and said, "I'll think about it, and I'll let you know Monday morning." I stood up and left him with my usual tag line when he went away to meetings: "Have a good time, learn something, and cross the street very carefully." He collapsed without warning on Sunday in the airport in Philadelphia, and he died six days later, apparently never regaining consciousness.

Notes

* This chapter was published previously as Ellen Pinsky, Mortality, Integrity and psychoanalysis (Who are you to me? Who am I to you?). *The Psychoanalytic Quarterly*, 2014 (83)1, p. 1–22.
1 There are exceptions; for example, see Feinsilver (1998), Hoffman (1998, 2000), Morrison (1990, 1997), and Silver (1990, 2001).
2 For example, some clinicians keep a sealed list of patients and their phone numbers; the list can be located by colleagues appointed to contact them in the event of an emergency.
3 To the great psychoanalytic thinkers who have articulated this ordinary/extraordinary paradox, we can add Loewald: "Analysis is not and should not be like ordinary life, although it is a replica of it in certain essential features, while it is fundamentally different in other respects" (1962, p. 259).
4 Elsewhere I write: "Perhaps Freud means by 'no model' that for none of these other objects of transference is the position as fully stylized: a stringency limiting reciprocal action and seductive behavior (the analyst's abstinence) along with a non-judgmental receptiveness to everything the patient expresses (the analyst's benevolent neutrality)" (Pinsky, 2012, p. 37).

References

Blum, H. (1989). The concept of termination and the evolution of psychoanalytic thought. *Journal of the American Psychoanalytic Association, 37*: 275–295.

De Masi, F. (2004). *Making Death Thinkable*. P. Antinucci (Trans.). London: Free Association.
Feinsilver, D. (1998). The therapist as a person facing death: the hardest of external realities and therapeutic action. *International Journal of Psychoanalysis, 79*: 1131–1150.
Firestein, S. (1978). *Termination in Psychoanalysis*. New York: International Universities Press.
Freud, S. (1915a). Observations on transference-love. *S. E., 12*. London: Hogarth.
Freud, S. (1916a). On transience. *S. E., 14*. London: Hogarth.
Freud, S. (1916d). Some character-types met with in psycho-analytic work. *S. E., 14*. London: Hogarth.
Freud, S. (1917e). Mourning and melancholia. *S. E., 14*. London: Hogarth.
Friedman, L. (2007). The delicate balance of work and illusion in psychoanalysis. *Psychoanalytic Quarterly, 76*: 817–833.
Friedman, L. (2012). Personal communication.
Galatzer-Levy, R. (2004). The death of the analyst: patients whose previous analyst dies while they were in treatment. *Journal of the American Psychoanalytic Association, 52*: 999–1024.
Hoffman, I. Z. (1998). *Ritual and Spontaneity in the Psychoanalytic Process*. Hillsdale, NJ: Analytic Press.
Hoffman, I. Z. (2000). At death's door: therapists and patients as agents. *Psychoanalytic Dialogues, 10*: 823–846.
Houlding, S. (2013). When a patient dies. In: A. Edelman & K. Malawista (Eds.), *The Therapist in Mourning: From the Faraway Nearby* (pp. 107–117). New York: Columbia University Press.
Klauber, J. (1981). The identity of the psychoanalyst. In: *Difficulties in the Analytic Encounter* (pp. 161–180). New York: Jason Aronson.
Loewald, H. (1960). On the therapeutic action of psycho-analysis. *International Journal of Psychoanalysis, 41*: 16–33.
Loewald, H. (1962). Internalization, separation, mourning, and the superego. In: *The Essential Loewald: Collected Papers and Monographs* (pp. 257–276). Hagerstown, MD: University Publishing, 2000.
Loewald, H. (1978). Transference and love. In: *The Essential Loewald: Collected Papers and Monographs* (pp. 549–563). Hagerstown, MD: University Publishing, 2000.
Macalpine, I. (1950). The development of transference. *Psychoanalytic Quarterly, 19*: 501–539.
Meisel, P., & Kendrick, W. (Eds.) (1985). *Bloomsbury/Freud: The Letters of James and Alix Strachey, 1924–1925*. New York: Basic Books.
Morrison, A. (1990). Doing psychotherapy while living with a life-threatening illness. In: H. J. Schwartz & A.-L. S. Silver (Eds.), *Illness in the Analyst: Implications for the Treatment Relationship* (pp. 227–250). Madison, CT: International Universities Press.
Morrison, A. (1997). Ten years of doing psychotherapy while living with a life-threatening illness: self-disclosure and other ramifications. *Psychoanalytic Dialogues, 7*: 225–241.
Novick, J. (1982). Termination: themes and issues. *Psychoanal. Inquiry, 2*: 329–365.

Orgel, S. (2013). A patient returns. *Journal of the American Psychoanalytic Association, 61*: 935–946.
Pinsky, E. (2002). Mortal gifts: a two-part essay on the therapist's mortality. *Journal of the American Academy of Psychoanalysis, 30*: 173–204.
Pinsky, E. (2004). Contribution to "Symposium on the Dead." *Threepenny Review, 24*: 28–29.
Pinsky, E. (2011). The Olympian delusion. *Journal of the American Psychoanalytic Association, 59*: 351–375.
Pinsky, E. (2012). Physic himself must fade: A view of the therapeutic offering through the lens of mortality. *American Imago, 69*: 29–56.
Schwartz, H. J., & Silver, A.-L. S. (Eds.) (1990). *Illness in the Analyst: Implications for the Treatment Relationship.* Madison, CT: International Universities Press.
Shakespeare, W. (1600). A Midsummer Night's Dream. In: *The Comedies of William Shakespeare* (pp. 485–545). New York: Modern Library, 1994.
Shevrin, H. (2012). Personal communication.
Silver, A.-L. S. (1990). Resuming work with a life-threatening illness—and further reflections. In: H. J. Schwartz & A.-L. S. Silver (Eds.), *Illness in the Analyst: Implications for the Treatment Relationship* (pp. 151–176). Madison, CT: International Universities Press.
Silver, A.-L. S. (2001). Facing mortality while treating patients: a plea for a measure of authenticity. *Journal of the American Academy of Psychoanalysis, 29*: 43–56.
Winnicott, D. W. (1949). Hate in the countertransference. *International Journal of Psychoanalysis, 30*: 69–74.
Winnicott, D. W. (1955). Metapsychological and clinical aspects of regression within the psychoanalytical set-up. *Internationl Journal of Psychoanalysis, 36*: 16–26.
Winnicott, D. W. (1969). The use of an object. *International Journal of Psychoanalysis, 50*: 711–716.

Retirement

Chapter 9

A note on retirement and mortality

Sybil Houlding

"Are you thinking about retirement?" This question occurs with some frequency once one approaches seventy. As psychoanalysts, we ask each other, casually or seriously, trying on the word, trying to locate ourselves in a new phase of living. It becomes clear, in speaking with colleagues, that "thinking about" does not necessarily mean "planning to." The topic sometimes leads to assertions that the speaker has no plans for retirement, plans to keep working . . . indefinitely. Some confess that they would not know what to do without working. Others report thinking about retirement without a specific plan, but with confidence that with time they will have a fuller idea of what is both possible and desirable. While it is true that people in other professions have complicated feelings about retirement, ranging from "I can't wait" – when work is a necessity but not a pleasure, to the wish to "die with one's boots on", the analyst has, I believe, special circumstances to confront. Certainly the wish not to interrupt ongoing treatment is one.

But I suspect that the centrality of our analytic identity adds a layer of complexity to the decision to retire for people in our profession. The thought of not being an analyst seems, in fact, very close to not being at all. These thoughts have been very much on my mind as I recently turned seventy, and watched older colleagues slowly reduce their patient load, eventually limiting their work to teaching and writing. This second option makes the possibility of retiring from clinical practice less final, and allows for the continuation of generative capacity that is the hallmark of successful aging.

It is the "not being" – the intimation of mortality and death – that I suspect causes some analysts to continue to practice long after they are capable, and to convince themselves that this is best for their patients. Rather than facing their own aging, diminished capacity, and most difficult of all, their imminent and inevitable demise, these analysts leave their patients with the task of caring for them by continuing to remain in treatment.

We rarely hear accounts from inside the treatment room, a protected and private space. But we have all seen old (note I did not say "older") analysts, sometimes physically frail, continue with a few remaining patients. We may wonder, or at times ask colleagues if "X" is still practicing, but often "X" is a beloved teacher from one's own training. This arouses complicated feelings of loss, or perhaps disappointment that a former idealized teacher has been affected by time. We have committees to deal with compromised analysts but we find them difficult to use. It's too close, too personal. Alerting a senior colleague to the need to discontinue his or her practice is too much like killing the parent.

And what of the patient? Perhaps the intimacy of the relationship, often a long one, makes the analyst's decline harder to see, or to register. Perhaps the analyst does function at her highest level in this setting. Perhaps the patient thinks she is capable of keeping the beloved analyst alive.

A few vignettes

As we approached her termination date, a woman who had had several episodes of treatment with me over a period of years blurted out that "On the way over I thought that if I didn't stop coming, you wouldn't retire." With tears in her eyes she confessed that she was aware that I knew her as no one else did, and that I was – in that sense – her best friend. I heard her fear that I would retire as a fear that not only would I be dead to her as her therapist but also that I would die. This woman was herself waiting impatiently for the moment of her retirement from a job she found increasingly difficult and humiliating, transforming her profession into a function, one that could be easily replaced. She had also recently lost a sister to death, a death that revived pain she experienced on the death of her mother from cancer, when she was an adolescent, one with no opportunity to actively mourn. Then, her father turned to alcohol, and the prevailing taboo about mentioning cancer left her alone and bereft as none of her teachers, the clergy, or extended family acknowledged the loss of her mother. Now, these feelings were revived on the death of her sister, and the presence of a sympathetic listener enabled her to process them and to put them to rest.

This piece of work was the occasion for the recent round of treatment. So it was clear that the themes of retirement and mortality were very much a part of her mental landscape, perhaps leading to her wish to keep me alive by continuing to work with me. Necessarily, these thoughts became part of my mental landscape as well. How could they not? Immersed in her inner world in the treatment situation, her retirement became my retirement, the death of her loved one became my death – in reverie – and the reality of my own retirement, if not now, soon enough to make it an issue in her termination, stayed with me even as she was able to leave me. This patient was able to access her fears of both retirement and death in my presence, and she stimulated my own thoughts on termination and mortality. I have heard other patients allude to the fear of my death both glancingly and more directly.

A patient who I had seen weekly for ten years moved to another state. She requested Skype sessions "for as long as you're available" – leaving the question of why I might not be available unspoken. A year later, she married and had a child. She was now able to request diminished sessions of monthly rather than weekly meetings. Her request allowed me to suggest the possibility of termination. This patient was able to acknowledge that her attachment to me was her primary reason for continuing, and my suggestion that we consider termination inaugurated a process of thoughtful leave-taking.

An analytic patient, for whom separation and loss were prominent sources of anxiety, wondered from the outset how she would know when it was time to end. This new beginning with me immediately summoned thoughts of ending. Later she wondered if she would be allowed to attend my funeral, and if she would even know if I were dead. Perhaps my patient would hear of my death, and attend my funeral. I, on the other hand, could not.

Another patient became more aware of my benign essential hand tremor and found the courage to inquire about my health. She too had been in a long and useful treatment, one which continued as she confronted her aging mother's failing health. I am younger than her mother, but the transference was certainly colored by the reality of her next question: "Are you planning to retire?" (Are you going to die?)

These vignettes underline my patients' sometimes unconscious, sometimes completely conscious fears of mortality in general and my mortality in particular. My patients' fears of losing a crucial relationship are stimulated by consideration of a future moment of retirement – one that seems more real to each of us as I age. However, the denial of aging and the possibility of the analyst's retirement are more typical than their acknowledgement. Indeed, the denial of time passing is a hallmark of analysis, for patient and analyst alike, unless at least one party is alert to the reality of aging as time goes by.

How does this happen, the mutual failure to note the signs of aging over many years? The phrase, "gradually, then suddenly" comes to mind. An analyst and an analysand meet frequently, if not daily, over many years. An analysand might notice a change in her analyst's hairstyle, increasing baldness, perhaps a slightly different carriage – a slight stoop, the presence of a cane, but the setting remains essentially the same – unchanged by time. Add to this the mandate to look inward, and the lack of vis-a-vis conversation. The backdrop for these failures to notice is the resistance – the desire not to give up a familiar way of responding to the world which is so much in conflict with the desire for change. Add to this the analysand's anxiety about loss in general and in particular, the loss of the relationship with the analyst. One might wonder how an analysis ever ends.

Her training helps the analyst, her understanding of the signs that termination is imminent alert her, despite her own temptation to deny the passage of time and wish to continue what has become to her as well, an important relationship. And when all goes well, most analyses do end.

We acknowledge that a successful termination is a critical part of the analytic process. Some institutes require a terminated case for graduation.

But with the analyst's aging, she may find herself less alert to the time passing, to her own eventual "termination." It may take a patient saying, "Are you alright?" as she nods off, or repeats herself, to call attention to the passage of time and the fact that the aging process has reached its final stages.

Analysts cross a long series of thresholds in the course of training. The decision to apply for training often coincides with the beginning of an analysis – psychoanalysis itself is a process that tends to ignore time. In an analysis, process counts more than product; it is a long journey with an uncertain time frame, one where wisdom counts for more than technique, and one which demands continual scrutiny and evaluation. Moreover, analytic training fosters a protracted period of being in thrall to the older generation. Graduation can feel like an endlessly receding horizon and psychoanalysts may be well into their forties, and sometimes their fifties before they can begin to practice as fully fledged members of the profession.

When applying for psychoanalytic training, one's anxiety centers upon being acceptable to enter what can sometimes feel like a secret society rather than a profession. This ritualized process undermines a clear sense of beginning and ending a specialized training, one that has clear markers. Applying for training can also feel like a referendum on one's own mental health. Changes in our field including increasing transparency have greatly modified the "secret society" aspect of analytic training. The number of candidates has diminished over time, in a profession where few expect to earn their living exclusively through the practice of psychoanalysis.

Graduation, and the freedom to practice without supervision, marks a developmental milestone for the future analyst. Certification, and becoming a training analyst if the analyst chooses this route, follow. After approximately ten years, one is ready to be fully fledged, and to continue the journey of clinical work, while undertaking teaching and supervising candidates. Retirement signals the end of the line. Is it any wonder that analysts are reluctant to give up a practice so hard won? And is it surprising that psychoanalysts, who reach independence at an advanced age compared to practitioners of other areas of specialization, may be reluctant to give up after only a few decades of practice?

I believe that something else is at play as well, and that is the link between retirement and mortality in the mind of the practicing analyst. Because analysts live close to instinctual life, and dwell, of necessity at times, in the "timeless" unconscious, retirement may signal both the waning of instinctual life and the cessation of conscious being. Retirement punctures the fantasy of timelessness and the denial of aging that analysis cultivates, and registers, unconsciously, as retirement = mortality. We cultivate the denial of time and aging in a way that may not be quite the case for other professions. While physicians, or priests, or artists, for example, may well feel that their profession is central to their identity in ways that are similar – just as once one becomes a parent one is never not a parent even when the children are grown and possibly not even alive – I think that perhaps analysts, for the reasons I have been discussing, are somewhat more vulnerable to equating working with living. The privacy of the work, the interior focus, perhaps the transference which makes us the focus of our analysands' wishes that we have magical powers, add to our vulnerability in this regard. For these reasons, retirement and mortality may be both linked and denied more readily in our profession. To the extent that retirement signals "not being" – if not now, then soon – the analyst needs to acknowledge on a personal level, her own finite nature, and needs the support of a community that respects, acknowledges, and facilitates dignified retirement.

But how is such a community created? In our personal lives we often come across the moment when we, as adult children, must discuss with our parents the possibility of relinquishing a driving license, or considering moving to assisted living. Certainly the longer life span of the population in general makes these conversations more necessary – at least in the minds of the adult children. The elders are sometimes receptive to these suggestions, sometimes even take these steps on their own. But more often we hear of the situations that do not work so smoothly. Anger and denial are usually in the forefront. Oedipal wishes and fears may be activated in both parties. Early conflicts, long quiescent, may reemerge as parent and child struggle for dominance.

Another possibility is that the adult child does not want to see the parent as compromised. Individual families are left to find their own way. How different is this in our analytic community? It is true that many institutes set a cutoff age for taking on a new candidate in analysis, and some require retirement from their education committee at a fixed age. These responsible steps suggest a beginning. They allow younger colleagues to acknowledge the potential diminishing capacities of their former analysts and supervisors, and this promotes their ability to foresee their own aging and diminishment. And the same conflicts that infuse family dynamics continue between one generation and the next in the analytic community as well.

The cessation not only of one's analytic identity but also of one's "livelihood" is a tremendous loss. The simple definition of livelihood, from the Merriam-Webster dictionary, is "a way to earn money in order to live." Economic needs may well influence when we decide to retire from clinical practice. But if livelihood is equated with earning money to live, does retirement suggest not living? The decision not to continue to earn one's way has emotional significance perhaps beyond the loss of income. The very word "livelihood" connotes liveliness, vitality, being alive. Analysts are fortunate in being able to continue working in their community through teaching and writing. Yet, not earning one's way can signal a lack of efficacy, even potency, especially in a culture that places great value on productivity, and, one might add, youth.

The death of one's analyst, or her retirement from practice, will ignite feelings long dormant – grief, triumph, the proximity of one's own future ending. We, as a profession, honor our dead in public and private ways that are meaningful and contribute to the intergenerational transmission of our values. Through memorials, through writing, through gatherings, we console ourselves.

These rituals provide solace. But I think we collectively avoid the recognition that retirement is not an exclusively personal decision, as it affects our patients, but also our collective stance toward facing the reality of the finiteness of life.

I am not suggesting that fixed dates for retirement offer any kind of solution to the larger psychic problem of confronting retirement and mortality, although they are a recognition that attention must be paid to the aging process. Some analysts will be able to practice productively for many decades. These practitioners can be an inspiration – a mind still sharp with much to offer into the ninth decade. But these are the exceptions. I suggest that our role in the community requires a responsible and responsive dialogue about this neglected topic in our field, and a recognition that for analysts, given the trajectory of our training, the close link between retirement and mortality in the unconscious may make this dialogue a difficult one to begin and sustain.

I have emphasized the difficulties some analysts might face when the time comes to close the practice space, the external symbol of the analytic identity, and have speculated on why this might be. I have described the possibility of an unconscious link between retirement and mortality. The capacity to face reality is central to analytic thought and practice. In Freud's beautiful essay, "On Transience" – a fictional account of a conversation with a young poet – Freud emphasizes that because life is finite, its beauty is more valuable. But this is the long view, necessary to our understanding of what gives life meaning. It does not speak to the question, "Are you planning to retire?" with which I began this essay. Facing one's mortality is the ultimate reality test.

The difficulties that individual analysts face are reflected in the difficulty our profession has in addressing these concerns. It doesn't seem as urgent, or perhaps as interesting, to our profession to think about a dignified retirement, or the frailty of our beloved leaders, as it is to create new theories, or to debate how to preserve our field. We don't hear of – nor should we – the gentle help that some analysts receive from colleagues when ending has been hard to face. But these tactful, and I suspect rare personal moments are not a substitute for our field taking on the meaning of retirement and with it, mortality.

I have also ignored in this essay those analysts, many of my colleagues, who plan thoughtfully for retirement, indeed look forward to it, and offer a model on how to live on. And I haven't mentioned some of the significant markers which must be traversed – for instance the decision to stop taking analytic patients, or the last session with one's last analytic patient – on the way to retirement. I think our field would benefit if more analysts could write about these experiences. It may not be exciting, but it's a profoundly moving moment, one we would benefit from hearing more about as we anticipate our own ending.

Reference

Freud, S. (1916a). On transience. *S. E.*, *14*. London: Hogarth.

Index

abandonment 19, 51, 102, 115, 120, 144
Abraham, Karl 143–144
abstinence 117, 149
adolescence: awareness of mortality in 81–84; risk-taking in 83–84; young teenagers 75–78
adults: awareness of mortality 84–86, 90–91; awareness of mortality in late adulthood 86–88
afterlife, professional 11
afterlife beliefs 11
aggressive drive 50–51
aging: analysts' experience of 26, 30–32, 35–38, 163; attitudes toward 29–34; and forgetfulness 29–30; and mental deterioration 21, 30, 150–151; positive aspects of 26
agoraphilia 47
Akhtar, Salman 10, 11, 12, 19
Almighty Power hypothesis 92–94
American Psychoanalytic Association 122
American Psychological Association (APA) 28
analysis, termination of 65–66, 129, 136–137, 144–146, 162, 163–164
analysts: aging experience of 26, 30–32, 35–38, 163; awareness of mortality 110–112; colleagues' reaction to death of 141–142; colleagues' reaction to illness of 109–110, 122–124; concern for patients by 102, 104, 114–115; death of 8, 15, 19–20, 27–28, 124, 141–144, 150, 155, 165; and defenses against mortality 12–14; denial of death in practice 19–21; and the facilitation of patient material regarding mortality and death 14–19; illness of 25, 99–104, 110–112, 120; impairment of 21, 30, 150–151; patients' reaction to illness of 104–109, 120–121; and the relational turn 37–38; relationship with own mortality 9–12; responsibility of 146–148; retirement of 161–167; role of 7, 9
analytic function 15, 118, 147; loss of 151
anxiety attacks 61–62, 77
attachment 37, 69n8, 49, 51, 52; to analyst 28, 63, 163; avoidance of 51; libidinal 123
Atwood, George 28
avoidance 7, 9, 15, 20, 28, 51, 142, 147, 152

Balint, Michael 35
Becker, Ernest 11, 27
bereavement: in children 35, 69n6; and guilt 35
Berger, Barbara 26
Bergman, Martin 66
Bernays, Edward 32
Boesky, D. 115–116
Bolgar, Hedda 26
bone marrow transplant 100, 101, 102, 103
borderline personality 50
boundary violations 148–149
Braque, Georges 68
buddy system 21, 124

Cannon, Walter B. 74
castration 15, 19, 54
children: awareness of mortality 74–75; bereavement in 35, 69n6; impact of

parental loss on 45–55; and mourning 18; as patients 102; psychic pain of 66; *see also* parental loss
closeness-distance conflict 51
cognitive decay 21, 30, 150–151
cognitive reframe 34
Cohen, Phyllis 35
colleagues: and the "buddy" system 21, 124; reaction to death of analyst 141–142; reaction to illness of analyst 109–110, 122–124
Collins, Billy 29
commodification of the symptom 31
consumerism 32
Cooney, Elizabeth 83
countertransference 16, 37, 66–67, 121, 148; *see also* transference
creativity 27, 33, 67–68; and generativity 34–38

De Masi, Franco 7, 146
death: accidental 19, 35, 134–136; of the analyst 8, 15, 19–20, 27–28, 124, 141–144, 150, 155, 165; awareness of 13, 28; confrontation with 13; defenses against 7, 8, 13, 21; denial of 2, 7, 8, 12, 13, 19, 31; facilitation of patient material regarding 14–19; fear of 15, 17, 19, 54; idealization of 54; from illness 20, 131–132; middle knowledge of 13; of patients 129–137, 143, 152–153; reality of 31, 35; of spouse 133–134; sudden 144, 150; *see also* death anxiety; mortality
death anxiety 7–8, 14–15, 19, 21, 27, 88–89, 90
death instinct theory 8, 86–88
death terror 27; *see also* death anxiety
defensive capacity 3
defensive strategies 7, 8, 13, 21
denial 2, 7, 8, 12, 13, 19, 31; of dependence 48–49
depression 17, 37, 63; in survivors 36
developmental intervention 58
dissociation 13, 18

ego rupture 48
ego strength 3
Eisenstadt, J. M. 35
Eissler, K. 7
enforced disclosure 101
Erba, Annalisa 35

Erikson, Erik H. 17, 26, 27, 86, 87
Erikson, Joan 26
ethical misconduct 148–149
exceptionalism 28, 31

Fair, Eric 36
family formation 85
fantasy 52, 53, 64
fathers: abandonment by 59; child's relationship with 87; death of 18, 44, 46, 55, 61, 74–75; *see also* parental loss
Firestein, Stephen 145
forgetfulness 29–30
"Forgetfulness" (Billy Collins) 29
Freedman, A. 124
Freud, Anna 50, 57
Freud, Sigmund: on abstinence and neutrality 149; on death and mortality 7–8, 9, 10, 13, 27, 33; on death instinct 86; on forgetting 30; matrem nudam 69n1, 43; on maturation 31; on melancholia 142; on mother-child relationships 47–48, 87, 93; on mourning 33, 45–48; on psychoanalysis 33; on repression 141; on the role of the analyst 148, 152; on Seelenshmerz 47; on superego 82; "On Transience" 146, 166; on unconscious wishes 115–116, 119
Friedman, Lawrence 152
Frommer, Martin Stephen 1, 3–4, 18–19, 21–22, 27
Furman, Erna 68, 74

Galatzer-Levy, Robert 145
generativity, and creativity 34–38
geriatric populations 25–26
gerotranscendence 26
Ghent, Emmanuel 33
gratifications 17, 26, 32, 33, 36, 52, 67, 86–87, 88
Greenspan, Stanley 26
grief 34, 45–46; *see also* mourning
Groopman, Jerome 119
Grotstein, James 32
group dynamics 122–124
guilt 19, 82, 90, 114, 122, 123, 153

Hacket, T. P. 13
happiness 33: nature of 32; pursuit of 31

Harris, Adrienne 18, 99
Harvard Childhood Bereavement Study 69n6
Hedges, Chris 84
Hoffman, I. Z. 7, 8, 10, 17–18
holding environment 58
homosexuality 52, 62
horizontal split 13
Houlding, Sybil 143
Howell, Nathaniel 50
human exceptionalism 28, 31

idealization 48–49, 148
immortality 10–11, 32; literal 11; symbolic 11; yearning for 12; *see also* mortality
intellectualization 7, 16

Jensen, Frances 83
Jung, Yudit 27

Kantrowitz, Judy 120
Kasper, A.M. 15
Kernberg, Otto F. 33, 35, 52
Klauber, John 145–146
Koenigsberg, R. A. 84
Kohut, H. 17
Krystal, Henry 88

Lacan, J. 33
Lichtenberg, J.D. 33
limitation 31, 33, 34; acceptance of 34
Lippman, Paul 3
Loewald, H. 119, 145, 150
love-hate economy 51

Macalpine, Ida 152
majority privilege 38
Makari, George 31
manic defense 48–49
McCabe, Marilyn 34
melancholia 142
mental helplessness 47
mental pain 47–49
Messer, S. B. 31
metapsychology 31
Miller, Arthur 32
Mitchell, Stephen 13
Morrison, Amy 110
Morrison, Andrew 101
mortality: acceptance of 22; of the analyst 145; attitudes towards 53–55; avoidance of 147; awareness of in adolescence 81–84; awareness of in adulthood 84–86, 90–91; awareness of in late adulthood 86–88; children's awareness of 74–75; confrontation with 25; defenses against 12–14; denial of 152–153; facilitation of patient material regarding 14–19; relationship with 9–12, 32; and religion 92–94; and retirement 161–167; symbolic 11; young teenagers' awareness of 75–78; *see also* death; immortality
mothers: anger at 90; child's relationship with 87–88, 93; death of 2, 44, 46–47, 55, 56–57, 59–60, 61, 63, 132; *see also* parental loss
mourning 67, 142, 146; in children 18; normal 35; ongoing nature of 34, 45–46; for a patient 132; as work 33; *see also* grief
Multi-Trends Theory of Aggression 86–88

Nagel, Thomas 18, 21
narcissism 12–13, 18, 33, 52
narcissistic imbalance 46, 49–50
near-death experience 1
Nemetz, Joseph 153–155
neutrality 117, 149
Newman, David 27
Novick, Jack 145

Oedipus complex 35, 52, 82, 116, 121, 165
omnipotence 12, 18, 19, 34, 48–49, 57
oral fixation 52
Orfanos, Spyros 33
Orgel, Shelley 152–153
Ornstein, Anna 88
orphanages 59, 68
orphaned adult treatment: discerning defences against awareness of pervasive impact of the loss 60–64; interpreting defensive uses of orphan status 64–65; managing countertransference 66–67; providing a greater amount of 'illusion' and 'holding' 57–59; termination and post-termination phases of treatment 65–66; validating

Index

the importance and 'unfairness' of loss 59–60
orphaned child treatment: attitudes towards one's own mortality 53–55; continued intrapsychic relationship with the dead parent 45–47; disturbances in subjective experience of time 52–53; disturbances in the aggressive drive 50–51; mental pain and defenses against it 47–49; narcissistic imbalance 49–50; problems with love and sexuality 51–52; variation in individual responses 55–57
orphans: examples of famous 69n9; paucity of references to 43–44; various language expressions for 44; *see also* orphaned adult treatment; orphaned child treatment; parental loss

panic attacks 61–62, 77, 81
Parens, Henri: escape from detention camp 72–74, 78–81
parental loss 45–50, 67–68; ameliorative influences 56–57; and attitudes towards one's own mortality 53–55; and continued intrapsychic relationship with dead parents 45–47; and disturbances of aggressive drive 50–51; and disturbances in subjective experience of time 52–53; mental pain and defenses against it 47–49; and narcissistic imbalance 49–50; and orphaned adults 57–67; and problems with love and sexuality 51–52; psychopathological consequences of 55–56; *see also* fathers; mothers; orphans
patients: bereavement of 146–148; death of 8, 129–137, 143, 152–153; illness of 8, 131; informing of analyst's illness 101–102, 106–109, 116–119, 120–121; notification of analyst's death 19–21; reaction to analyst's illness 104–109, 120–121
penis envy 52
Pine, Fred 47
pleasure principle 31
Plotkin, Daniel 26
positive psychology management 33

professional afterlife 11
professional will 28
projection 15, 51, 52, 115
psychology, positive 33
psychopathology 7, 50, 55

reaction formation 51
reality principle 31
Reisner, Steven 31
relational turn 1, 37–38
religious belief: and awareness of death 12; as coping mechanism 10; and mortality 92–94
repression 7, 12, 15, 50–51, 64, 141
retirement 161–167; patients' reaction to 162–163; thoughtful preparation for 166–167
Richman, Sophia 27
Rodin, G. 13
Rolland, Romain 93
Rosenbaum, Elana 103
Ruitenbeek, Hendrik 33

sadism 75–76
Schachter, Joseph 66
Searles, Harold 9
Seelenshmerz 47
self-acceptance 26
self-destructiveness 51, 63, 86
self-esteem 11–12, 49, 56
self-neglect 51
self-psychology 33
self-sabotage 51
separation anxiety 47, 67
sexuality 37, 45, 51–52, 67
Shabad, Peter 11, 34
Shevrin, Howard 151
Silver, Ann-Louise 104, 110, 145
Slater, P.E. 17
Slavin, Malcolm 27
Smith, Tracy 112
Soldz, Stephen 38
Sossin, Mark 35
Spira, Marcia 26
spouse, death of 133–134
Stark, Martha 33
Stevenson, Adlai 35
Stolorow, Robert 3
Strachey, Alix 143–144
Strenger, Carlo 33
substance abuse 135
suicide 133–134, 137

Summers, Frank 31
superego 77, 82
survival guilt 35; *see also* guilt

terminal illness 27, 36, 124
termination 65–66, 129, 136–137, 144–146, 162, 163–164
termination theory 146
terror management theory 11
Tessman, Lora 120
therapists see analysts
therapy see analysis; termination
time, subjective experience of 52–53
transference 76, 117, 130–131, 145; *see also* countertransference
transience 9, 17, 22, 146, 150, 152, 166

unconscious wishes 115–116
undoing 35, 51
unhappiness 33, 130

van Raalte, Peggy 27
vulnerability 3, 15, 19, 52, 65, 67, 89, 99, 110, 112, 119, 123, 147, 165

Watson, John 32
Weissman, Avery D. 7, 13
Whitaker, Carl 101, 112
Winnicott, D.W. 34, 147, 148
Winokur, M. 31
Wolf, E. 33
women: and penis envy 52; postmenopausal 26; *see also* mothers

young teenagers, awareness of mortality 75–78

Zilboorg, Gregory 12, 13
Zimmerman, C. 13

For Product Safety Concerns and Information please contact our EU
representative GPSR@taylorandfrancis.com
Taylor & Francis Verlag GmbH, Kaufingerstraße 24, 80331 München, Germany

www.ingramcontent.com/pod-product-compliance
Lightning Source LLC
Chambersburg PA
CBHW052023290426

44112CB00014B/2346